Born on the 19 February 1987, Dar
Bristol, England before moving to Ply1
to study BSc Geography. After complet
left England for six years, working anc
different countries around the world. ⌐₁   ⌐
outdoors, Daniel's writing reflects his love for the natural world.
He recently returned to Bristol and is planning his next adventure.

A
Walk
to the
Water

Daniel Graham

SilverWood

Published in 2015 by SilverWood Books

SilverWood Books Ltd
14 Small Street, Bristol, BS1 1DE, United Kingdom
www.silverwoodbooks.co.uk

ISBN 978-1-78132-422-6 (paperback)
ISBN 978-1-78132-423-3 (ebook)

British Library Cataloguing in Publication Data
A CIP catalogue record for this book is available from
the British Library

Set in Sabon by SilverWood Books
Printed by Imprint Digital on responsibly sourced paper

For Jake

Contents

Overview Map

1

Bristol to Dover

0 to 404 kilometres from home

ROUTE FINDING

'Why?' she asked inquisitively. We sat with our legs dangling over the edge of the harbourside. A white swan bobbed on the water below, pecking at the algae-stippled walls and then ducking its head decisively into the pantry of weed on the dock bed. As I looked up, she pushed her dark auburn hair over her shoulder, revealing an earring that spun, pine-green and gold, in the November breeze.

'Why?' I took a moment to gather my thoughts. 'Someone told me a story.'

'A story?'

'Yes.' The swan lost interest and pushed through the murky water towards a small wooden jetty on the other side of the dock.

'What do you mean? A story?'

'I was in New Zealand, somewhere in the North Island. I was sitting in the kitchen of a hostel when a man wandered over. Arne, I think his name was. He was stocky, with a large nose and big earlobes. I don't know why I remember that, but they were massive – the biggest I've ever seen!'

Claudia laughed, holding the frame of her black glasses to stop them falling forwards.

'You know what it's like with backpackers: everyone chats to everyone,' I continued. 'He started talking about this walk he had done in the United States, the Appalachian Trail. I'd never heard of it.' I had told this story many times over the previous two years and was used to people losing interest long before the end. But Claudia held her gaze, nodding slowly as she played with her hair, as if to say, 'Go on. Then what?'

'He told me he had flown over from Holland with his girlfriend,

11

and they had walked for four months through fourteen states, Georgia to Maine. He talked so passionately about it – forests, hills, bears, boredom, elation, rain, sun, rations and his relationship. He talked about it all, and I could see it had affected him. After an hour or so, he looked up at me, his eyes were glazed, and he had this sort of fire burning in them. Then, on the brink of crying, he said, "It was both the best and worst experience of my life." I remember a chill going down my back, and that's when I knew I wanted that experience too.'

'And Jake, he thought the same as you?'

'Well, he's an adventurer. Does there have to be more of a reason than that? A lot of the time, people justify their decisions because they think they have to. I mean, once we had both decided we were doing it, we came up with a few more motives, but they were afterthoughts really. We told people it was a charity walk, a physical challenge, and an opportunity to get to know our surroundings better. All the kind of things that people want to hear, you know. But the truth is we're doing it because we feel an urge to. Sometimes it's good to go with your instincts, no matter how big the challenge.'

I had only met Claudia a few days earlier, but she trusted my justifications and didn't dig for weaknesses in our plan. She appeared excited beyond conversational politeness and queried further. 'So why walk? Why so far? Where will you sleep? Do you think you will get a tattoo afterwards? Will you take a teddy bear?'

We talked for hours, watching the swan drift off towards Prince's Wharf, beneath the looming metalwork of the old industrial cargo cranes. As the light faded, we parted with the docks and sought refuge from the evening's chill within the comforting walls of the Bristol Ram, where we drank cider that smelt of the countryside, and danced awfully until our feet grew sore.

One month earlier, on 14 October 2012 at exactly 11.06am, I had looked at Jake and reciprocated his broad smile. I remember focusing on my brother more intently at that moment than I had ever done before, as if it was an occasion I subconsciously wanted to remember.

With just twelve minutes separating our births, Jake and I bear many similarities – brown hair, hazel-coloured eyes, aquiline noses, and built lightly on a frame of bones several inches below six feet. To the more trained eye, however, there are differences: Jake's face is a little longer than mine, his nose slightly more freckled, and his hair less curly. On his lower lip is a small yet permanent swelling obtained from a misplaced elbow in a football match, and in the iris of his left eye a deep black speck resides.

Having spent eighteen years side by side, it wasn't until our late teens – as Jake ventured to the west coast of Wales to begin a three-year study of marine and freshwater biology, and I boarded a plane to Hong Kong – that we both experienced our first real taste of independence, not just from Bristol and our home but also from our family and, most poignantly, each other.

I returned to England the following year and moved to the south coast, picking up a degree in geography before setting my sights abroad once more. Meanwhile, Jake's love of all things aquatic took him back to Bristol where he acquired a job in the local aquarium, inspiring the next generation of shark lovers and jellyfish admirers. Jake spent three years amongst fish and crustaceans, cephalopods and reptiles until one day, following my return from Western Australia, I asked him to join me on an adventure.

'So, we're doing it then?' Jake said softly.

In six months, we would leave our jobs and step out on the path. Everything was in place – everything except for one or two minor details. We had to decide where we would begin our walk. In fact, we had to decide where we would end it too, and how far we would hike, and on which continent. Indeed, it seemed that two years of mental preparation had done little more than convince Jake and me that the walk was a good idea. It was time to buy a map.

With the world on our dining room table and the smell of filter coffee in the air, we scoured the lands. I saw Jake running his finger along the western coastline of North America. 'How about the Pacific Crest Trail? It's long and goes through the Rockies!'

'Could do. What about visas? They might be a bit of a hassle,' I replied, leaning over a cluster of Antipodean islands.

'Good point.'

Somewhat unjustly vetoing Asia and South America for little other reason than that my coffee cup was sitting on Brazil, and Jake's body lay across Russia and China, our focus turned to Europe.

'The Alps,' we uttered simultaneously, both drawn towards a heavily shaded section of the continent where the map's terrain folded and the road networks thinned.

Jake and I had spent much of our lives sharing, from the confined walls of our mother's womb to a bedroom, a classroom, a football team and, in our more recent years, an overwhelming love for ground-crumbling, snow-topped mountains. We were by no means mountaineers – indeed, Jake suffered from vertigo – but we enjoyed hiking immensely and craved the awesomeness of a massif and the thrill of a summit.

My nose grazed the map as I traced a chain of peaks down into the Swiss foothills, where I wound north and then east towards Austria and Slovakia with no structure or purpose, remembering that anywhere was an option. Whilst walking held the advantage of freedom, it was proving an oddly restrictive mode of transport as we struggled to decipher a worthy route.

A lapse in concentration, or perhaps the exact opposite, saw my eyes settle on a female blackbird on the apple tree in the garden. She was splendidly beautiful.

'Let's start in Bristol,' Jake said as I turned to see that he too was staring at the bird. 'From our doorstep and down into Europe. It would be brilliant!' Jake suddenly seemed very excited. 'No transport, no preliminary journey, just straight into it! What do you think?'

Jake was right: what reason did we have to begin the walk anywhere other than home? With such wonders on our doorstep, it would have been foolish to consider passing them at anything other than walking pace.

'Yes!' I said, with a widening smile. 'Begin here, in Bristol, and walk to the Alps!'

'Or over the Alps? And then down to the Mediterranean. What's better than the ocean to drag us to the finish when our legs are buggered?'

And that was that. With a little more fine-tuning, involving the linking together of various long-distance European footpaths, we decided on our route. We would leave Bristol and head east via the Kennet and Avon Canal and the North Downs Way, dipping south of London and into Kent. From England's south-eastern waters, we would sail the North Sea to Ostend and continue on towards the rising sun, through the flat farmlands of Belgium and the Netherlands, and then on to the city of Antwerp, before finally arching south. With eight countries on our route, the path would then drop into the hills of the Luxembourg Ardennes and along the banks of the Meuse River, beyond the castles of the Vosges Mountains and the gorges of the Jura Range in France's far east, before falling into Switzerland and onto the shores of Lake Geneva. From this point, the trail would ascend into the mighty Alps, where Hannibal and his unlikely elephants once passed, before rolling us blistered, battered and exhausted into Menton and the French Riviera, where our feet would eventually feel the licking waves of the Mediterranean Sea.

Our estimations, based almost entirely on a length of string stretched along the route, told us that we had approximately 3,000 kilometres to walk which, at an average of twenty kilometres a day, would take us roughly five months to complete, or six if we were being particularly generous.

We would camp where possible, immersing ourselves in the resounding splendour of Europe's biota. We would cook our own food, use paper maps, and have no access to the internet, save for the occasional glance when passing through the larger towns or cities. And, to prove that this was not some sort of rebellion against society and the modern world, and more importantly to keep our mother happy, we would take an old mobile phone.

GREENSLEEVES

It was a crisp spring morning in mid-April 2013. The air was fresh and the gardens colourful. We walked silently towards the end of the street, turning every five steps to wave goodbye to our family who stood on the wall and road camber outside our house. I tried to control my welling tears with deep breaths that wobbled on each exhalation.

Reaching the corner of the street, we stopped for one final farewell. The fifty metres that Jake and I had put between us and our family had rendered their expressions unreadable. How very sad I felt. And then they were gone.

15

Several moments passed before Jake spoke. 'Well, that was pretty tough.'

I struggled to find any words.

Just before we had left our house, the local Bristol station, *Heart Radio*, had aired a thirty-second interview with Jake about our walk to the Mediterranean. In spite of the wealth of questions they had asked – probing into our motivations, our greatest fears and the fundraising for WaterAid which we had decided to include in the venture – the editor had chosen to broadcast an uninformative clip on our thoughts about the weather we were expecting over the five-month trip. Listeners would have learnt little of our pending journey, but, to the editor's credit, the piece did tie in nicely with the meteorological forecast that followed. Our sister, Jessy, a self-employed painter and decorator, often listened to *Heart Radio* as she worked, and I knew that our brief moment of local stardom would have amused her.

Unfortunately for Jake and me, with our family now behind us, we didn't feel much like smiling. The smell of fermenting yeast sugars and cooling loaves wafted out from the windows of the Split Tin Bakery, and, a little further down the street the Bird Table Café stirred with early Sunday risers.

Submerged in deep thought, I failed to notice a loop on the lace of my right boot latch itself onto one of the buckles on my left. Lurched violently from my contemplation, I stumbled uncontrollably forward like a running toddler, waiting to feel the pain of the concrete pavement on my hands and knees. To my surprise, with the aid of a flanking garden wall and some neat footwork, I was able to remain upright, suffering only from a substantially increased heartbeat and a heavy dose of embarrassment. At this rate, statistically, we would suffer another 14,400 stumbles, trips and falls before the end of our trip, at least one of which would surely end in either serious injury or death. I was suddenly appreciative of the travel insurance that our mother had insisted we took out, and glad for the early lesson: tie laces properly.

Parting gifts from our father had left Jake and me carrying a pedometer each. Mine sat quietly on the hip of my shorts and had clocked 2,000 steps by the time we had reached the end of Cranbrook Road. Jake's, however, provided us with our second lesson in as many kilometres: never take a singing pedometer on a 3,000-kilometre hike. In fact, never take a singing pedometer off the shop shelf. *Greensleeves*, sounding like it had been played on the buttons of an old house phone, rang out from the small device, gasping momentarily to catch its breath before hurling itself once more into a chorus of irritating beeps.

Somewhat conspicuously – courtesy of our large packs, relentless melody, and garishly white WaterAid T-shirts – we marched along familiar pavements into the city centre, where we joined the muddy waters of the River Avon, turning east to follow the winding course upstream and out of Bristol.

We had chosen to use the towpath of the Kennet and Avon Canal for the first part of the journey, allowing us a trouble-free introduction to life on the trail, with easy navigation and almost no elevation changes. Efficiently dissecting the counties of Bristol, Somerset, Wiltshire and Berkshire, we then planned to drop south from the canal into Hampshire, picking a route through the farmland towards the town of Farnham and the beginning of the North Downs Way. With the footprints of pilgrims leading us through Surrey and the hop fields of Kent, we would dip beneath the sprawl of Greater London, towards the far south-east of England and the Port of Dover. According to our small piece of distance-measuring thread, we had roughly 400 kilometres to cover, a journey that, dismissing navigational mishaps or injuries, was set to take us somewhere between three and four weeks to complete. Put neatly and concisely into a short paragraph, the first month of our walk sounded simple and undemanding.

As the morning crept by, we rarely strayed from the river and stopped only to eat cold falafels from our leaving dinner the night before. A dense blanket of cloud spread across the sky, and, as afternoon set in, the comforting breeze on our cheeks strengthened to a disconcerting wind. Not even the ostriches and wallabies of the Avon Valley Country Park on the opposite side of the river could lift the oppressive atmosphere that had descended.

I looked down at my Mammut Mercury boots, their untarnished graphite and dark green exterior pacing along the dry soil. I wanted them to be worn, dusty and cracked, with kilometres beneath their soles, and tales of mountains climbed, rivers crossed and ancient pathways walked. But they were fresh and inexperienced.

With a stroke of good fortune, I had seen my Mammuts on the shelf of an outdoors shop a couple of months back, tried them on once, and bought them without a second thought. Jake had been subjected to a slightly bumpier experience. Dark grey and splashed with red, his boots were the result of half a dozen returns, refits and experimentations, eventually seeing him slip on the Regattas with an exuberant yelp of relief: 'They're the ones!'

Following the acquisition of boots, we had turned our attention to rucksacks. After hours of adjusting straps, examining features, and querying prices from North Bristol to South, we discovered the Lowe Alpine Appalachian. It was the perfect fit, complete with external pockets, and, considering its potential to pack 85 litres of gear, relatively light. We got one of each colour: Jake's clover-green and mine chilli-red. With most of our gear budget gone, we bought several more important items – including a pair of walking poles for Jake, a cooking stove and a tent – before raiding our wardrobes at home for fleeces, shorts, waterproofs and thermals. Finally, we had a set of belongings that would get us comfortably and painlessly to the Mediterranean Sea.

Drizzle fell as the honey-coloured limestone buildings of Bath began to dot the riverside. The thin rain dusted our hair white and gave Hemingway and Charlie, our walking mascots, their first taste of the perils of the outdoors.

With patched fur, small ears and a subtle smile, Hemingway the teddy bear had been posted to us a few days back as a good luck gift from a friend. With the parcel was a note:

Hello!
My name is Hemingway. I am lightweight and bendy so able to squish into very small spaces! I am here to be your muse, to remind you of nice things and loved ones, as someone to break the ice when you get bored of talking to each other. Please take me with you. I would love an adventure.

Now lassoed to the back of my red pack, I was glad to see that, in spite of the rain, Hemingway still bore his gentle smirk.

Jake's mascot, Charlie, was an orange, white and black clownfish given to him by his colleagues as a leaving present from Bristol Aquarium. Squashed into Jake's netted side pocket earlier in the morning as a last-minute talisman, Charlie's expression was less friendly than Hemingway's. I felt sorry for the little chap, knowing that if ever we needed to reduce the weight of our packs, which was a more than likely scenario, he would be the first to go.

By the time we reached Bath, Jake's pedometer, which if nothing else had increased in volume, had racked up a hearty 40,000 steps – some thirty kilometres. Relieving the strain of having to find a campsite for the night were two friends of ours, Ryan and Maria, who met us in the centre of Bath and walked us to their house.

'Bit sore, are you?' Ryan teased through a broad grin as we began to lag behind.

My hamstrings were so tight I could barely bend my knees, and instead I had adopted an odd gait that saw my legs swing wildly out to the sides before looping back into my stride. Our waists were bruised from the hip belts, and our shoulders were chafed.

'It's a good thing,' I returned. 'Our exhaustion, I mean. Aches and pains merely contribute towards a strengthening body. Don't they?'

We spent the evening watching *Match of the Day* as our stomachs digested a bowl of kindly prepared spaghetti bolognese and a sleep-inducing can of Carlsberg.

'I'm sorry, guys, it's going to have to be the living room floor tonight,' Ryan said through a yawn. 'Bath house prices and all that. Now, do you need any bedding?'

'If we said yes, I think we would be screwed for the next five months,' Jake replied. 'We'll be alright. Gives us a chance to test out the roll mats!'

Five minutes later, I was in my sleeping bag. 'We're ditching that bloody pedometer, Jake. It'll drive us both mad,' I whispered.

No reply.

Turning to face him, I noticed that his eyes were closed, and a healthy pool of dribble had already formed on his makeshift pillow.

SCROGGIN

We climbed gingerly out of Bath in warm sun, glancing every now and then over our shoulders at the city which gradually faded to a quarry of merged Roman and Georgian architecture, dotted with steeples that reached for the sky.

I was hungry and suddenly remembered the trail mix that we had stuffed into our side pockets as we prepared our packs earlier in the morning. 'Scroggin?' I said to Jake, tossing a bag into his hands.

'Why do you call it that?'

'I've always called it that. Mr Wright used to say it all the time. It's from New Zealand apparently,' I replied, thinking back to my school years.

When I was fifteen, I took part in Ten Tors, a hiking competition in south-west England. Mr Wright, my secondary school's head of geography and a keen hiker, was our leader, and dedicated days off to taking a gaggle of skinny teenagers over the hills of the Quantocks and up the slopes of the Black Mountains in a bid to get us trail fit for the challenge. With dark, spongy hair, a little like the top of a microphone, studious eyes, oval glasses, and remarkably toned calves, Mr Wright addressed impressionable ears. 'Now,' he said, huddling us into a group beside the minibus after our first training hike, 'scroggin is undoubtedly one of the most important elements of Ten Tors. It'll put fuel into your step, OK?'

I took Mr Wright's advice seriously and spent hours before each preparatory hike concocting spectacular bags of sweets and dried fruit. Each week, I refined the component ratios until, finally, the perfect mix of high-energy consumables was achieved.

I remember the moment that darkness fell over Dartmoor at the end of the first day. We had been climbing and descending for fourteen hours, from one ground-splitting granite tor to the next, over tussocks and heath, peat bogs and rivers. The clouds wept tirelessly, and the wind pulverised our weak adolescent bodies whilst Royal Air Force helicopters patrolled the skies, hoisting kids with broken ankles, hypothermia and exhaustion to safety. As we stumbled down towards the meander of a river to camp, I began to feel that perhaps one of us would be next.

In spite of our numb fingers and exhausted minds, we were able to erect the tents, managing a brief sleep before waking early the following morning to a cacophony of squabbling alarms. With packs the size of their bearers, we continued on over the moors through the relentless rain until, eventually, just shy of our ninetieth kilometre, and with quivering knees, we crossed the finishing line. Completing Ten Tors was one of the proudest moments of my life, and I never doubted that the well-balanced fusion of scroggin was the difference between our success and the deployment of a rescue helicopter.

With each walk that followed Ten Tors, I noticed a maturing of the scroggin. Jelly sweets were replaced with nuts, whilst liquorice was removed altogether. Bag weight was reduced from an intimidating 1,000 grams to three more manageable bags of 300 grams. And, finally, I learnt that the addition of 'padding' (a less tasty ingredient such as muesli) gifted a little fibre and carbohydrate to the mix – boring, but valuable for smooth-running bowels.

With the rooftops of Bath now hidden by trees, I tucked into a splendid plethora of scroggin ingredients, where Golden Grahams cereals were complemented with banana chips, cranberries and Sherbet Lemon sweets.

Jake seemed less pleased with the mix. 'We could do with a few more boiled sweets in here,' he said casually, obliterating over a decade's worth of fine-tuning in one fell swoop.

A path fell from the roadside through beech forest heavy with wild garlic and down to the Dundas Aqueduct, an innovative section of the Kennet and Avon Canal designed to bridge the turbulent River Avon. Bobbing with ducks and the ashen reflections of the forest's bare trees, the aqueduct looked tired and worn, no doubt the consequence of a long and wearisome history.

In the fourth millennium BC, King Menes of Upper Egypt was building navigable artificial waterways at a time when the practice of writing was just beginning to be established. In 1810, almost 6,000 years later, the Kennet and Avon Canal was completed after sixteen years of construction. The channel offered a direct and unimpeded route between Bath and London, and consequently began to flourish. By the 1820s, canal trade was booming, with its prosperity evidenced by the sixty-tonne barges of coal and stone that cruised the waters.

However, the glory didn't last. Just twenty years on, the Great Western Railway (GWR) was built, drawing trade away from the milky-coffee-coloured canal and onto its finely tuned baulks. 'God's Wonderful Railway', as it soon became known, had transformed the thriving artery of canal trade into a forgotten scar in the land. Sections of the waterway fell dry, and locks began to deteriorate.

Nevertheless, despite its condition, the canal struggled on through the twentieth-century, avoiding closure as tireless campaigners fought and government reports spewed. Restoration began in the late 1960s, with the repair of the dilapidated locks and the rather affectionately named 're-puddling' of the dried-out sections of the course, returning the Kennet and Avon Canal to its former – though certainly less industrial – splendour.

We traipsed along the towpath, once patterned by the metal shoes of hard-working horses that heaved barges to and fro. Hoofprints had been replaced by the tracks of a pushbike that wound playfully along the gravel, hidden every now and then by the shadow of a naked deciduous tree.

Bath lay in our wake, and we pushed on towards the next town, Bradford upon Avon, which, despite its close proximity to our home, we had rarely visited. In fact, aside from the first few kilometres through Bristol and our bisection of Bath's centre, we realised how very little we knew of our surroundings.

'Oh, we don't go far anymore. Too old, you see,' Pam said as her thin grey hair caught a breeze. We had been stopped in our tracks by a small white dog that sniffed enthusiastically at our boots, and its owners, Pam and Noel. 'But we used to love walking in the Lake District. You're going a long way. What's your incentive?' The inquisitive couple were particularly interested in WaterAid and quizzed us on the charity's objectives.

'Well, they aim to improve global access to safe water, hygiene and sanitation,' I informed the pair with a certain element of rigidity that implied I had learnt the line off by heart, which of course I had.

Whilst Jake rambled on about elephant pumps and gravity-fed water systems, I glanced over at Noel who had dipped two wrinkled hands into the pockets of his navy blue corduroys. After pulling out various items, he finally produced a five-pound note which was thrust our way. 'It's all we have on us.'

The water banks led us with little fuss north of Trowbridge and then south of Melksham, the overcast sky threatening a downpour. The canal was a social place, and we rarely passed a soul without breaking into conversation. David, a lethargic cyclist with a round nose and stringy grey hair, whose ambition for the day was to encounter some wildlife, pedalled slowly alongside our drained legs, pausing whenever the leaves rustled or twigs snapped. We stopped to admire a nesting swan and then a foraging blackbird before David probed us on our ginormous packs. 'So, which path are you walking?'

'At the moment, the Kennet and Avon Canal, then we're going to cut down to the North Downs Way in about three days,' Jake declared.

'You're finishing in Dover then?'

'Well, no actually, we're walking to the Mediterranean.'

'The Mediterranean? Blimey!' David blurted, erupting from the docile persona we had met a few minutes earlier. 'Feel free to tell me to bugger off, but do you mind if I cycle on and take a photo of you?'

We accepted the request, and two minutes later saw David clamber from his bike fifty metres up the track, propping his Digital SLR onto the handlebars. Seemingly looking for the perfect shot, he must have mounted and dismounted his bike half a dozen times, on each occasion clicking furiously away at the trigger before cycling on once more. Eventually, he disappeared off around a bend shouting, 'Until next time, which will likely be just around the corner!'

We didn't see David again.

The rain that had looked imminent earlier in the day never came, and we arrived at the Sells Green campsite dry but most certainly in need of a hot shower. The owner of the campground was so shocked that we had not brought our own teabags that she gave us a small handful. Neither Jake nor I drank tea, but we took them out of politeness before following her to a patch of boggy grass, unsurprisingly devoid of other tents.

Jake walked like a duck with cramp to the shower block, returning sometime later with washed socks. He hung them on the guy ropes of the tent, and then we sat on the wet grass and cooked couscous with a few leaves of wild garlic picked earlier in the day.

By late afternoon, we were still the only campers in the grounds, though the number of motorhomes had increased ten-fold, and with it our entertainment. A gentleman in a striped dressing gown, squeaking blue sandals and a washbag in hand strolled by our pitch with his nose raised high as if sniffing the air.

A second camper with matching attire, save for the blue sandals which were instead pink, scampered swiftly in his step. When she got too close, the tail of the husband's gown would get caught beneath her feet, provoking him to turn his head in disapproval, at which the poor wife would fall behind once more.

'Perhaps we should have packed our dressing gowns?' Jake mused, as the peculiar pair creaked off towards the showers.

THE CHRISTENING OF TED

The Sells Green church bells sounded early and were soon accompanied by tenor cows and soprano geese. It had been a wet and windy night, but a quick assessment of our sleeping bags suggested that the tent had held strong.

Clambering tentatively from the warmth generated by a night of body heat, we stood on the cold, damp grass and looked down at the shelter.

'It needs a name,' I said, eyeing up the contours of the structure. Predominantly dark green in colour and splashed modestly with black and orange, the 'Vango Tempest 200' blended in well with the countryside, but was not so inconspicuous that our sleeping bodies would never be found (or so we hoped). A small, triangular vestibule took the flysheet to its highest point, at which it met a perpendicular pole that curved to the ground on either side. The curve was maintained along the body of the tent, gradually tapering to a smaller pole at the foot end, and from here the material stooped towards the ground. The man in the shop had overwhelmed us by regurgitating tent acronyms, numbers and jargon. Apparently, the Tempest had 'reflective webbing', an 'internal brace system', a 'groundsheet hydrostatic head of 6,000 millimetres' and a 'Venturi Vent System', which frankly sounded like something you would find in a car, or perhaps even a spaceship. However, most intriguing of all was the 'waterproof Portex HC polyester flysheet' which, according to the expert, could take 5,000 millimetres of water before it began to drip. We didn't really know what this meant, but it sounded like a lot, so we bought the tent.

'Ted,' Jake said. 'He looks like a Ted.' And so it remained.

Our socks hadn't dried overnight, so we looped them through the elastic on the back of our packs and reunited ourselves with the canal. We had planned to start our journey slowly, beginning with days no longer than fifteen kilometres, or at the most twenty, before progressively building to a heartier length as we strengthened. However, our excitement had intervened, and since leaving Bristol two days earlier we had covered sixty kilometres, almost doubling the proposed distance. Our toes were aching, our muscles were stiff, and our hips had turned to the colour of gazpacho soup.

The path was flat and straight, yet held glimpses of modest pleasure: a swan's beak skimmed the water's surface, a pike stirred, and a wood pigeon cooed. Stretches of the canal lay untamed and bleak, but would soon become studded with moored narrowboats, their chimney smoke eddying. The elongated boats were colourful and intriguing, and we found it difficult to pass without peering into their dusty porthole windows, or announcing their names: 'Moonfleet', 'Dottie B' and 'Rose of Hungerford'.

We trod unhurriedly along the path, which lay scattered with sawdust, small piles of prepared wood and ankle-high heaps of ash, and we patted the backs of the dogs as they came to play. The boats would multiply like strings of chromosomes lining the banks, then bundle into dockyards where I couldn't help but feel a sense of inequality: whilst some felt the head of a hammer and the lick of a brush on their hull, others lay dry on the levees, dilapidated and forgotten.

A sign on the side of the track told us we had merged with the White Horse Trail, a 144-kilometre path running through the heart of Wiltshire, so named because of eight white horses carved into the surrounding chalk hillsides. Keen to spot the horses, we browsed the slopes, stopping to squint at anything that looked remotely white.

It appeared that life on the canal required a slow heartbeat. Sparrows rummaged quietly in the leaves, and the air bubbles of the canal's tench and bream popped on the water's surface. Herons stalked, never quite pouncing, and peacock butterflies drifted majestically through the tepid air. Indeed, the only creatures willing to exert themselves were the moorhens, forever nervous and forever busy, deserving their nickname: 'skitty coots'.

I had acquired three blisters since leaving Bristol, one on the inside of each of my big toes and a third on my heel, not yet painful but glowing with potential. Jake and I had both experienced bad blisters in the past and were distinctly aware that, if severe, they could sap the enjoyment from any experience. I thus adopted a forced limp in an attempt to reduce the friction, a gait which, on only our third day, began to worry me.

'There!' Jake pointed through the bare branches of a particularly gnarled hawthorn tree and up towards a white figure on the side of a nearby hill. It was the Alton Barnes White Horse.

With the blister on my heel beginning to tingle with ferocity, I was glad of a distraction and squinted up at the horse. In 1812, John Thorne – a journeyman painter known locally as 'Jack the Painter' – was paid just twenty pounds to design and then cut the animal into the hillside. Thorne left before the job was completed, leaving Mr Robert Pile, the Alton Barnes landowner, both out of pocket and with half a horse chiselled into his hill. Though it was a curious sight – big, white and clearly out of place – we proceeded to pass by without any more mention of its existence.

Before leaving Bristol, we had researched a number of campsites along the early stages of our route and marked them onto our 1:50,000 *Ordnance Survey* maps. The Barge Inn at Honey Street was irrefutably the most anticipated. A consistent winner of the 'Crop Circle Pub of the Year', and labelled somewhat confidently as 'the most popular pub in the universe', our expectations were high as we approached the large Georgian building, hugged to its west by a small, triangular field.

Rule number thirteen of the pub's campsite, as detailed on a piece of tattered paper stuck to the wall of the portable toilets, asked all pending visitors to 'Check the alien abduction threat level prior to pitching and follow the precautionary advice'. Without internet, we had no way of knowing the threat level. Thankfully, as we wandered aimlessly around the hummocky grass beside the canal, a message came through on Jake's phone: 'Barge Inn alien threat level: moderate, possible UFOs. See you shortly, Dad.'

We pitched Ted and made our way to the pub.

Sitting in the window away from the locals, most of whom had a pint in one hand and newspaper in the other, we covered our wooden table with maps and notes as the smell of freshly-poured cider filled the air. The pub was decorated as one would imagine – aliens, galaxies, UFOs – and was steeped with tales of its infamous crop circles which attracted hundreds of extra-terrestrial enthusiasts every year.

Looking up from my journal, I caught sight of a smiling face in the window beside us, thankfully not that of a boggle-eyed, green-faced alien, but of the hairless head, dark eyes and exulted smile of our father.

'You look shattered!' Dad exclaimed, eyeing up our rosy cheeks and drooping eyes as beer and pub food, already a welcome break from our high-calorie trail diet, replaced our maps at the table.

'We *are* shattered,' I returned. 'Last night, we were asleep by eight. It's nine now!'

'And physically?'

Jake lifted his T-shirt and showed Dad the contusions on his hips. 'It's pretty painful around the waist, but it'll get better. Shoulders are a bit tight, soles sore, but that's about it. Oh, and Dan's got blisters.'

'Well, the beginnings of them,' I added, lifting up my sandal and flashing my foot towards Dad. 'We're fine apart from that. Just want to be a few more days into it, you know, so it feels like we're really underway.'

I could see Dad assessing our fatigued bodies. 'Do you think you can do it?'

'Yes, we can do it,' Jake assured him. 'Of course, we can.'

Seemingly content with this response, and with the aid of a particularly dark beer, the tension in Dad's shoulders relaxed. Conversation gradually drifted away from walking, and we were soon hearing about the drinking sessions our father undertook many years back in the hollows of the Barge Inn, the best pub in the universe.

THE CROSS KEYS

I woke feeling a little sad. The stagnant canal and the low pressure of the morning left the sky looking grey and sullen. For three days, I had struggled to forget the waving hands and the smiles of our family as we stepped miserably towards the end of our road back in Bristol. Dad's departure brought it all back. Once on the Continent, we would be on our own.

Unwilling to let my mood drop, Jake reminded me that we would be seeing Dad again when we were closer to London, and before that Mum, her partner Paul, and half a dozen willing friends. 'And by the time we leave for Europe, we'll be hardened walkers. Solitude and the wilderness will be our best friends.' He smiled encouragingly.

We left Honey Street having experienced no alien interactions, aside from the scatological activity lurking within the camp's temporary toilets. The blanketed sky muffled the blue tit's song, and the smell of the boats' burning wood eased my tired mind. Bulrushes piled at the water's edge like oversized matches, whilst reflected bridges filled my vision with red-brick circles, broken only by the elegance of a gliding swan.

The thatched roofs of Pewsey's unimposing outskirts guided us away from the canal towards the village centre where we passed a chalkboard outside the French Horn pub which read: 'Save our planet, it's the only one with beer'. Nearby, the village's own welcoming sign, 'Pewsey – The Oldest Carnival in Wiltshire, 1898', confirmed that the residents of Pewsey had their priorities right: beer and carnivals.

We bought a bag of pastries and breads from Marshall's Bakery, which we ate before acknowledging that a 10.30am lunch was perhaps a little premature. Then, for the first time since leaving Bristol, we checked our map to shortcut us back to the navigation-friendly canal.

We instantly got lost – not altogether surprising considering that both Jake and I had yet to learn how to use a compass. Arguably, this was something that we should have mastered before beginning a 3,000-kilometre trek across Western Europe, but we were so ill-equipped in many other ways that compass logistics were the least of our worries. Of course, this was an easy statement to make on a warm spring afternoon in central Wiltshire, when our notion of lost was being 100 metres from our desired location.

After various twists of the compass dial and the hurdling of several fences, we soon tumbled out onto the familiar linearity of the Kennet and Avon Canal.

'Hey, Jake, we are about to pass a place called Clench,' I sniggered childishly. He found this amusing, so I continued, 'And then Cuckoo's Knob and Crowdown Clump!' With both of us in a rapture of giggles, I returned the map to the comfort of my bag, delighted with the discovery that Britain's detailed *Ordnance Surveys* were not only set to provide us with a reliable means of navigation but also moments of substandard yet highly rewarding humour.

Campsites were sparse along the Wiltshire section of the canal, so after seeing a bed and breakfast sign outside The Cross Keys at Great Bedwyn, we decided to call it a day. The two-street settlement – reportedly the site of a great battle in 675AD – was quiet and comprised the usual services of a rural village in South England: a post office, a bakery and two pubs.

We entered The Cross Keys, fronted with a chalkboard of daily specials and large sash windows, to learn that the building had a ghostly past. Susan, the owner of the pub, had a reassuringly glowing smile and weathered cheeks. 'But don't worry,' she confided with a Midlands accent, 'we've not seen it for some time, and all it does is open and close doors. Now, tea?' she digressed.

Not for the first time, we accepted the offer of a hot drink out of courtesy and were left by a fire that danced amber and black, its licking flames warming the sleeping bodies of Hendrix and Dylan, the pub's resident dogs. Great Bedwyn's history hung from the walls, with paintings, photographs and the wooden spokes of a horse-drawn cart, whilst the ceilings were slatted, like the ribcage of a carpenter's whale, with seventeenth-century dark oak beams.

Through the bar and up a set of creaking stairs, Susan showed us to a room of sloped floorboards and jaunty dado rails. 'This is where the ghost was last seen,' she warned with raised eyebrows.

After a moment's rest, I found the bathroom, leaving Jake staring vacantly two metres from the television at a surfacing blue whale, with David Attenborough's soothing words in his ears.

I draped a wet Ted over some chairs and then stepped into the hot shower to feel the water soothing my aching body. Over the previous weeks, both Jake and I had worked tirelessly to prepare our bodies for the journey ahead, carrying twenty-kilogram rucksacks filled with water bottles wherever we went – to work, the shops, and even the pub. As I hobbled awkwardly out of the shower, I began to think that perhaps our efforts had been futile.

Disgruntled at my accidental use of all the hot water, Jake's mood was quickly remedied as a knock on the door saw Susan bearing bowls of hot soup and bread rolls.

'This is on the house.' She spoke softly, with an expression of empathy as she placed the tray on the bedside table. 'I know how you feel. My sister, Angie, and I walked from Land's End to John O'Groats a few years ago.'

'Really?' Jake exclaimed. 'Were you as wiped out as we are now?'

'Every day.'

'I'm not sure if that's good news or bad.'

'Yes, well, at least it feels like you've put a good day in. And people were so kind to us on the path, which took away the aches and pains even more.'

'How far did you walk in the end?'

'Oh, 1,000 miles perhaps. Anyway, enough questions. I'll let you guys get some rest.' Susan bade us goodnight and shut the door behind her.

We were woken abruptly from our sleep by a rap on the door. I checked my watch to confirm the hour: 9.30pm. 'Hello?' I croaked timidly, not sure if I had dreamt the noise or, worse still, I had been woken by The Cross Keys' ghost. 'Come in.'

The door creaked open, and in the dim light I saw a head poke through the gap. For several moments, I assumed it to be Susan, but as my eyes adjusted, I realised that the lady bore subtle differences. 'You must be Angie?' I whispered, sitting up.

'Yes, that's me. Hey, I know you guys must be tired, but I think you ought to come downstairs. Something rather special has happened.'

'Special?' Jake queried.

'Yes. It appears that the teams from our pub quiz would like to donate their winnings to your charity. I think you should come down. They'd love to meet you.'

Half asleep and on tender feet, Jake and I slipped on our evening clothes – socks knitted by our Auntie Les, long johns, T-shirts and pullovers – and made our way downstairs, entering the pub through the bar. A soft hum of chatter, followed by light applause, greeted us. Then, as we stepped further into the room, heads turned and people stood. Welcoming hands were thrust towards our sides. I moved from one outstretched palm to the next, only at the final shake realising that mine were trembling with gratitude.

We didn't deserve this. The idea that the pub quiz would contribute a little money to the cause was enough of a gesture, but why such generosity towards Jake and me? We had only been walking for four days.

Angie leant through the crowd and tapped me on the shoulder. 'These guys have raised over £200 for you this evening.'

I was dumbfounded – verbally helpless in showing how beholden I was to these kind people. Our decision to hike through England's south could have been justified by this evening alone. How outrageously proud we felt of our homeland, and how well we slept that night when we finally returned to bed.

BLISTERS

'Have you got lunch for today?' Susan asked as we laced up our boots in the sun on the steps outside the pub door. We shook our heads and were subsequently handed a bag filled with lunchtime delicacies.

Angie was waiting down on the canal with her husband next to their red and white narrowboat. A final gesture of kindness saw her push a bunch of bananas into my hands. 'They'll give you energy.'

I strapped the fruit to the outside of Jake's olive-green pack. Then we waved goodbye, following a pretty string of primroses that lined the water's edge eastwards.

'I'll write a piece on you in the Bedwyn newsletter,' Angie cried out. 'And you're welcome back anytime!'

Angie and Susan were what Jake and I had come to know as 'Trail Angels', an American term which we had discovered when researching long-distance walks in the United States, referring to kind-hearted people set on treating hikers and pilgrims, with no motive other than to ease the burdens of the path.

Over the following few days, I thought often about the people who had supported us during the preparation of our walk, and how many more it might take to drag us to Menton. Trail Angels, to me, were not only generous strangers but also my family, my friends and, undoubtedly, Claudia who, after meeting me in the fading days of summer half a year earlier, had stuck by my side with an abundance of love and support. Trail Angels were those who told us we would make it, and, perhaps more significantly, those who reminded us that persistence without enjoyment was more of a failure than to reach the sea without a smile.

We skirted the northern fringes of Hungerford, leaving Wiltshire for Berkshire, before stopping to break at a point where the canal's muddy waters became suddenly translucent turquoise. I rummaged through the lunch bag Susan had given us, finding ham and cheese sandwiches which I ate while watching Jake stoop over the edge of the grassy bank to observe the swimming frogs. Large tussocks of bouncing grass bathed their thirsty roots in the clearing waters. Decorated with colourful aquatic weeds, the roots were the corals of the canal.

Rain came as afternoon set in, soon accompanied by groans of thunder, infecting us with an anxiety which we had always known we would suffer. All that we owned was in our packs – home, finance, food, literature – and we were distinctly aware that a dampening of these items could lower the spirits. But rain was inevitable, and we pulled our orange waterproof covers over our packs, knowing that it would be a procedure well-practised by the time we reached the Mediterranean.

Concentric rings rippled where the raindrops met the water, and leaves sprang cheerfully with each received drop. I was certain, as their melodies held strong, that the birds felt rather more partial to the shower than Jake and I did.

Gradually, the storm subsided, and soon only strands of cirrus clouds remained. It was then that I remembered the growing blister on my heel. I slipped off my right boot to reveal a large red patch just below my ankle. The skin at the centre was the texture of wet tracing paper. Preventative measures were required.

To the likely dismay and judgment of the threads of oncoming walkers, I was forced to replace the abrasive boots with my campsite sandals – visually inoffensive until slipped over a pair of white walking socks. I was deeply appreciative of Jake, who found the courage to tread for eight kilometres alongside such a patent faux pas, through the populous town of Newbury and on to the industrial estate of Thatcham.

Said to be the oldest town in Britain, Thatcham did well to hide its history amongst a heap of A-roads and warehouses. We passed through the estate briskly (as briskly as was possible in socks and sandals), before veering away from the main road, up through a field and towards the hilltop mansion of Colthrop Manor.

'We're planning to be on the path for five months and don't have a lot of money. Could you do us a deal?' I asked after ringing the bell on the front door. Mariola, the owner of the Georgian house, was very accommodating and knocked five pounds from our bill. Even so, we were aware that this was our second bed in as many nights – an expense we would have to curtail if our funds were to stretch across Western Europe.

Pushing our bank balances to the back of our minds, we quickly settled in, acquainting ourselves with the room's simply outstanding multifunctional shower. It sang, steamed and shot jets of water at my body from every angle imaginable. In fact, it provided so many services, controlled by such an abundance of buttons, that I was unable to determine the temperature of the flow and subsequently ended up burning my bottom.

On a wet Friday morning, we left the last few warehouses of Thatcham behind us, noting that the buildings of Britain's oldest town looked even more youthful in the rain than they had a day earlier. In spite of the drizzle – which was now filtering through the gaps in my sandals and the fibres of my socks – an air of excitement filled our lungs as we traipsed along the towpath towards a dammed section of the Kennet and Avon Canal. After 160 kilometres of strong easterly progress, we arrived at lock number ninety-four.

We had grown used to the humble nature of the waterway and been thankful for its easy passage through the central counties. However, signs of London were creeping onto our map, and we knew that it was time to dip south and avoid the noise.

Within two days' walk sat the start of the North Downs Way, one of England's most renowned long-distance footpaths. With the compass needle pointing south, a somewhat ambiguous track took us away from the canal and through farmland into the county of Hampshire, where the sun split the sky and the rain was swiftly forgotten. A pair of roe deer bounded across the newly dried soil, kicking puffs of dust into the drying air as they fled for the cover of a nearby forest.

It was just past noon when we stepped out into the pre-Roman village of Bramley. We made our way along the main street, past pruned gardens and red-brick houses, arriving shortly at the Bramley Inn.

Almost immediately, we were ambushed by a woman with shoulder-length, barley-coloured hair, whose eyes were shadowed beneath a russet cap, and a man equally shaded, whose hat disguised a silver ruff of curls and deep blue eyes. It was our mother and her partner, Paul.

We spent the evening listening to the mellifluous plucks of a Spanish guitar at the Raven Hotel, responding to the same questions that Dad had asked a few days earlier. 'Yes, we're going to make it,' we said, with growing conviction.

'There'll be ticks, won't there?' Mum fretted, anxiously fiddling with the pearl-white earring in her left lobe.

'Where?' Jake queried.

'Everywhere. Do you not remember that one Danny got in his head as a child?' She looked over at me with advising eyes. 'You got it playing in a field of long grass in the Lake District. A big fat tick it was. They had to cut it out, after they'd tried to freeze and burn it out!'

'Well, we've got Vaseline and a penknife. If we spot any, we'll be sure to get them out safely,' I consoled her.

'And what about mountain goats?'

'What about them?'

'You'll have to be careful that you don't get charged, like Jake did when he was a little boy. And watch out for dogs too,' she added, raising her eyebrows. 'They can be very dangerous if they're trying to protect their property.'

'We'll watch out for charging goats and biting dogs, Mum,' Jake said. 'And dragons too.'

'I'm being serious. People die from these sorts of things. Just remember that there will always be a doctor nearby if you need one. You're insured too, so don't worry about the money.' Jake and I couldn't hide our smiles. Even if Mum was right, which in all likelihood she probably was, it was typical of her to worry.

'Well, find me a mother who wouldn't be apprehensive about sending her sons across Europe on foot,' she urged, before warning us that, on a sunny day, our Casio watches would become fire hazards.

Early the next morning, we said our goodbyes to Mum and Paul and made our way to Hook's train station to welcome Claudia, along with three friends – Phil, Beth and Johnny – all keen to sample life on the path.

It felt wonderful to have the company of such enthusiastic friends alongside us, each with the same objective – to reach Farnham by the end of the day – but with entirely different motivations. Claudia, forever an admirer of the little things, gleaned feathers from the trackside and threaded them into her dark ponytailed hair whilst Phil analysed the map with a scrutiny that epitomised his seemingly irrepressible hunger for discovery. Beth, who had given Jake and me our mascot, Hemingway, focused on the pint of cider that was waiting to be poured in a cosy Surrey pub, and Johnny played with a piece of wire he had found on the floor, perhaps a straightened coat hanger, with the kind of concentration that only Johnny could conjure. Jake, I assumed, was in the same state as me: lapping up the companionship, for we knew it might be an occurrence seldom repeated as the months passed by.

Deep in conversation, Phil and I found ourselves several furlongs ahead of the others, the resonations of their laughter turning a horse's head and a rabbit's ear as we made our way through Surrey's docile farmlands and sleepy hamlets.

'So, do you feel like you're into it now?' Phil asked, the map case swinging about his broad shoulders with each striding step.

'I think so. We have a rhythm, or a routine at least. When we started, we kept wishing we were a few weeks in, you know, so it felt like walking was our lifestyle. That's where we want to be. And, to be honest, if it wasn't for all you lot reminding us of home,' I joked, 'I think we'd be getting there.'

'I hear you,' Phil chuckled. 'Speaking of visitors, if you make it to the Alps, I'd love to join you for a few days.'

'If we get that far, that'd be awesome. I'm sure we'll be sick of each other's company by then. Hey, maybe you could be our yak? You know, give us a bit of a break from all the weight. In return, we could treat your blisters?'

'It's a deal!'

THE NORTH DOWNS WAY

'You're going the wrong way,' a frizzy-haired lady shouted from her upper window as Jake and I, alone once more, turned down a residential road just thirty seconds after beginning the North Downs Way. The amused lady pointed us along a smaller street which led out onto a stony track and down to an engraved bench by the banks of the River Wey: 'North Downs Way National Trail, 153 miles (245 kilometres) to Dover.'

'Look, a bluebell!' Jake cried, crouching to confirm his discovery. 'Spring's arrived!'

One flower soon became two, and two a cluster, until by the time we reached the northern trees of Crooksbury Common, the bunches had merged entirely, sweeping the forest floor with a quilt of violet-crested shoots. Jays arched under the budding branches, deer grazed, and a fox – fiery and intrepid – stepped boldly across the path with the sun at twelve shining down onto its fur.

Without the social anaesthetic of our friends and family, the aches and pains of the path had returned, not least with a growing discomfort that had begun to niggle at Jake's left ankle.

We were, by no means, strangers to injury. A life of sport and the outdoors had inflicted numerous muscle pulls, back problems and broken bones upon our bodies. Not long before we left Bristol, I had broken my hand in three places playing football, resulting in the insertion of a metal plate and seven screws. Jake, meanwhile, had been subjected to a round of steroid injections with just weeks to go before our departure in a bid to strengthen a recurring knee problem. 'Now,' his doctor had said with a studious tone following the treatment, 'I am required to advise that a 3,000-kilometre hike is probably not the ideal remedy for an injury of this kind. Of course, I don't expect you'll listen to me, but that is my recommendation.'

But an injury at home was not the same as an injury on the trail. A bad ankle could be the difference between achieving the adventure of a lifetime and going home early. Jake became despondent, in his familiar stubbornness staying quiet rather than verbalising his pain.

'Do you want to take a photo?' I asked him, as the path rejoined the willow-flanked banks of the River Wey just south of Guildford.

'No.'

And that was that. Jake loved photography. I knew this rejection meant he was struggling.

With my brother limping miserably at my side, we left the waymarking of the North Downs Way and moved silently through Guildford's bustling centre, soon becoming lost amongst a maze of clothes stores and cafés. We stopped several times to ask strangers for directions, on each occasion being pointed back along the road from which we had just come, until eventually, with the aid of a few Horse and Groom regulars, we found the Yew Tree bed and breakfast tucked down a nearby side street.

It was a comfortable lodging, and we quickly made ourselves at home, grateful for the bounty of food, the deep enamel bath, and a slightly peculiar documentary about a herd of homicidal elephants which appeared, quite miraculously, to medicate Jake's damaged ankle.

Two orange ear plugs lay on Jake's pillow in the morning. Assuming I had subjected him to a night of snoring, I fashioned a braided loop by way of apology, tethering it to a zip that had broken on his pack several days back. It turned out the culprit wasn't me at all, but a burly roadworker from next door whose display of guttural gasps and high-pitched whistles had reverberated throughout the night.

Relieved of all snoring guilt, I revelled in the April sunshine as we navigated empty golf courses and woods of box and yew. Jake's limp had all but vanished, and he rolled his T-shirt sleeves up over his shoulders. 'Dan, guess what?'

'What?'

'This is our tenth day of walking.' I could hear the pride in his voice. 'Double figures. It's by far the furthest I've ever walked.'

'Further than the South West Coast Path section that we did?'

'Definitely!'

'That was a tough walk.' I sighed, thinking back to the training hike we had completed five months earlier.

In the darkening days of November 2012, Jake and I, along with Mike, a fellow geographer and hiker who I had met whilst studying at Plymouth, agreed to go on a training walk. Physical preparation for our trek to the Mediterranean had been minimal – we had both done one or two multi-day hikes before, and we owned a sleeping bag each, but that was about it. Keen to assess our gear and bodies, we chose to walk from Falmouth to Plymouth, a 125-kilometre section of England's longest waymarked trail, the South West Coast Path.

The weather was atrocious and the endless peninsulas ensured that with each knee-jolting descent came an equally arduous, thigh-burning climb. We were shocked at our lack of fitness but knew that, with the right training over the coming months, it was something we could overcome. Of greater concern was the suitability of our gear. So when we arrived at the first campground, dripping wet and chilled to the bone, and were offered a luxurious yurt free of charge by the kind-hearted owner, we couldn't help but feel a little guilty as we left our tents in our bags and happily accepted. 'I know we should be testing our gear in the rain, but this is rather nice,' I had said. 'Perhaps we'll get another chance tomorrow.'

Sure enough, after a blissful night's sleep next to a snapping fire, we faced three days of torrential rain and swirling wind, finally arriving into Plymouth with cauliflower toes, which quite frankly smelt as bad as they looked. Nonetheless, the preparatory walk had achieved its goal: we had been taught some valuable lessons. We learnt that single-man tents are restrictive and antisocial – Jake, in his slim single-man tent, spent most of the three nights trying to understand the muffled chatter coming from the two-man tent in which Mike and I slept. We discovered the heavenly relief of talcum powder on pruned toes at the end of a long day in the rain, and the waterproofing qualities of plastic bags. We decided that carrying a day bag on your front not only looks ridiculous but jeopardises back stability, and, finally, regardless of how much you like them, it's never a good idea to pack a kilogram of carrots.

Jake was in a mathematical mood and, having remembered the torridly damp South West Coast Path experience, continued to fractionise. 'We're one sixteenth of the way to the Mediterranean, or less even, and by the time we reach Folkestone we'll be one eighth of the way there!'

For the next few days, we trod the spine of the North Downs chalk ridgeline, where sheep, cattle and rabbits maintained the grasslands and heaths. Farm fires sent soft scribbles of smoke into the air, meeting the April sun and hazing the surrounding hills, whilst the delicate purple thimbles of harebells flickered. We spent a night in the garden of Tanners Hatch Youth Hostel, where a dusk walk led me into the National Trust grounds of Polesden Lacey. I jumped the fence and sat alone in the amber-dusted gardens of the Edwardian house. Light refracted through the wings of flies – irritants by day, magical Diptera by dusk. The night-time calls of a tawny owl comforted me back to the tent, where I found Jake immersed in a deep sleep.

The following night, we were forced into our first wild camp after a campsite owner told us, 'We don't allow tent pitches until the high season.' Initially exasperated, we found a beautiful spot two minutes later amongst holly, beech and bluebells in Furzefield Wood. We were so close to the campsite that we could hear the clanks of cooking utensils coming from the static homes, alleviating our isolation and adding comfort to the pitch.

Jake sat with his back to the trunk of a large, moss-hugged beech tree, resting his eyes as dinner time passed. With his lightly freckled face bathed in the forest's half-light, he looked so utterly relaxed that I didn't dare disturb him. Instead, I listened to the song of the robin and the great tit, and watched ants crawl across my legs. Then my eyes fell upon the curled tip of a shooting fern: the foetus of the forest waiting with the rest of spring's patient organisms to stretch its newborn limbs.

OLD GIT WIT

The melodious warbles of the blackbird woke us, and were soon joined by the robin and the wren. A heavy mist covered the silhouetted branches above our heads as we crawled from the tent.

'Fifty minutes,' I announced after pulling my bag over my shoulders. 'That took us fifty minutes to pack away. We're getting quicker.'

Delighted with Ted's first free night, we left the flattened twigs and the forest's resident birds to rejoin the sunken lanes and well-trodden bridleways of the North Downs Way, pulling us clear of the morning fog.

Pasture gave way to forest, and forest opened up to more pasture, where kestrels hung from invisible threads above their grassy hunting grounds, and bundles of soft marjoram leaves scented the air. We climbed a steep road fringed by ivy-strangled oaks, and celebrated at the top of the ascent with an apple. Jake, never a man to waste food, ate the entire fruit, core and all, nearly dying as he choked on the stalk.

I too was experiencing an unpleasant misfortune, although certainly less life-threatening than Jake's gasping splutters – I was losing hair. Not from my head, but from my ankles, the insides of my thighs and, more unsettlingly, not far from my groin. It appeared that I was balding wherever fabric and movement combined. If nothing else, the gradual epilation at least gave me the opportunity to experiment with the lubricating qualities of our small pot of Vaseline, finally justifying the twenty grams of weight that it added to our packs.

Feeling a little sorry for ourselves, we decided we deserved a night indoors. As Surrey became Kent, we diverted from the waymarkers and made our way down Chestnut Avenue. A few minutes later, we arrived at The Old Farmhouse, an aptly named sixteenth-century brick and flint building, where we were met by the owners, Roger and Carol, a well-spoken couple whose cheeks were flushed bronze.

The dining room and kitchen, indented with deep inglenook fireplaces, were spread with ornate rugs and low timbered ceilings, both cluttered with antiques of English charm, most notably a proud grandfather clock that had been chiming every hour on the hour since 1740.

Upstairs, two fluffy, white dressing gowns lay waiting for us on our beds. Absorbed by the soft, comfy cotton, I sipped on a steaming cappuccino whilst reading *Old Git Wit*, a book from the house library, in which Helen Hayes had written, *'If you rest, you rust.'*

I was not an old git. However, after a night of outrageous comfort – which included a scalding, candlelit bath, multiple cappuccinos and hot chocolates, and a twelve-hour sleep – followed by a delicious breakfast of smoked salmon and eggs, I felt that perhaps we had rested too well, too long, too luxuriously. I was keen to lace my boots. Jake glanced briefly across the table, confirming that he too was ready, so I pulled my wallet from my walking shorts and began to sift through it for the necessary notes to settle the bill. Putting her hand across my wallet, Carol passed me a note:

Danny and Jake,
Eighty-five pounds to be donated to WaterAid,
Carol and Roger

The idea of rusting had got to us, and our legs moved quickly through the sodden grass, past fields of broad-leaved dock and seeding dandelion. On another day, the nearby Down House, once home of Charles Darwin, would have lured us in. However, not even *On the Origin of Species* could have inspired a diversion today, as a volley of diagonal rain swept onto our numbing faces.

We moved briskly from one wood of oak and beech to the next, climbing to the crest of the chalk Downs before dropping once more to the valleys below. When afternoon came, the rain subsided and streaks of warming sunlight cut through the empty clouds. The forest floor glimmered with a patchwork of bluebells, snowdrops, archangel and garlic, and butterflies twirled in the drying meadows.

'Do you think Doritos are crunchier than Kettle Crisps?' I asked Jake whilst we lunched on a colossal pork pie atop a grassy hill, looking south over the rooftops of Dorking.

Jake momentarily contemplated. 'I think we may have run out of conversation already, Dan.'

A rabbit emerged from a nearby hedge and sniffed the air. I considered Jake's point.

'Doritos,' Jake muttered several minutes later. 'Doritos are definitely crunchier, aren't they?'

Three consecutive nights in the tent correlated with an increased consumption of instant mashed potato and two-minute noodles. Additional energy was gained from an ample supply of tent snacks – usually sweets, crisps and biscuits – which we ate in the comfort of our sleeping bags. We slept before the sun sank and woke gratefully with the birds, beginning, as much as was possible in Surrey's empty campgrounds and village-studded trails, to attune more closely with the wildlife that surrounded us.

On one particularly serene morning, where droplets of dew covered the landscape, I sat with my legs outside the tent porch and read a poem that Claudia had sent me: *Stopping by Woods on a Snowy Evening* by Robert Frost.

With Claudia's voice bouncing around the walls of my head, I looked at my naked feet, cold and white in the crisp morning air. The night before leaving Bristol, she had decided to paint the small toe on my right foot with a lick of pink nail varnish by way of recording time. The gloss shone garishly in the light. Already, I could see that a distinct gap of unpainted keratin had opened

41

up between my cuticle and the lower end of the pink varnish. In terms of nail growth, we had been walking for just over half a millimetre.

Jake also had a body calendar, courtesy of his girlfriend Rose who had run a pair of clippers over his head the day before our departure, leaving a pile of brown strands on the conservatory floor. Every now and then, he would pass his fingers through his hair and say, 'I think it's getting longer.'

One day on, as light rain fell and our path crept up to the southern boundaries of Greater London, we began to notice unavoidable evidence of the swinging city. From a viewpoint on a hill just south of the unfortunately named village of Knockholt Pound, we were treated to a glimpse of London's central business district. Canary Wharf, the Gherkin and the needle head of the Shard strove for the clouds through a soup of miasma. Along the outstretched tendrils of the M25, the M26, the M2 and the M20, cars moved in slow motion, conveying commuters into Western Europe's largest metropolis.

With the growing urbanisation, we increasingly found ourselves tramping along A-roads, beneath concrete flyovers, and through the overflow of north Kent's expanding towns. Along the A20, we cut through the heart of Larkfield, named after the flocks of skylarks found in the surrounding fields. But, despite the promise of the town's name, we couldn't have left Larkfield quicker, after receiving a bout of verbal abuse from a mob of teenagers in a Vauxhall Corsa. With the car skimming the kerb of the pavement, we were forced into a roadside bush, robbed of the chance to respond to the jeers.

'What tossers!' Jake said, as we edged away from the town. 'Well, I'm never coming here again!'

'Wow, you really know how to reap your revenge,' I joked. 'But, yes, tossers.'

Eventually, the path leached away from buildings, reuniting us with rural Kent as we followed a wide dirt track through White Horse Wood, where woodpeckers hammered, and crab apple and oak grew alongside birch and ash.

'Are you feeling it again, Jake?' I asked after a few minutes of silence.

'Yep.'

'I wonder what it is?'

'Dunno. I guess we're just more tired at the end of the day,' Jake proposed, referring to the lull that typified many of our afternoons on the path. 'In the morning, we're fresh and the light is nice, more wildlife too. I guess all those things distract us, and in the afternoon we have camp on our minds.'

We were both relieved to see a sign just beyond the small village of Charing: 'Dunn Street Farm Camping'. A series of wooden pens with bleating spring lambs and several foraging goats led us up to a gate. Pushing through the field entrance, we plodded heavily towards the brow of the hill, stopping abruptly as we reached the crest.

A huge white canopy, supported by large timber poles and thick ropes, sat in the middle of the field. Three elaborate oak shields, each embellished with emblems of rearing horses and intricate crowns, hung above a gap in the tent, through which I could make out a long wooden table topped with a gallimaufry of food and drink. Men, women and children stood about the buffet, some prattling with their neighbours, whilst others played and danced. Away from the marquee, a crowd had formed around two figures moving quickly from side to side. It was then I noticed that the men had swords, and every person in the field was dressed from head to toe in medieval clothing. A whole minute must have passed before I turned to Jake, whose expression was a twist of surprise, confusion and intrigue.

'Um, do you think we can just go over there?' I questioned timidly, pointing to a corner of the field away from the jousting blades. We began to creep towards the hedge, still unsure if we had just gatecrashed a medieval community yet to be discovered by the world.

'LARP!' a man shouted, running aggressively towards us. Bearded and with a sword under his leather belt, I deemed the attacker to be a genuine threat to our lives and began to reach for the sandals that hung from my pack, with my method of defence presumably being some sort of flurry of offensive slaps. But, as the aggressor drew closer, I realised he was smiling and his blade was wooden.

'LARP! We're a LARP group. Sorry, we've sort of taken over,' he said, catching his breath with one hand on his hip and the other weakly grappling at thin air for some sort of imaginary support.

'No, don't worry. We were just a little confused. Is this a campsite?' I asked.

'Oh yes, it's a campsite. Your best bet is to pitch over there.' He signalled to the far corner of the field.

'OK...thank you. Sooo...?' I hinted for an explanation.

'Sooo...?'

'So, what is this?' I eventually blurted. 'I mean, what are you guys up to?'

'Oh sorry, I didn't even explain,' the man bumbled with a sincere tone. 'We're running a LARP. It stands for Live Action Role-Playing. We come here every year – sing, dance, whatever people want to do, but in character. We're just finishing off now actually.'

'Oh,' Jake said, his confused face now a little less distorted. 'Like fancy dress?'

'Kind of,' he replied politely, though I'm pretty sure a different response was running through his head: 'No, not like fancy dress. Fancy dress is for children. Why do people always say that? This is role-play, for adults, you ignorant morons!'

'Oh, sounds like fun.'

'It is. Anyway, been nice talking. I must go!' And with that, he went.

True to his word, the tables, chairs, canvas and poles were efficiently contorted into a number of cars that left the campground in dribs and drabs until all that remained was us.

With our entertainment gone, we settled into a well ordered chain of tasks refined over the previous two weeks of walking. Once the camping spot was determined – based on ground firmness, slope and view – we pitched Ted, and then filled him with roll mats, sleeping bags, warm clothes and books. As I showered, Jake rested, making the most of his time alone by jotting a few notes in his diary or examining our maps. An exchange of roles then saw Jake wash as I began to prepare dinner. Noodles, instant mashed potato or couscous were the popular choices, not for their taste but for their minimal weight in our packs, low cost, and quick cooking times. We ate outside the tent unless the rain fell, discussing the day or abstaining from conversation altogether when our surroundings spoke to us. The dishes were then washed or, if water was scarce, wiped with our yellow Shammy cloth. With the evening chill, we found refuge inside the tent, dragging the rest of our gear into the relative shelter of the porch and covering it with the two orange rain covers from our packs. We then had until 7.30pm to enjoy a number of tent activities – journal writing, eating and reading (we had two books, *Clear Waters Rising* by Nicholas Crane and *Into the Wild* by Jon Krakauer) – after which the dimming of daylight obscured our vision and lulled us to a deep sleep before the bells chimed eight.

GOODBYES

Our route through Europe had been plucked from an almost infinite labyrinth of footpaths that etch the topsoil of the Continent. Whilst rummaging through a section in Stanford's map shop in the centre of Bristol six months earlier, we had learnt that the longest footpaths, which comprise hundreds of smaller trails, are known as E-Routes, established by the European Ramblers Association in a bid to encourage cross-border walking. Of the many routes, it was the E2 – running north to south through Western Europe – that attracted our attention. 4,850 kilometres in length, the route comprises many of the areas Jake and I wished to hike through. With the added incentive of a traverse of the Alps and a spectacular finish on the shores of the Mediterranean Sea, the E2 was the perfect backbone for our trip. A purist hiking the E2 trail would have first tied their boots in Galway (though the route through Ireland is incomplete) and would have half a dozen weeks of walking under their loose-fitting belts by the time they reached the E2 signpost that we now stood beneath, midway through the Kent countryside.

After a quick photo shoot with the blue and yellow emblem above our heads, we continued on, dodging the swinging nine irons of the Downs' prim golf courses, and passing the wrought-iron gates of scores of lavish houses and pillared estates.

Approaching the village of Wye, we stopped at the sight of a hillside carving, not dissimilar to Jack the Painter's horse seen a week earlier in Wiltshire. However, unlike Jack the Painter, the students who had cut a huge crown into the chalk hillside of the Wye College Estate to commemorate Edward VII's coronation in 1902 had finished the job.

We sat in a strong breeze above the chalk figure and watched as a toy train shuffled through the checked crops of the valley below. Closer to our pew, the wheat fields folded with the wind, the breeze making the invisible evident like watercolour on a damp page.

'What's that?' I said, standing suddenly and pointing south.

'What?'

'Over there, on the horizon. Can you see?' I squinted to reveal dozens of rotating blades, each planted into a grey nebula on the horizon. 'Wind turbines,' I confirmed. It took me several seconds to acknowledge the significance of the enormous offshore structures. 'And the sea! We can't be far from Dover now!'

Jake's eyesight was poorer than mine but he seemed happy to trust my observations, so I joined in his celebratory dance, stopping moments later as a particularly flamboyant twirl induced a mild yet worrying twist in my left knee.

With a cautious hobble, we left the Wye Crown as the glamorous manors of Kent gradually gave way to its more charming countryside. The smell of manure ran rich and sweet. Old wooden cowsheds with corrugated roofs became a canvas for a swift's shadow that lost focus as the bird arched away. We moved east, through islands of forest and beyond the conical rooftops of Kent's oast houses. I preferred this environment. It felt honest. And my affection for the area only grew as I read a tattered sign that hung with rusted nails on the decaying beam of a farmhouse gate: 'Horse owners are stable people'.

'Oh, I remember those roofs,' Mary said with her thick Essex accent. We sat at a table in the corner of the Kings Arms in Elham at the end of the day. Dad had driven from Bristol, collecting our grandmother, Mary, on the way, before meeting us for a farewell pint and a thorough education in the long and eventful history of Kent's hop industry.

'Yes, my parents used to take us on 'oliday there. Leave London for a few weeks and enjoy the end o' summer in Kent. We'd work in the fields, o' course. Not really an 'oliday, but the sun shone and people seemed 'appy.'

I loved Mary's stories. She had so many to tell and, in spite of just having turned ninety, could summon a sight, smell or sound from decades earlier without a moment's thought.

'Did you enjoy it?' I asked as my weathered cheeks began to feel the warmth of the pub.

'Well, we used to go down in a lorry, you see. And we didn't have a suitcase, no! We were, well, we were poor. We used to wrap our clothes in a sheet, all bundled up, and throw it in the back of the lorry as we climbed in.' I could tell Mary's mind was not in the Kings Arms amongst the timber beams, beer-stained carpet and table stools, but in the back of the hot, dusty truck as it rumbled through the smog of London and south-east towards Kent.

'We camped, which o' course meant we needed to take a bed. Mum would roll a mattress. Then we'd use it to cover the floor. When we came to going 'ome, it was all mucky. Don't know what Mum did with it. Cleaned it, I guess. She did those sorts of things.' Mary paused briefly, marking her glass with crimson lipstick as she sipped her red wine before a hint of a smile crept across her face. 'Oh, I didn't like it. I used to 'ate it, in fact. I wasn't much good at it. Esther loved it, my sister. She used to sit on the bin and pull 'ops over her shoulder.'

Agricultural mechanisation in the 1960s soon rendered hard-working holidaymakers such as Mary redundant, meaning they had to go elsewhere to enjoy their holidays – something I'm sure Mary was pleased about.

'All this talk of hops is making me thirsty,' I exclaimed. 'I need a drink!'

A burly chap with dishevelled sandy hair and cider-veined cheeks propped up the bar, eyes squinting and mouth curled, the kind of glare that only a local could muster. His gaze fell upon my feet, at which point I remembered that I was wearing my sandals over the pair of thick woollen socks, striped maroon and brown, that our Auntie Les had knitted me for Christmas. 'Nice socks,' he grumbled sarcastically, returning to his pint of bitter as I scarpered away from the bar.

'Your grandmother seems particularly amazed by your haircut, Jake,' Dad whispered behind a hand as she left for the toilet. Usually the length of his thumb, Jake's new hairstyle made him look younger.

Mary had not stopped gawping at it since we met her outside the pub. 'Look at that 'air! I can't believe your 'air!'

'I suppose it'll be long and straggly again by the time you reach Menton,' Dad remarked. 'It'll be like you never left!'

'I can't believe his 'air!' cried Mary as she returned to the table. She shook her head with astonishment. 'I really can't!'

'He's done it before, Mum,' Dad urged.

'Has 'e? Well, I still can't believe it, I really can't!'

'This isn't easy, is it?' I said to Jake as Dad's car pulled away from the kerb with Mary's face pressed up against the window.

'I know,' he returned quietly.

Having both spent time away from our family before, we were used to saying goodbye, and the five months that we had put aside for the walk was far less than we had spent on previous trips. But, for some reason, this one felt different. It was hard to imagine the next time we would see Dad and Mary, and for this I was sad.

A short day's walk took us through the thinning countryside until soon the infrastructure of the south-east's coastline met our sides. If ever there was a sign that we were on the right track to the European mainland, the rattles, grinds and rings of the Eurostar were it. We crossed a splaying of tracks and motorways over a quaking bridge before continuing on to Folkestone, where a series of backstreets led us towards the town centre and the blissful smell of the seaside. We had reached the English Channel.

'Excuse me!' a voice called to us as we strode purposefully down Bouverie Road, several streets up from the water. We spun around to see a waitress emerging from the glass doors of Paul's Restaurant. 'Are you Danny and Jake?' A little perplexed, we confirmed the woman's suspicions at which she invited us in through the entrance to a dining area busy with customers. 'I hear you've walked from Bristol? Your girlfriends told us you would stand out!'

'Oh, is this Stay 2a?' I asked, finally remembering the name of the bed and breakfast that Claudia and Rose had booked us into.

'Sure is.'

'We were that obvious then?' I uttered to Jake, looking at our muddy boots, then smelling my shirt.

'I'll show you to your room,' the lady interjected as I withdrew my nose from my armpit. 'You might want a wash before the girls arrive.' On almost any other occasion this comment would have warranted a defensive, 'I beg your pardon?' But we gladly let the remark slide on the grounds that she was unquestionably right.

Claudia and I had been given the room 'Love Letters' whilst Jake and Rose had 'A Walk in the Park'. It all felt very relevant until I learnt that Stay 2a's third bedroom had been christened 'Burlesque' and featured a section of wallpaper strewn with a dozen half-naked women.

The room was spectacular – no doubt the consequence of letting the girls book the accommodation – and I felt a little guilty as I pummelled the dirt and grime from my clothes in the spotless ceramic sink.

Once the washing was hung, I scrubbed my body and dressed into my smart evening clothes: a blue checked flannel shirt; a thin striped sweater; a maroon T-shirt; thin canvas trousers, already too big for me as a result of my thinning waistline; black boxer shorts; knitted woollen socks; and sandals. Incidentally, I also wore my smart evening clothes at camp after a day of walking, and in bed when the night-time temperatures dipped towards freezing. All I could do to diversify my look was to layer the garments in a different order – sweater over shirt, shirt over sweater – not quite a full-body makeover, but a makeover nonetheless.

Claudia and Rose arrived at dusk, and for two days we were able to forget the pleasures and pains of the path. Claudia and I sat on the beach in the sun, pocketing pebbles and pieces of rounded glass whilst we talked and joked irrepressibly of things that neither mattered nor made sense. We ate wonderfully and shopped with little intent other than to absorb the company that would soon be torn from us.

With twelve kilometres of our England section still remaining, Jake and I threw our packs into Claudia's car and practically ran along the grassy clifftops from Folkestone to Dover. Reuniting with the girls two hours later, we wandered down to the water's edge as ferries chugged in and out of the world's busiest port.

Midway along the promenade, we found the official beginning/end of the North Downs Way – a line of shining marble engraved with the word 'FINISH' – and, to accompany it, a circular slab of iron that read: 'Farnham. North Downs Way National Trail. Dover. An inspirational journey through Kent and Surrey'. For most, this would have been a moment of elation, relief and a time to reflect. After all, we *had* just completed one of the great long-distance footpaths of England. But I didn't feel elated, and nor did Jake. I felt drained, devoid of any sense of satisfaction, emotionally on edge, and not ready to let go.

To watch Claudia drive away that night pushed my heart into my throat. My hands shook and my breathing wavered. Yet, with all the anguish that plagued me, I knew that our parting was unavoidable, necessary and unerringly motivational.

'I can't watch anymore, Dan. Can we go?' Jake said as the car disappeared off around the corner, Rose's hand still waving.

2

Dover to Antwerp

404 to 686 kilometres from home

THROUGH THE STRAIT OF DOVER

'Piles,' Claudia confirmed down the phone. 'It sounds very much like piles.'

'Really? Piles?' I blurted, suddenly lowering my tone as a dog walker turned his head to identify the foul-mouthed offender. 'Lovely,' I continued in a hushed voice. 'So, what exactly does that mean?'

'Are you sure you want to know?'

'Well, at least give me a vague outline. If I've got them then I should probably know what I'm dealing with,' I returned begrudgingly.

'OK. Well, the article I read used the word "swellings" a lot, along with "lumps" and "hanging". Apparently, "fourth degree piles can't be pushed back in".'

The words Claudia had carefully filtered from the webpage were, at best, unpleasant, and I soon began to feel nauseous at the thought of my condition. 'Alright, cool. Well, not cool, but I get the picture. I certainly haven't had to push anything back in, so that's good. Causes?' I queried further.

'It says here, regular lifting and straining, irregular bowel habits and low-fibre diets, and a lot of other stuff about being pregnant, but I assume that doesn't concern you. It says that you can often treat them by taking fibre tablets, so I suggest you do that.'

'Well, that certainly sounds like a less traumatic remedy than I was expecting. Sorry this had to be our first conversation since you left. Not exactly romantic.'

The pharmacist handed me a bottle of fibre pellets that looked and smelt like hamster food.

'I may as well have a couple too,' Jake said as we left the shop

51

and followed Biggin Street down towards the water. 'So, we're on the supplements. All we need now is to lose three-quarters of our gear and we can consider ourselves lightweight walkers!'

The day was already hot, and I could taste salt on my upper lip as we made our way along the seafront to the western side of the port. 49,000 tonnes of steel bobbed in anticipation whilst cars, vans and trucks manoeuvred slowly into the vessel's lower cavity.

We had initially planned to bridge the North Sea to Belgium via the Ramsgate-Ostend ferry, but just days before leaving Bristol had discovered the somewhat fundamental obstacle that the crossing only caters for freight and those travelling by car. Thus, our only option was to cross the English Channel from Dover to Calais and walk the four days to Ostend instead. After all, relatively speaking, four days was nothing.

We found a bench on the top deck of the P&O Ferry and watched as the Cliffs of Dover, striped black and white with flint and chalk, disappeared into the distance. More and more passengers joined us, each as jubilant as the next as they shoved the heavy fire door open to the outside world. Within ten minutes, the deck was jammed like a livestock market. Parents shouted, and children bleated. Hordes of people posed for cameras, clutching, hugging and caressing the blemished metalwork like it was a family member of their own. We must have been in the background of several hundreds of pictures; our disgruntled faces soon to be cropped out in a post-holiday editing session.

As the engines throbbed, my eyes drifted away from the bodies and fell upon a seagull that had emerged from behind the billowing smoke of the central funnel. I watched as it sat on the air current, only occasionally pushing its wings, until a voice interrupted. 'Where are you going?'

Jake and I looked up from the bench to see a fair-skinned man with sunglasses propped atop a head of short strawberry-blonde hair standing awkwardly beside us, like the new boy in school.

'Calais, then up the coast to Ostend,' I answered, one hand shielding my eyes from the glaring sun. 'And you?'

'Holland, on my bike. I'm Chris by the way,' he replied with a confidence that contradicted his demeanour.

'Holland?' Jake said. 'We're going that way too. Got a route sorted yet?'

'Well, it's northish from Calais, so I'll go that way.' It sounded like Chris had adopted the same navigational strategy that we had chosen for our stretch up to Ostend: keep the water on the left and the road on the right, and it should be impossible to get lost.

The Port of Calais wasn't designed for foot passengers. The vast infrastructure of the docks spread up the coastline, forcing us to stumble through a maze of tunnels and roads before climbing over numerous barriers and fences that led through deserted building sites and gravel car parks overgrown with weeds.

After some time, we emerged from an underpass onto a quiet slip road and pulled out our new map, squinting at the unhelpful cluster of lines and symbols that represented Calais.

'We could be anywhere,' Jake fretted.

Our last-minute decision to walk the coastline had left us poorly prepared. I remember rushing down to Stanford's map shop a few days before we left Bristol. 'I need maps!' I had demanded.

'Well, that's what we sell,' the middle-aged lady had returned dryly. 'You'll need to be a little more precise.'

'1:25,000 *IGN* maps for Calais and the coastline up to Ostend. Do you have any?'

The lady searched the computer database as I waited anxiously, finally concluding that, 'Nobody walks in that area, so we don't stock the maps. We do have road atlases though.' Both elements of this response were cause for concern: our coastal stretch from Calais to Ostend would not only comprise abandoned paths but inappropriate cartography too.

'*Je suis perdu,*' Jake said to a bearded man with dark aviator sunglasses as he thrust the 1:100,000 *IGN* road map through his car window. '*Où sommes nous, s'il vous plaît?*'

The man shrugged, perhaps unsure of our location, or more likely unable to decipher Jake's accent.

'You lost already?' a familiar voice called. Chris smiled down to us from the hard shoulder of the N216 motorway above the slip road. Pedalling slowly, he appeared to be unfazed by the grunting and revving vehicles that blurred behind him. 'North's that way.' He pointed straight ahead, after spotting Jake with his head and map in the stranger's car window. 'At least, I think it's that way anyway. I don't know!' He sounded almost excited at his

53

ignorance. 'You coming?' he bellowed, putting his foot down and accelerating away.

'Yeah, we're coming!' Jake yelled, having returned from the car. We began to scramble up the grassy road bank, grappling at the dry shoots until we reached the top. 'Enjoy your ride!' Jake shouted through the noise of the traffic.

'And you your walk!' Chris responded over his shoulder with a flailing hand dangling in the air.

With the raised motorway as a vantage point, we were able to gather our bearings. We had passed through the Strait of Dover, and the English Channel was behind us. This was a landscape dictated by the North Sea. A sweeping beach arched first to the east and then to the north, its berm backed with a string of sand dunes, their depressions thick with rich vegetation.

Our best bet, we decided, was to get to the beach as quickly as possible and then follow it until we were forced into another decision. We jumped the motorway barrier and then ran across the road and down the bank on the opposite side. Almost instantly, we were wrapped in thick scrub and knee-high grasses. Trails shot this way and that, each linked inextricably with the next.

'There's a lot of rubbish here,' Jake voiced at an unclear junction. I looked around and observed the piles of bottles, plastic bags and torn clothes. 'It's a bit weird,' he continued, eventually opting for the right-hand turn.

Through the dense foliage, I thought I saw the outlines of a makeshift tent, tattered and unkempt, but I couldn't be sure. We continued on quietly around the base of a dune, following its lower contours. A second shape appeared. A closer look revealed a large sand-dusted sheet draped over a bleached stick protruding from the ground. The shelter was surrounded with yet more rubbish.

'What was that?' Jake stopped abruptly.

We stood motionless as the sun beat down upon our loaded bodies. My pack felt heavy and my cheeks hot. I listened intently. Through the light breeze and hissing marram grass, I could hear voices.

'Let's just get onto the beach,' I told Jake. We began to move again, passing another two or three tents, each awash with scraps of metal and plastic. A particularly large shelter, made from blue tarpaulin and sheets of corrugated iron, creaked in the breeze, and

54

two men surfaced from within its shadows. Their skin was dark and weather-damaged, their clothes were dirty, and their expressions indefinable. Scared? Curious? Offended? Angry? We quickened our pace, increasingly desperate to escape the confined sand walls. But, instead, we found ourselves moving deeper into the squat, where more faces turned, each with the same perplexed look. We climbed on, warm sediment spilling in through the lips of our boots with each step, and crested another horizon, at which point my heart rate doubled. Camps huddled wherever space allowed, and groups of men, all men, lingered unobtrusively. One or two of the migrants spotted us and began to walk slowly up the rise of the dune, their calmness frightening and their intent unknown.

'That way.' Jake pointed, leading us away from the bodies. I followed Jake's hasty strides, winding over and around the energy-absorbing hills until, finally, we toppled out of the labyrinth and onto a hard flat beach, three kilometres east of the Port of Calais. The retreating tide had taken the North Sea out of sight. At pace, we walked across the seemingly infinite beach, deserted and barren.

'I need to stop,' Jake announced five minutes later as we approached a half-buried tractor tyre in the sand. He dropped his pack and began to pull at the sleeves of his red fleece.

I gazed over the desolate landscape. My eyes followed our footprints back towards the dunes where I noticed three figures standing on the sandy horizon. My heart rate had returned to a more familiar beat, and I began to think about the migrants. It was likely that they were waiting for their chance to sail to the divine shorelines of the United Kingdom: genuine refugees, desperate and tortured. They were not dangerous people, I knew that now. A torrent of guilt gushed through my body. Like us, they too were temporary nomads. Whilst we had chosen our path, it was likely that theirs was one of necessity.

'I hope they make it,' Jake said, as we left along the beach with the sun continuing its arc across the sky.

SAND UNDER FOOT

For four days, we traipsed along the beach as the sun beat down, one step sinking and the next not, energy leaching from our bodies. World War II bunkers lay toppled on the sand, their foundations dragged from beneath them by the dynamism of the dunes. We scrambled over the eerie ruins, discovering further buildings behind – shelters, barracks and an observation tower – each clad with graffiti and straddled with rusted barbed wire.

We passed fields of jellyfish polka-dotting the sand and crossed banks of razor clam shells that freed the smell of the sea as they crunched beneath our boots. On occasions, when the rising tide cut our route, we were forced inland. These were times of caution, for our map lacked the appropriate detail and our compass skills were still questionable. Relocating the shoreline thus brought relief and a less encumbered mind. Joy came, albeit quietly, whenever there was concrete underfoot, for we knew our step, allowing our muscles to relax. The pavement led us along esplanades, lined with hotels and *tabacs,* where shopkeepers advertised their postcards, papers and cigarettes with shouts and jingles.

'Everyone speaks English in France,' we had been informed by friends and family before leaving England. This was a hypothesis yet to be proven, for our broken French was summoned often and our confused shrugs perfected. With each town we passed – Grand-Fort-Philippe, Gravelines, Loon Plage, Grande-Synthe, Dunkirk, Bray-Dunes – came linguistic challenges, but so too the delights of a lunch stop of bread, sausage and cheese, and the beginning, it seemed, of our sandwich revolution.

Two days north of Calais, I saw Jake dart towards a sign, then turn to me with the most wonderfully euphoric smile. 'It's a *GR120* sign, the *Grande Randonnée*! We've found it!' On a wooden post beside him were two splashes of paint, a stripe of white above a stripe of red. The symbol represented the *Grande Randonnée* (GR), Western Europe's most prolific network of trails. Indeed, France alone has 100,000 kilometres of *GR* paths. It felt reassuring to know we were on the right track, so to speak, even if the subsequent waymarking of the coastal path did turn out to be, at best, vague.

'I think this is it,' Jake exclaimed to me a few hours later. 'The Franco-Belgian border.'

We were standing, rather indistinctly, nowhere in particular. There was sand, a few shells and the sea. We had crossed nothing, yet things felt different. People greeted us, '*Bonjour*' or '*Hallo*', and some even asked us questions, to which we invariably mumbled inappropriate answers. The streets were wider, cleaner, and planted with trees, whilst gardens flourished with flowers that scented the air.

'The dogs bark less here too,' I said to Jake. 'I think I like Belgium already.'

Campsites along the Flanders coastline were abundant, basic and cheap. However, unlike the English ones, we soon learnt that they didn't provide toilet paper. Folk would tuck rolls under their arms, or swing them proudly in loosely-clasped hands as they journeyed to the ablutions block. Some campers even had special toilet roll holders – portable, waterproof and designed with a hook to allow freedom to hang on almost any toilet wall, be it cubicle or long-drop. Unwilling to get caught short, we bought a multipack of toilet paper the following day, stuffing the hood of Jake's rucksack with a rather overambitious eight rolls of *Le Trefle*.

Our penultimate night on the coast was spent camped in the dunes at Koksijde, where we ate a floppy carrot that had been with us since England, and a packet of instant noodles. A period of do-it-yourself then followed as I sewed a button back onto Jake's popped shorts whilst he spread superglue over a hole that our plastic water bladder had developed earlier in the day.

The next morning, we scrambled up the hot sand of High Blekker, the tallest dune on the Flemish coast and, at thirty metres, the highest we would climb for another two weeks. After absorbing the new perspective, we descended into Oostduinkerke-Bad, a beautiful town of thatched roofs and flowerpot road signs built precariously into the sand. We stopped to watch an old lady pause to smell the perfume of a jasmine vine, her eyes closed and her smile sublime. Then we marched on, once more meeting the sea as the coastline began to curve north, away from its easterly trajectory.

'This has been a long day,' I huffed, as the sun began to drop. 'Sand makes me tired.' We had been walking for ten hours along beaches and over dunes, and were weary as we entered the suburbs of Ostend. My left knee was sore, grinding with each step, and the ache in Jake's soles had forced him to limp. According to our map, we were close to a campsite, but a quick spin on the spot revealed nothing but a jungle of apartment blocks and roads.

We sought help from an obliging lady in a nearby *pharmacie*, who was kind enough to circle a campsite on our map as she sold me a knee support. 'Now you both have one,' she chirped, nodding towards the white brace that wrapped Jake's knee.

'Oh,' Jake stuttered, looking down at his leg. 'I forget I'm even wearing it. I've had it a long time. Recurring injury,' he elaborated, to which the lady smiled sympathetically.

Frustratingly, the campsite was an hour's walk back towards the border, and it was dusk by the time we arrived at a huge plot of tightly packed caravans and motorhomes.

By the way the day was going, I was not the least bit surprised when a woman at the entrance told us that they were a sales company and had nothing to do with camping. 'Right, let's just get back into the city and pay for a hotel,' I told Jake, whose weariness was mounting.

'OK, but can we just go in the first one we see? I'm not in the mood to be choosy.'

After another hour of walking, we found ourselves back in the Ostend suburbs walking alongside a tramline where we spotted a promising-looking sign beneath a block of newly built apartments: 'Restaurant de Wandelaar'.

'*Wandelaar!*' I exclaimed. 'That means walker, doesn't it? That's us!'

Assuming that a cheap bed and hot shower were now simply a matter of time, Jake took a deep breath. 'I'll go.' He lifted a foot over the chain that separated us from the establishment. However, before I could grab him, a tired leg had hooked itself onto the metal rings, making him drop like a sack of potatoes onto the tramline below, the full force of his pack not far behind. Without a sound, Jake got up and, with blood trickling from his knee, walked slowly away. I figured he was screaming inside, 'Bed! I just want a bloody bed!'

It was not until we finally released our packs, after another hour of searching, onto the floor of a room in the Hotel Pacific that I realised Jake's true problem. 'It's my arse,' he said as he hobbled towards the shower and stopped by the door. 'I mean, yeah, my feet hurt and my knees are playing up. Oh, and my ankles are killing me, and my back and shoulders too. But it's my arse that's giving me the real problem.'

'Your arse? What do you mean?'

'I don't really want to talk about it, Dan. But I think boxer shorts were a bad idea. The material's kind of latching onto stuff. I think I need the scissors,' he said with a frown before closing the bathroom door behind him.

THE LAKE OF LOVE

We took a plastic bag down to the buffet breakfast and, between servings, filled it with sachets of Nutella, pots of yoghurt, croissants and fruit. 'It's easier to justify the money that we spent on the beds when lunch is included too,' I whispered across the table to Jake as he downed a glass of orange juice.

As with many of my overseas adventures, I saw our walk as an investment, exchanging money for experiences that we could relive fondly in our minds until the day we die. I had worked for almost three years in Australasia – picking apples in the foothills of New Zealand's Southern Alps and walking tourist camels on the northern beaches of Western Australia – with each job remembering that one more hour behind the wheel of the tractor, one more bucket of fruit or one more pruned tree would make life on our walk to the Mediterranean a little easier. We loved the thrift of camping, not to mention the wildlife and the fresh air, but sometimes a splash of money on the comfort of a bed and the reassurance of a roof was much appreciated. Still, one night in a bed could pay for a week's worth of food, and so, as I tucked the bag of goodies under my T-shirt and nipped quietly out of the dining room, I didn't feel as ashamed as perhaps I could have.

'Now I would walk 500 miles, and I would walk 500 more...' a man sang to us with a thick Dutch accent as he whizzed by on a recumbent bike, laid back and legs circling. We had joined the Kanaal Gent-Oostende, an artificial conduit connecting the Belgian coastline with Bruges a day's walk away, and beyond that the medieval city of Ghent, East Flanders's largest settlement.

The canal, wider and more pristine than the Kennet and Avon, was paralleled on each side by towering beech trees. Their rattling leaves blinked silver and green in the morning wind. Hundreds of small waterways fanned out from the main channel like the veins of a broadleaf, irrigating a quilt of arable and pastoral land that spread to the horizon. Perhaps this is Belgium in a nutshell? I thought as an enormous barge inched past us on the otherwise deserted waters.

'A lot of cyclists here,' Jake mumbled through a mouthful of newly replenished scroggin, now containing jelly beans, white chocolate, 'roll-over' (old scroggin) and, quite peculiarly, Bombay mix. 'Look at them all!'

Enticed by the straight, flat towpaths, bodies wrapped tightly in colourful Spandex flew past, some alone and others in teams of six or eight, shouting words back and forth. I couldn't understand the language and could only assume they were bickering over whose Lycra was the prettiest or the tautest.

Our route to Bruges was as the crow flies – direct and studded with small food-foraging breaks. We replaced the 1:100,000 *IGNs* that had guided us loosely up the coast with a new set of 1:50,000 topographic survey maps. The small-scale Belgian charts were detailed and informative, and we quickly formed the unsurprising hypothesis that an inappropriate map, such as the 1:100,000, would inevitably lead to anxiety. It felt good to be walking with more detailed cartography.

We approached Bruges from the north-west of the city, dropping away from the uneventful waters of the canal and into the curved streets of the Kristus Koning suburbs. The roads were narrow and cobbled, and pinched in the middle by a central gutter. Buildings bunched intimately on the roadsides, their overhanging terracotta roofs, four or five storeys up, shielding us from the afternoon sun. With each corner turned, the walls grew taller and the ways became busier. Pushbikes, mounted with wicker baskets and wide handlebars, accidentally sounded their bells as they rippled over the cobblestones between ambling pedestrians, whilst vans unloaded fresh fruit and vegetables, chinking crates of beer, and bags of bread into the restaurants and cafés that resided wherever our eyes fell. It was, for a local, just another day in Bruges.

'This place looks alright,' Jake said, stopping to analyse the price list outside the brick facade of a large hostel.

'You think?' I retorted sceptically. A reverberation of drums and generic guitar chords blared out from the building's large arched windows.

'Let's just check it out. If it's no good, we can go elsewhere.' I could tell that Jake was eager to explore the city, so accepted his proposal.

Tables and chairs cluttered the sticky floor, and the walls were packed with framed posters of Willie Kent, Phillip Walker and a host of other American blues artists. We made our way past a string of stained pool tables over to a circular bar, where the smell of stale beer oozed out from the stool cushions as we sat.

It must have been ten minutes before a brunette lady in the corner, who I had assumed was a customer, sauntered over to us. Her face was decorated with layers of make-up, through which I could just make out an expression of disinterest. She wore tight black trousers and a white shirt that I presumed, by the way her cleavage was being displayed, had been left in the dryer too long.

'*Bonjour, Madame, je voudrais un...*'

'A room?'

'Um, yes please, a room for two please. *Combien?* How much?'

'Fifty-five euros,' she responded bluntly, the smell of cigarette smoke piping from her mouth. As I looked to Jake to confer, I was interrupted for the second time. 'Everywhere else is full. There is a festival. So, do you want to stay or not?'

'Let's just take it,' Jake directed my way. 'Then we can get out and see the town.'

'OK, room seven,' she hissed, before dropping the keys onto the bar and returning to her table to light another cigarette.

The room was basic, but had its own sink and a view of the street below. The communal lavatories, however, were not quite as pleasant. After battling through a crowd of screeching teenagers in the hallway, most of whom had apparently just discovered alcohol for the first time, I found an empty toilet which opened out intimately into the throng. Without a lock, and with gravity pulling the door ajar, I was forced to lean awkwardly forward as I did my business, clinging to the handle as a succession of rattles, raps and yanks fell repeatedly upon the doorway.

'We may need wine tonight,' I told Jake as I closed the bedroom door, finally muting the cries of the howling youngsters.

Standing beneath a fluted black lamp post, forked like an oversized candlestick holder, we decanted a three-euro bottle of wine into two plastic bottles, so as not to offend, hid the evidence in a nearby bin, and then celebrated our day's walking with a hearty swig each.

The bulb above our heads flickered gently on, followed by a second lamp to our left, until soon Burg Square was glowing amber, road to roof. The streets hummed with the sound of chatter and the snap of cameras, their lenses drawn towards the six grand windows and embossed biblical figures of the Stradhuis, Bruges's fourteenth-century city hall. We watched a horse clip-clop by, pulling a wooden cart over the intricate floor. Holding the reins loosely in her palms, a lady with long brown hair and a straw hat steered the carriage through the crowds, bellowing out city facts to the overweight couple that sat behind her. The pair, who must have been profoundly uncomfortable bouncing over the corrugated ground, were red in the face and wobbled in their seats.

With the taste of cheap wine swilling around our mouths, we strolled lethargically down a side street, glad to be moving without the burden of our packs.

Soon, the alleyway opened out into a second square. Grote Markt, bigger than Burg Square, was framed with restaurants and cafés: their tables, chairs and aromas sprawled romantically out across the stone and towards the Belfry of Bruges – a medieval bell tower teetering eighty-three metres skywards.

In a moment of subtle rebellion, we bought a burger and chips from a takeaway at the end of a long line of exorbitantly priced restaurants, and then ambled from one waterway to the next, sipping on the vinaigrette-like wine as dusk birds hauled their final catches for the night. A heron tiptoed through the shallows, paused, and then shot its head through the surface, appearing moments later with a wriggling fish in its bill. With the sky a deep blue, we followed the dimly lit canal south, addicted to its mirroring waters, until we reached the Minnewater – 'the lake of love'.

The evening strollers had retired to their beds, and the lake was quiet, save for a distant laugh here and the *ting* of a pushbike there. We stepped onto an arched bridge and leant over its walls to stare into the treacle-coloured water as it ebbed quietly against the banks. The silhouetted branches of horse chestnut, oak, poplar and willow pulsed delicately on the lakeside whilst dozens of swans floated below on the opaque surface, near motionless with their necks upon their backs, white on black.

ASPARAGUS

The hostel had kindly added eight euros to our bill, assuming we wouldn't be able to resist their award-winning breakfast of a bag of white bread, a toaster and an empty coffee pot. Unwilling to leave the 'bed and breakfast' hungry, we stuffed a slice of bread into our mouths and left with several more wedged conspicuously into the pockets of our shorts.

It had not rained for five days and, as one drop of water tapped on my shoulder, then another on my hand, I began to feel a wave of energy percolating through my body. Dust sprang from the stone pavement, with each falling bead releasing that divine smell of rain on parched ground. The light peppering soon evolved into a downpour, and we dashed across Grote Markt, seeking shelter beneath the tarpaulin of a fruit stall.

Despite the weather, the Wednesday market was thriving with locals and tourists who browsed the colourful berries, bags of hanging citrus fruits, and the rotating chickens, with eyes eager for a bargain. We dodged the prongs of several jousting umbrellas, escaping the chaos via a small alleyway in the southern corner of the square, before crossing a humped bridge where I admired the resilience of sightseers who seemed determined not to let a little rain spoil their day. A canal boat tour shuffled towards us with two dozen purple umbrellas on board, each popped and adjoined with the next like a giant tumbled boysenberry. The brollies moved subtly in unison, following the guide's gesticulations as tracks of rainwater patterned their bulbous skin.

We left Bruges with the flat chimes of the city bells and, after a quick stock up in an out-of-town supermarket, joined a regional trail where strokes of red and yellow paint marked on gateposts, trees and walls took us east into the countryside.

We still knew little about the area we were walking in. After analysing the maps, it became clear that our route to Antwerp was set to be unorthodox, comprising an eclectic mix of regional *GRs*, canals, country lanes and roads which would, we hoped, lead us through West Flanders into East, and on to Belgium's second most populous city.

I often found myself drifting ahead of Jake on the path, and would turn every now and then to let him catch up. At first, I was anxious, assuming he was struggling. Maybe his knee was hurting or his ankle playing up again? I had a good understanding of Jake and knew that he would endure a considerable amount of discomfort before he voiced his anguish. But this wasn't a game of football or a day's walk. If he had a problem, I should know about it. 'You alright, Jake?' I asked tentatively, turning to stop once more until he was at my side.

'Yeah, bit thirsty though. Can you pass me the water?'

Jake carried most of the liquid in the water bladder on the back of his bag, forever watched over by Charlie, the beady-eyed clownfish mascot. I unthreaded the tubing from the elastic strap, pulled the nozzle over his shoulder and put it in his mouth. 'No, I mean, are you OK, your knee, your back, is everything OK?'

'Uh-huh.' He nodded, sending air bubbles through the blue tubing as he gulped. 'Why shouldn't I be?'

'Well...you're always behind me, aren't you?'

'I guess sometimes I am. Not always. But I'm smaller than you!' he announced matter-of-factly. Acknowledging my bemused face, he elaborated. 'My legs are shorter than yours and, therefore, so are my steps. I have to take more than you.'

In hindsight, this was a simple and logical explanation. Although we bear many similar features, Jake, at one metre and seventy-one centimetres, is two centimetres shorter than me. I started to watch his step against mine. From a synchronised stride, I noticed that his leading foot began to hit the ground moments before mine, until we were totally uncoordinated. I counted about 150 paces before our legs, once again, were striding like those of two well-disciplined soldiers. Based on an average step length of fifty centimetres (normally larger, but for the weight of our packs and the relief of the land, particularly in the second half of the walk) over a distance of 3,000 kilometres, I was due to take six million steps before we reached the waters of the Mediterranean. Jake, and his minutely shorter legs, would take 39,000 steps more than me, equating to an entire day on the path.

As we crossed from West Flanders into East Flanders, the land maintained its flatness. We cut through fields of Belgian Blue cattle and bands of quiet forest, leaving the red and yellow stripes of the regional trail for the *GR131*. With little in the way of altitudinal stimulation, I found myself looking at the ground with more purpose. Buttercups, daisies and dandelions grew opportunistically in the flooded meadows, between the cracks in garden walls, and under the cloven hooves of a bullock. And 'toilet plants' – a name that Jake, Jessy and I had conjured up as children to identify the peculiarly scented cow parsley – frothed with small white flowers along the roadsides and into the trees, where squirrels scampered and rabbits sniffed.

The rain began to ease in the afternoon, and soon all that remained of the storm were a few magnolia petals on the neatly trimmed lawns west of Maldegem. We sat for lunch on the side of the path and, for the fifth day in a row, ate a baguette, this time crammed with cream cheese and salami. The meal did little to satisfy my insatiable appetite, and I was forced, by Jake, to eat more scroggin.

'We will *not* go hungry,' Jake iterated. 'That's what we've always said. We're going to get blisters, back problems, and all sorts of aches and pains, but we are not going to go hungry.' This had been our philosophy from the moment we left Bristol. Food was the one constant that could satisfy us, the one luxury that we could look forward to no matter what the situation. We were even putting food ahead of water – a dangerous game, of course, but Jake and I had never been big on hydrating anyway. Food was our pleasure, our priority. But we were paying the price.

'Twenty kilograms is the point of significance,' Jake declared. 'Any less and it's manageable, sustainable. Any more and I start to feel it. I'm pretty sure we're over twenty now.'

'I heard that you can get away with carrying one third of your body weight,' I said. 'That would allow us a few more kilograms.'

'Well, I read that anything over fifteen is too much.'

'That's about the weight of our bags at the moment, isn't it? Until you pile on all the food, that is,' I added.

'Well anyway, it doesn't really matter what other people say. If you can carry it and you're not killing yourself, then it can be as heavy as you like. I reckon twenty kilograms is our tipping point, or mine at least.'

'We'd better eat more of this food then. I think we may have been a bit overzealous on the resupply!' I concluded, eyeing up the small bunch of bananas that swung from Jake's green pack.

We had not climbed a hill all day. In fact, after a brief assessment of the map, we learnt that we had stayed pretty much consistently at an altitude of five metres since leaving the coast, which was less than the climb from my front door back in Bristol to my bedroom at the top of the house. In spite of our lack of ascent, I was tired and my soles were sore.

We had been walking north for the best part of the day, and after crossing the wide levees of the Leopoldkannal, over a bridge and onto the opposite bank, we spotted a large red and blue sign on the roadside, clothed with a jacket of ivy that shuddered in the strong afternoon wind: 'Netherland'.

The village of Eede, lying just inside Holland's serrated border, comprised a small grid of characterless streets, like an empty noughts and crosses game devoid of symbols. We had heard that there was a campsite somewhere in town and followed the triangular tent icons, each of which was footed with the word '*Asperges*', down clean wide roads and alongside picket-fenced houses, their repetitive tones making me wonder if *Asperges* was indeed an almost literal translation.

'No, asparagus!' exclaimed the pursed-lipped lady at the campsite. 'It means asparagus. We grow it here and sell it in the farmhouse behind me.' Her accent was almost indefinable, and we were once again relieved that our limited Dutch – 'yes', 'no', 'hello' and 'thank you' – was not called upon. I looked over her wiry grey hair, and absorbed the bustle of workers behind, each dressed in a white apron and matching hat, calmly sorting the floret-headed sticks into piles of varying quality. 'We have white ones too. Yes, that's how we eat it usually. It's more tender and more tasty.'

'How do you grow them?' Jake queried.

'In the dark. We cover the shoots with soil and pull black plastic over the beds. Come and look. I will show you to your spot.'

We crossed a lawn, following the quick steps of the asparagus lady, before entering a small cluster of soft-needled pine. 'This will shelter you from the winds. They come from the south here and blow pretty hard.'

A couple of moments later, the trees opened out into a large field of dirt, their peaks and troughs rolling off towards a farmhouse in the distance.

'Over there,' the lady pointed to our right, 'we have wrapped the field in black lining.' Five or six men, Indonesians perhaps, were standing alongside one of the beds. Two of them pulled at the plastic whilst the remaining four gently cut the white shoots from the soil, clutching them delicately in their hands before placing them into a crate. 'They are the white asparagus. It's harvest time. May and June normally. And here,' she looked back at the deeply ploughed ground in front of us, 'here are the green asparagus.'

To me, the field looked entirely unfruitful. But once I saw one shoot, another came into view, and soon I could see thousands.

We washed our socks and underwear, and then hung them between two trees on a line of thin rope that we had found on the floor earlier in the day.

Whilst Jake voiced his pride in teaching himself a new slip knot, I stepped into the trough between two beds and ambled languidly along its line in the setting sun. Three crows jostled in the low light before departing for the comfort of a nearby fir tree. I looked back towards Ted and Jake. A chicken, no doubt attracted by our ample supply of biscuits and chocolate, tiptoed about the guy ropes and pecked the ground around Jake's feet.

On my walk back, I snapped a shoot from the soil and bit the head from the stem. The asparagus was sweet and juicy.

HOEVETERRAS DE VLIENTHOEVE

Violet clouds bowled above our heads, driven by a stiff breeze that saw us tug our woolly hats from our bags. Jake's was dark green – a useful garment when trying to camp imperceptibly amongst the trees – whilst mine was Persian blue – beneficial when being searched for by a mountain rescue team. I liked wearing my hat, when the weather permitted. It was comforting and protective, and it muffled the outside world. I often fell into a trance of nothingness, where my surroundings blurred and my mind went blank. These moments were neither good nor bad, but perhaps necessary. They gave me time to myself – something that was difficult to come by.

We had thought about taking a phone each. This would have allowed us to be more independent perhaps, but in the end I ditched mine before we left England, and Jake kept his so that we could call home from time to time. With just one phone, an old black-and-white-screen Nokia, and one set of maps between us, separation on the path would have been a bad idea. Thankfully, Jake and I had spent the best part of our lives together and were not afraid of sharing each other's company. Still, if a piece of headwear could give me a few minutes to myself then I was happy to take it.

We spent the first few hours of the day slapping boots to concrete, returning to Belgium as we strode uninterrupted and without the map alongside the Leopoldkannal. It was a pleasant waterway, with steep banks, towering birches and hard-working coots, flanked on either side by an unsurprising arable expanse. In the distance, I caught sight of a tractor and its devoted flock of gulls, whilst the ploughed furrows close to the canal were streaked with pink blossom.

By midday we had left the Leopoldkannal's protective tunnel of trees and dropped onto the *GR5a* where the southern prevailing winds reminded us of their brawn. Gusts loaded with dirt and dust whipped around our bare legs and pushed our eyelashes onto our cheeks. With hoods pulled up and hats folded down, we moved silently across the asphalt until finally, as the road veered east, we arrived at a junction. On the other side of the street, there was a small plot of land studded with young spruces, each surrounded by bedraggled Christmas decorations blown from their perches by the unrelenting winds. The only building in sight was a café that stood beside the out-of-date festivities.

Eating in establishments was not a practice we indulged in often. However, our recent trip to the supermarket on the outskirts of Bruges appeared to have left us overloaded with chocolate and under-supplied with bread. In terms of nutritional goodness, we were most certainly lacking. We craned our necks at the chalkboard on the wall, enticed by the perfume of fresh baguettes and mussels that exuded through the café windows. But before we could make up our minds, a man's voice stole our attention.

'Oh sorry, we don't speak Dutch. French? *Francais?*' I replied, knowing full well that a response of '*Oui, francais*' wouldn't have furthered conversational matters.

'You're English?' the portly man blared with a thick accent through a joyous smile. His large shoulders and even larger stomach were not quite hidden beneath a huge Hawaiian shirt, undone enough to reveal a freckled chest. Next to the man sat a lady of similar age, about fifty-five and, dare I say it, similar stature, who I assumed to be his wife, for she smiled as keenly as he. 'Where are you going?'

'Boekhoute.' I pulled the *Zelzate* 1:50,000 *IGN* from my jacket and pointed at the map.

'Argh, we just come from here!' beamed the man. 'We are from the Netherlands, on a cycling holiday.'

We spoke to the delightful couple for several minutes about our trip and theirs, in which time I decided that, despite their claims, they were in fact not on a cycling holiday at all, but on an eating and wine-drinking holiday, where a bike was their only means of legal transport for getting from one bottle of red to the next.

'Well,' the happy Dutchman continued, 'Boekhoute is six kilometres that way.' He lifted a swollen paw and gestured up the road as a whirl of dust spun through the air. '*Bon voyage!*' he boomed with a wave of his hand.

'Yes,' Jake agreed some moments later, 'I think they're definitely on a drinking holiday. Boekhoute is two kilometres from here, not six.'

Sure enough, half an hour later, we found ourselves approaching a half-erected marquee in a small town square next to an oversized red-brick church. Two men with sunken eyes and bristly chins watched our steps as they sat on a pile of wooden boxes, one with a cigarette hanging from the corner of his mouth, and the other swilling back a beer.

If we expected less attention after entering Dany's Snack, a beer café across the road enveloped with glossy green tiles and the rearing white bull of Belgium's Juliper beer, then we were very much mistaken. At a table by the door, we sat and analysed the picture menu, instantly choosing a pizza bread – an easy decision as the shiny white base topped with cubes of reconstituted meat and red pepper was the only option without an 'out of stock' cross through its photograph.

The room was not quite full, but huddles of old men, who I assumed made up half of Boekhoute's population, congregated tightly around two or three of the tables. They turned to look at us, listening in with curiosity as we ordered our lunch from a lady with scruffy hair and a flowery dress.

A wooden hatstand cloaked with jackets and faded flat caps stood by the toilet door which, in keeping with the male-dominated inn, read '*Homme*'. The walls were hung with scores of framed black and white photographs, each depicting a beaming cyclist; local legends, no doubt, perhaps some of whom were sitting across the room retelling stories from the good old days.

Ping! The lady opened the microwave and dragged the ready-made breads onto two plates, which were then swiftly brought over and dropped in front of us.

As I picked at the sweet dough, I noticed a woman in the corner of the room crying through her words. A man sat opposite, his wispy white hair waving from the heat of the radiator beside him. He seemed to be trying his best to console the poor lady, whose solemn face made me feel terribly sad.

We left Dany's Snack with an adopted sorrow, wishing that the feeling would pass, not only for us but so too for the grave-faced lady.

The day was growing late and, after crossing into the municipality of Assende, where threatening clouds began to crowd the skies, we decided to start looking for a place to pitch Ted. Thick, unfenced forests appealed to us – discrete, wind-protected and dry. Instead, however, we were surrounded by fields, small roads and paint-flicks of woodland.

'Let's ask a farmer,' Jake said, after another dark green patch on the map turned out to be little more than a string of trees. 'I can't wait to get to the other side of Antwerp. There are actually forests there!'

'What about this one?' I suggested, stopping twenty minutes later at the entrance of a drive caked with manure. 'Look,' I said, spotting a small red and white sticker on the postbox, 'it says *"Grote Routepaden. Wandelaars Welkom"*. That's the Dutch *GR*, and it's telling us that wanderers are welcome, I guess?'

'We're wanderers!' Jake revelled.

'I know we are.'

Above the gate there was a larger sign: 'Hoeveterras de Vlienthoeve'. With desperate optimism, we approached the main building and aimed for a net-curtained glass door, bordered on either side by two rotund hedges. Peering through the windowpane, I could see a dozen wooden tables, each attended by the curved splats of four polka-dotted, white chairs that sat uniformly on a mahogany-coloured tiled floor. The brick walls were painted green and hung with chalkboards, each plentifully covered with swirling letters depicting the *'Zondag Specials'*.

The café was empty, so we knocked firmly on the door as we entered, unwilling to startle whoever might be inside. A swell of warmth and the fragrance of coffee and cake engulfed our senses. Grateful to be indoors, we took our hats from our heads in appreciation.

A lady smiled over from behind the counter. She had wavy blonde hair, turning subtly grey, and greeted us with words that we didn't understand but knew, by the tone, to be kind and welcoming. Still unsure of the appropriate tongue, we reciprocated the lady's smile, mumbled an amalgamation of English, French and Dutch, and then turned silent. She raised a finger as if to say, 'One moment,' and then signalled for us to sit down, before disappearing through a door between two lofty fridges loaded with bottles of beer and cider.

A minute or two later, she returned, accompanied by a tall woman with short auburn hair and slight eyes that told me the pair were mother and daughter.

'Hello,' the daughter said. 'You are English?'

'Yes, we are,' I replied. 'Sorry, we don't speak Dutch very well...or at all really. We were wondering if you had a space for us to camp tonight in your field? We've had a long day and there are no campsites in the area.'

'Yes, we can do that,' she said without a thought, 'but the grass is long and the cows are out. Will that be OK for you?'

We would have accepted far worse camping spots than the one Elsje directed us to. As we clambered over the electric fence behind the café, Lieve, Elsje's mother, clapped her hands to her mouth, uttering several words under her breath.

'She is worried that you will hurt yourself on the fence and nettles,' Elsje translated. 'Now, are you sure this is alright for you?'

Although the day had seen little in the way of rain, the knee-high grass was wet and quickly dampened our boots. 'It's perfect,' Jake said, no doubt feeling as relieved as I was to have a pitch for the night.

'The cows are calving.' Elsje pointed to a section of the field next to us that had been separated from the rest by a minimal fence of blue string. Four or five wide-bellied Friesians stepped wearily from one patch of grass to the next. 'They will be noisy in the night.'

We propped Ted up with his nose facing the prevailing gusts, only to see the wind direction alter once the final peg had been pushed into the ground. Our walking clothes were swapped for long johns, trousers, T-shirts and pullovers, before we slipped on our sandals and returned to the café.

'It's a *crêperie*,' Elsje corrected after we asked her about the coffee shop. 'My mother is an expert, and she wants to make you one. Oh, and it's on the house, no arguments!'

It wasn't long before our table was crammed with pots of sugar, bowls of fruit, bottles of Den Mulder beer, and two ginormous pancakes, so large in fact that we struggled to finish them. I was astounded to hear that the passengers of a pensioners' bus – who were regular visitors to the Hoeveterras de Vlienthoeve *crêperie* – often ate two pancakes in one sitting.

Elsje's husband, Luc, was out on the farm milking the cows whilst their two daughters, Marte – a playful ten-year-old – and her younger sister, Noor – shy yet full of kindness – nipped in and out of the room, joining us one minute and leaving us the next. Marnix, Luc's father, didn't speak English, but yakked away in Dutch as if we understood every word whilst Marte sang 'Three Blind Mice' and then counted to ten, 'One, two, three...' Indeed, Lieve appeared so delighted with the whole affair that she phoned the children's headmaster, who turned up an hour later with his wife just as Luc came in from the farm smelling of creamy milk and manure. The school headmaster appeared eager for us to try as many dark and, in my eyes, dangerous beers as possible, and was soon offering to drive Jake and me through the 'boring bits' of Belgium and into Antwerp.

'We don't mind getting in cars,' I exclaimed, 'but we have to return to the point where we left the path. That's our rule: we walk every step of the path.'

'OK, OK,' he finally accepted, before going on to talk about the great Belgian floods of 1953.

The whole family smiled as they chattered and listened intently no matter what the language or the story. It was our first Trail Angel experience since arriving on Mainland Europe, and one that reminded me of the power of spontaneous and unprovoked altruism.

'Would you like to feed the calves?' Luc asked.

Moments later, we were in the yard with buckets of milk and the company of the family dog, whose limp showed his age. 'We have 120 cows,' Luc said proudly over the calls of a pen of calves. 'They are milked in the morning and the evening for three hours, fifty at a time. After three days, the milk is collected – 4,000 litres of it – and taken to a nearby farm to be used. We have about thirty or forty farms in the area which work together and help each other out. Production is good at the moment because these guys have just come out.' Luc pointed at the calves, each now sucking enthusiastically from a contraption made of buckets and plastic bottles, designed to mimic their mothers' udders.

'They're only a few days old,' he continued, still looking at the calves, 'but they already weigh forty-five kilograms. In two years, they will be ready to milk.'

'You must work hard. You have the café and the dairy farm. Do you get tired?' I quizzed.

'We do potatoes too. This year is a good year for us because the rest of the country had a dry summer. The weather here was good so we get twenty-five cents a kilo compared to our normal rate of ten to fifteen cents. Find me a farmer who doesn't get tired!'

FROM ARABLE TO ANTWERP

During the night, one of the cows gave birth, though, perhaps as a result of the eight per cent beer, I didn't hear her discomfort.

Elsje had prepared a profusion of breakfast ingredients – bacon and eggs, strawberries and yoghurt, and another monstrous *crêpe* – which we ate with freshly made coffee. By way of a parting gift, Jake plucked Charlie the clownfish from the side pocket of his bag and handed him to Marte and Noor, who accepted the soft toy cheerfully, suggesting it would go well with the other clownfish they already possessed.

We left the farm in the rain, much to the dismay of Lieve who brushed a trickle of water from Jake's pack, and then pulled the collar of my fleece up to protect me from the cold.

For the next two days, we teetered on the border between Belgium and the Netherlands, passing through Sas van Gent, Langelede and the Dutch city of Hulst – a settlement surrounded by battlement walls, shaped like the leaf of a holly tree. At times, we were forced to wade through meadows of deep grass and toilet plants, where green-veined orange-tipped butterflies battled through the saturated air and nettles snapped at our bare ankles. At the end of one field lay another, and at the end of that one more again. Motorway crossings, quite miserably, were a highlight: a moment of relative excitement amongst a landscape as sullen and dripping as they come. Our elation, therefore, as we grew closer to a pasture of tulips could not have been greater. White and orange, pink and red – we stood beside the streaks of colour for some minutes, visually absorbing the pigmentation before reluctantly walking away.

'I always stop to chat to walkers!' Karel told us with one foot on the floor and the other on the pedal of his bike. Karel, like most of the Belgian and Dutch population, was obsessed with his bike, and spent the best part of ten minutes guiding us systematically through the functions on his cyclometer. 'Ninety-eight kilometres I've done today,' Karel sang, 'and it's only just noon!'

And then there was Phillip, another avid conversationalist, who called us over through the wire of a tall fence. '*Hallo, hoi!*' he hollered, with one finger poking through the metal like a deprived zoo animal. He had a spade in one hand and was standing next to a large hole. The more we spoke to Phillip, which in truth wasn't long, the more he struck me as the kind of guy who dug holes in the rain. In fact, I wouldn't have been surprised to learn that Phillip had every intention of refilling the holes at the end of the day. 'It rains a lot in England, yes?' he said through a fixed grin, water gliding along the peak of his cap before dropping to the floor, 'and you like to shoot rabbits? I like to shoot rabbits too!'

We spent the rest of the day trudging through wet farmland, discussing the roles that JRR Tolkien's Fellowship would have if they were to join us on our adventure. Jake eventually concluded that, 'Strider would have to carry the scroggin because Sam would just eat it all!'

We had been walking for almost forty kilometres, and were grateful finally to be amongst the infrastructure of Antwerp, the largest settlement on our route to the Mediterranean. Climbing to the rise of the A14 motorway, we darted between the traffic, catching a glimpse of the emblematic Cathedral of Our Lady on the skyline before dipping back down through the city's outskirts and on to the Scheldt River.

SWAPPING BOOTS FOR WHEELS

We spent two nights at Camping de Molen, a basic yet pleasant campground of patchy grass and broadleaf trees, placed on an acute meander of the Scheldt River: the first in the tent, and the second in a static caravan with flat tyres and an algae-mottled exterior. The campsite owner, a young bearded man, offered us the accommodation upgrade free of charge. Apparently, he didn't like the thought of us spending a second night beneath the plane tree which, despite the relatively clear skies, had dripped incessantly with stored rainwater, and with the occasional thud of a pellet of wood pigeon guano.

Antwerp was supposed to have provided us with a day of rest, giving Jake's ankle a chance to relax and my heel blister, which had now developed its own heartbeat, time to settle. Instead, we spent our respite day trudging through the Sint-Annatunnel below the Scheldt – where 1930s wooden escalators clanked – and into Antwerp's centre. We bought food, sent letters, picked up pharmaceutical necessities (mostly Compeed, a gel-like blister protection pad) and did our best to glean any information that would help us along the next leg of our journey.

'Internet café?' the small-headed man repeated over the top of his spectacles in the information centre. 'You want an internet café? Well, there are none in Antwerp.'

'None?' I exclaimed. 'So, there's nowhere for us to use the internet?'

'Everyone uses their phones now. There is no need for internet cafés anymore.'

We left the information centre and stood below the two dozen flags that fluttered from the walls of the town hall. 'That might change things,' I fretted. 'I guess that means we'll be having even less contact with home.'

'We still have the phone if we need it, remember,' Jake consoled me, pulling the brick-like Nokia from his pocket and waving it in the air.

That afternoon, I lay on my stomach on a pile of rigid caravan cushions and opened my diary. The head of the page read 'May 13 2013'. We often spent the latter stages of the day in near silence, masking the moments of potential over-contemplation with chores such as journal writing, map analysing, cooking and washing. However, that afternoon, with all of our jobs completed, my mind began to wander until soon it was awash with thoughts of friends and family.

We had been on the path for one month. The last time that we had seen Claudia and Rose was eleven days ago, Dad fourteen, Mum twenty-two, and Jessy thirty. This was the first time I had quantified our time apart. I didn't like it and swiftly told myself that I wouldn't do it again.

I got up and found our watertight blue safety bag in the depths of Jake's pack. In amongst the wallets, passports, mobile phone and address book was a scrunched-up envelope, unopened, with holes at its seams. I returned to the cushions and read, for the umpteenth time, the words on the outside of the package:

> To Jake and Danny, sorry to have provided another necessary item, but this is an MP3 player full of messages and such from loved ones. Love Claudia and Rose.

Inside was an old AA-battery-run MP3 player that both Jake and I had resisted since leaving Bristol, unwilling to listen until the time was right. I unravelled the headphones, pushed them into my ears and pressed play: 'Hello, Danny and Jake.' I immediately recognised the soft, calming voice of Ben, our father's girlfriend. 'This is a little ditty for you called *The Walker's Friend*, inspired by Flann O'Brien. He's Irish, which is why I currently have an Irish accent.'

I listened to Ben's words as they pulsed from the headphones, each sentence more veracious to our journey than the previous.

Nearing the end of the poem, her voice slowed:

> When your blisters smart and your tent is damp
> And the shit has hit the fan,
> When your joints seize up and there is nowhere to camp –
> A pint of plain is your only man.
>
> When Menton seems like a distant dream,
> I'm telling you Jake and Dan,
> There's always hope, rough though it might seem –
> For a pint of plain is your only man.

I could hear Ben rustling around with the microphone before the recording stopped. I felt a tear leave the corner of my eye and wiped it away before Jake noticed, not out of embarrassment but because I didn't want him to think that I was upset. Of course, after listening to the poem, it would have been easy to go out and buy a crate of delicious Belgian beer, Duvel perhaps, drink the lot and then blame Ben for making us believe that a pint of plain would get us to Menton. But I was not sure if Flann O'Brien, or indeed Ben, meant the lines literally. Or perhaps they did? But I heard it metaphorically. My pint of plain was anything: anything that gave me hope, or a kick up the arse. And as we lay between the flimsy fibreglass walls of our complimentary caravan, I realised that my pint of plain was an 850-gram tin of ravioli. The gelatine-like tomato sauce and overcooked pasta may not have rivalled the gastronomy of Paris or Rome, but it filled my stomach and refuelled my muscles.

I took the MP3 player and wound the headphones around its body, placed it back in the envelope, and buried it deep into the bag of valuables, hoping that I wouldn't hear it again for some time.

Joining Jake by the smeared caravan window, we watched intently as a man tweaked a satellite dish he had propped up on a plastic chair outside his colossal-sized tent. He must have returned to the precarious structure ten times, on each occasion moving the dish one centimetre this way and two that way before finally settling down with a beer in his hand and a grin on his face.

3

Antwerp to the Luxembourg Border

686 to 1,040 kilometres from home

FIFTY CENTS TO SPEND A PENNY

On the first day of our second month, we spent one euro between us on a public lavatory. Included in the fifty cents' deal was a female toilet cleaner whose job comprised not only cleaning but also making every relieving male feel as uncomfortable as possible with her deep-voiced barks and a flying mop.

We left the toilets through the Antwerpen-Centraal railway station – a magnificent dome of stone and glass completed in the early years of the twentieth century – heading east, out through the city's cosmopolitan suburbs. The congested roads of Antwerp, lined with launderettes, kebab shops and the inevitable presence of the nation's *pharmacies*, eventually faded, giving way to pristine parks and grand manor houses garnished with rhododendrons, bougainvillea and wisteria.

After lunch, consisting not surprisingly of bread, cheese and ham, we began once more to enjoy the peaceful sounds of rural Belgium, with tweeting wrens and leaf-rummaging blackbirds. Using our fourteenth map, we joined the *Grande Randonnée 565* (*GR565*), relishing the comfort of the red and white symbols that guided us down wide, empty boulevards, bordered by elaborate, mansion-protecting gates, and into a forest of beech and holly.

Until now, we had been fortunate enough, with only minor detours, to spend a large number of our nights in campsites, where toilets flushed and, on the whole, showers ran hot. But we were aware that things were about to change. East Belgium, it seemed, was not quite as accepting of camping as the West. There was still an abundance of hotels and bed and breakfasts but we now had to choose: pay for comfort or camp out in the wild.

'Maybe we could walk to that bed and breakfast?' Jake suggested, pointing to a dot that we had marked on the map. We were stood in the well-maintained grounds of Park Schildehof, an area awash with artificial lakes, exercise apparatus and gravelled paths. The bed and breakfast was an hour's detour north.

'Or we could camp here?' I nodded into a thicket of tree branches beside us.

Jake sighed. 'I know we should. I just don't feel comfortable.'

'We're going to have to start doing it sometime,' I urged. 'We might as well get used to it.' I could see that Jake wanted to camp, but with the exception of our forced wild camp back in England, it was an unfamiliar practice, and the insecurity was getting to him.

'Come on then,' he announced, as the leaves beside us began to spring with the weight of rain. 'Let's get Ted up before it buckets down.'

By the time the last items of gear had been slung into the tent porch, we were soaked through. A thorough analysis of Ted's peripherals revealed that we were well camouflaged amongst coppiced beech, creeping brambles and hip-high nettles. Ted was so well hidden in fact that we were totally unaware of the Albertkanaal, whose industrial girth of channelised water lay just ten metres south of our pitch. Not even the hardiest dog walkers would have found us. Despite our invisibility, the procedure had left Jake in a foul mood, so I decided to give him some space.

Sitting by the park's central lake, I watched the thinning rain spread rings across the water's surface, blurring the dark brown outlines of several hundred gathering tadpoles below. When I returned to the tent, I cooked some noodles. Then we ate a packet of biscuits in our sleeping bags whilst watching slugs and insects busy themselves between the inner tent and flysheet. My knees felt hot from the numerous nettle stings suffered in our densely vegetated camp area, and my cheeks were rosy from the wind and rain.

'Sorry for being grumpy,' Jake said quietly before pulling the hood of his sleeping bag over his woolly hat and falling asleep.

GRAND RANDONNÉE CINQ

Whether it was the persistent rain, an overdose of nettle histamine or the apprehension of pitching in a park, I slept awfully and was deeply thankful when dawn finally broke. As we flicked molluscs from the tent, I could already feel drips of water meandering down my legs and into my boots.

The *GR565* strategically kept us away from the monotony of arable Flanders by linking one patch of fern-blanketed forest to the next. On a scroggin break (now comprising dried chickpeas and croutons, along with the usual ingredients), we stared up at Kasteel van Vrieselhof. Its spires, tall and elegant, spun with doves.

'It doesn't look like a castle, does it?' Jake said dismissively. Apparently, a clumsy translation turns a huge number of Belgian aristocratic homes into 'castles', of which Vrieselhof was one. Nonetheless, with its so-called Flemish Neo-Renaissance architecture of pointed slate roofs and ivy-covered red-brick walls, the building was marvellous to look at and distracted me from the confusing blend of chickpeas and fizzy cola sweets that had taken residence in my mouth.

Two hours after leaving camp, we found ourselves in the tiny city of Halle, where we ate a freshly baked *éclair au chocolat* in the rain whilst watching locals dash into and then out of the bakery, shielding precious boxes of cakes and buns under opened jackets and hunched postures.

There was no tap along the main street and as a result, twenty minutes later, I found myself stooping down to a small stream just north of Grobbendonk with two bottles in hand. Up until this point, we had found water easy to come by, filling our vessels from campsite facilities, bed and breakfast kitchens or gas station taps. But without our usual means of supply, it was time to adapt. The course was flowing fast, and a quick glance upstream revealed no dead sheep, so we left the purification tablets in our medical kit and glugged the mossy-tasting water without any more thought.

In spite of the rain, we felt a sense of positive anticipation as we made our way down Boshuisweg Lane towards a turning at the end of the gravel to see an askew timber post on the roadside. Cresting the sign were three arrows. The first finger pointed east, along the continuing course of the *GR565* towards the border of the Netherlands, the second north to Bergen op Zoom, and the third south along the *GR5* to Liège and on to Nice.

We had read a lot about the prestige and popularity of the *GR5* over the months leading up to our departure: 'The *GR5* is Western Europe's premier hiking trail' and 'one of Europe's most walked long-distance paths'. But the articles, websites and guidebooks seemed to skim over much of the 2,600-kilometre route, or disregard it altogether, solely praising the final section from the Alps, which for many was seen as the most beautiful part of the journey. In fact, the first half of the GR5 was so poorly documented that the only detail we could gather was the starting point of the route. Although even that appeared to be vague, with some sources (including the sign that we now stood beneath) stating that the path begins with the North Sea at Bergen op Zoom in the Netherlands, and others suggesting that it starts a little further north at the Hoek van Holland on the Nieuwe Waterweg shipping canal in Rotterdam's western suburbs.

'This is a big moment, Dan,' Jake shouted as he danced around the sign, using his walking poles for stability on the more ostentatious moves. 'This is the beginning of the walk. All that stuff that we've just done, that was like getting out of the car and finding your way to the start of the first hill. This is it now – 2,400 kilometres of southerly walking!'

Since leaving Bristol, we had walked 690 kilometres along a disjointed route of vaguely linked paths, beginning at latitude 51.45°, just 0.23° further north than our current location on Boshuisweg Lane. This fact meant that our southerly progress so far equated to no more than twenty-five kilometres – just 800 metres a day. An accomplished athlete could run the distance in less than an hour and a half, yet to get this far south it had taken over a month. Our arrival onto the GR5 thus signalled two momentous milestones. Firstly, we had joined a path that would take us, more or less, from the icy waters of the North Sea to the tepid waves of the Mediterranean, through Belgium, Germany, Luxembourg, France, Switzerland and Italy. And secondly, it was now time to part ways with our easterly trajectory and turn boldly south.

The GR5 was, to all intents and purposes, our new home.

'Perhaps we should get on?' Jake checked his Casio. 'The sign is cool and everything, but we've got a long day ahead.'

'Good idea,' I agreed.

The GR5 led us into the forests of Gobbendonk, where bunches of stringy daisies hemmed the path verges and poplar seeds snowed down from the turreted canopies above. We crossed the Albertkanaal, far wider than any canal we had seen so far on the path, and then continued onward through ploughed fields and along country roads. Each village we met reminded me of the previous one – nice lawns, nice houses and nice cars. Each, that is, except Bauwel, which stood out thanks to a man with a weathered face who yelled at us, blasphemously we assumed, from his car window. What offence were we committing?

However, with each bout of animosity hurled our way, we were treated to equal acts of kindness. With our forty-third kilometre of the day, we arrived in Noorderwijk, a pancake-flat town, just south of the Albertkanaal. In need of a little food, we found the local supermarket and got talking to a young guy in the queue, sporting a large floppy quiff and thick sideburns.

'I'm going to pay for that,' Bram told us, putting his hand in front of Jake who was rooting for cash in his wallet.

'No, don't be silly,' I responded weakly.

'People have done nice things for me in the past, so I'm going to give something back.'

THE ALBERTKANAAL

'I smell,' Jake said from beneath his hood. 'I really smell. And it's raining. Should you be able to smell yourself when it's raining? I don't think you should. Do you smell?'

It was another wet morning, and somewhat reluctantly I lifted my arm. Trickles of water migrated towards my elbow as I buried my nose into my pit. 'Yep, I smell.'

'We haven't washed our clothes for two weeks, apart from our socks and boxers, and that's a long time, even by our standards!'

Rain had been a familiar occurrence since we left Bruges over one week ago. Drying washed clothes was not an option so we just wore them dirty instead. On a personal level, this didn't really bother us, but as Jake so selflessly put it, 'I feel sorry for the people who have to smell us.'

It was one of those dank and miserable days when smelling your own armpit was likely to be the highlight. Streams ran down trees, and leaves that were not quite ready to fall fell. The one positive was that we made forty kilometres of strong southerly progress, finally arriving by late afternoon into the charming, but wet, settlement of Diest.

Relief from a cold and damp night in the tent came quite

unforeseeably through the purchase of a tube of athlete's foot cream from the local *pharmacie*. The two compassionate chemists decided it would have been a crime for us to camp in such atrocious weather and, with the help of a number of phone calls and a small hand-drawn map, directed us to the Hotel de Franse Kroon on the other side of town. On another day, the street lanterns and sixteenth-century buildings dressed with awnings and regional flags would have stopped us in our tracks. But with Jake's recently acquired foot fungus, his fragile knee, my frozen bones, and a fire of chafing sores raging between my legs, we decided to push on for shelter.

I was upset to find that my day diary, in which I wrote observations and quotes, was sodden, and so too was the gear inside our 'dry' bags. Indeed, somewhat ironically, the dirty clothes which I had stuffed into a plastic bag, the very same one that the dry bags had been sold in, were the only items that had remained dry.

There were no windows in the room, and the radiators were not working, but I didn't care, for the chipped and stained bath filled with steaming hot water heated me from the outside in. After washing, we sank into the double bed in front of the television, took account of our ailments, and agreed to take a rare day off from the path the following day.

However, when morning came, one look at our guilt-inducing boots saw the decision reversed, and we began to gather our things. My green walking shorts were the only item to have dried overnight. This anomaly was quickly dispelled at the buffet breakfast when I spilt a glass of orange juice over my lap whilst trying to shove *pains au chocolat* into my pockets for lunch. I made quite a scene, and felt the looks from the nearby tables to be both sympathetic and disapproving.

We stepped out of the Hotel de Franse Kroon, pulled our hoods over our heads, and left Diest in the pouring rain. Packed full with wet gear, my bag felt uncomfortably heavy. I began to think of all the items we were carrying. Was their use justified? Before we left Bristol, a sniffling cold had encouraged me to pack a handkerchief. I must have deemed it essential, but since leaving home it had not seen a single milligram of mucus and likely never would (especially having received a lesson from Jake on the effective art of 'snot spitting'). My sunglasses, and their accompanying hard case, had not been touched, nor had the floss, which we were certain we would use in times of boredom. Despite the rain, our waterproof trousers had never left our bags. We preferred to walk in shorts on the principle that the less we wore, the less we had to get wet. And, quite amazingly, our head torches had only been used once: we slept before dusk and, because of a curfew on fluid intake (nothing after 6pm), would more often than not sleep through until morning, making the torches redundant. The last and without doubt most pointless item was a small fabric tape measure. Its existence was a mystery – a mystery that made us think: perhaps we should keep it…you know, just in case.

Walking in the morning always made us happy. It didn't seem to matter that the rain came down in sheets, because the birds still sang, and there was a harmonious atmosphere in the forests, alongside the canals and beside the industrial estates, that often seemed to evaporate with the afternoon. We were heading once more for the Albertkanaal, a three millimetre-wide blue scar on the map, dissecting the north-east corner of Belgium. Since joining the *GR5*, we had skipped across the impressive waterway several times. Today, and for the next few days, we would take advantage of its direct 'kilometre-friendly' channelisation.

But before we reached the canal, something on the path ahead brought us to a halt. A large round bulge filled the horizon, jagged in places with pine tops, and smoothed in others with deciduous canopies. It was a hill. The towering mass peaked at a dizzying fifty metres, the highest we had climbed for weeks. It reminded our thighs that they did have a job to do on this venture. Indeed, our bodies were so in tune with East Belgium's *crêpe*-flat terrain that the climb aggravated the ankle injury Jake had sustained back in England. With each step more painful than the last, his stride became laboured. We took short cuts wherever we could, shaving two kilometres from our day, until we reached Hasselt, an important transport junction between Antwerp and Liège.

Deciding that a successive day on the canal would have done little but exacerbate Jake's pain-struck ankle, we checked into a cheap hotel for two nights in the centre of the city. Drying was the priority of the first evening. The room had a ceiling heater that projected a narrow band of hot air diagonally towards the floor. Not ideal but, with five weeks of walking now behind us, we had become resourceful. We fashioned a precarious structure out of bedside tables, chairs and walking poles, and then strung it with clothes, boots, bags, and a damp yet still simpering Hemingway. The construction strove for the ceiling, maximising every centimetre of the heater's output, wobbling and creaking in the hot breeze. By 7pm, the room was so humid that my pen had stopped working, and I was forced to put my journal aside and watch a German reality television programme that Jake had curiously chosen to be the best of the entertainment available.

On our second day in Hasselt, we completed a familiar routine of chores, and then spent the afternoon focusing on a tick Jake had discovered between two of his fingers. He smeared Vaseline over the tiny arachnid, then screwed it out with the penknife, squinting in the window light at its robust body on the end of the blade. 'Little bugger,' he muttered pensively.

It was a fine Sunday morning, and for the first time in days, we felt the warmth of the sun on our napes. With the last few pieces of damp clothing tied to the outside of our packs, we converged once more with the Albertkanaal. A flock of pigeons took to the sky, their twinkling wings catching the sunlight as they clapped against their bodies.

The canal, completed in 1939, was built as a transport link between Antwerp and Liège. In the 1960s, the 130 kilometre-long waterway was expanded to allow larger barges, some as heavy as 10,000 tonnes, to utilise the channel. Until now, I had considered the Albertkanaal to be mildly oppressive: a water-filled concrete wound flanked by timber stacks, saw mills, piles of sand and grit, tangles of shimmering scrap tin, and steaming red and white power plant chimneys. But, today, the aesthetics of industry held charm and intrigue.

To many, the long, hard winter was over. Fishermen with stretching rods dotted the poppy-smattered banks, whilst snorkellers in black wetsuits bobbed in the water. The towpath was busy with droves of cyclists, each rider as happy as the next to be involved in rain-free recreation. 'Hallo, goedemorgen,' they called to us as they whooshed by. To our surprise, we even passed the occasional day walker, a sight that had eluded us for almost three weeks.

If there was one lesson Jake and I had taken from our walk so far, it was that the loss of one bodily problem almost always meant another was on its way. My blisters were hardening, and we had both got used to the feeling of beaten soles at the end of the day. Jake's ankle, although initially appearing bad, had made another miraculous recovery, and our sense of smell had clearly decided that body odour was acceptable. Replacing these adversities was another agony: our abrasive hip belts.

This time, it was Jake's hips that were feeling the pressure. His rucksack had been comfortable in England and much of Belgium. However, as the pounds began to drop from his midriff and his belt gradually tightened, he found that his bag had reached its smallest setting. With no more strap to pull, the pack was slipping. Jake lifted his T-shirt up to reveal a large area of raw skin, like the grazed knee of a child.

'It's really uncomfortable,' he said with a grimace. 'What should I do?'

'You could try and make your hips bigger?'

'What do you mean? Bigger?'

'Bigger, larger, you know, to mimic a wider waist.'

'Good idea!' Jake dropped his pack and yanked his dry socks from the straps. After tying them around the hip belt, he hauled the bag back on, clipped up, and we were off again.

'Any better?' I questioned after a few minutes.

'No,' Jake said miserably.

By mid-afternoon, we had reached the Central van Langerlo, a coal and biomass plant defined by two thimble-shaped chimneys gushing with cooling water at their bases. We left the canal and dipped into a wood of young oak just south of Zutendaal and, in a square of dense trees between a grid of walking tracks, unravelled Ted.

Once our camp was established, I left Jake and pushed through several metres of branches before emerging onto one of the paths. Away from the dog walkers, I found a mossy log and took a seat, feeling its velvet on my palms. For the first time, I felt relaxed and content at the prospect of a wild camp. My eyes fell upon a puddle beside the log. It was then that I realised focus changes everything: the pool of water, at first a bed of leafy detritus, transformed with a lethargic blink into a mirror of swaying tree canopies, free and unhindered. This is how I had hoped it would feel.

I followed the large branches that I had left on the floor – more reliable than breadcrumbs – back to the tent. Feeling at one with the situation, I decided to dig a hole beside one of the smoother-looking tree trunks surrounding the camp. I bordered the dugout with snapped sticks to define its position, and then plucked a dozen broad leaves from the oak beside me, heaping them next to the primitive lavatory.

'I made you a toilet, if you need to go,' I said as I climbed into the tent to see Jake analysing tomorrow's section of the map. It was 8pm and the light was beginning to fade, so I scribbled a few more words in my journal and then lay on my back staring at the ceiling. The subtle shadows of the leaves danced joyously across the tent walls as the great tits sang like a tittering, buckled bike tyre.

'Right,' Jake said, scrambling out of the tent just as I was drifting off, 'I may as well use that toilet you spent so long digging.'

GEESE TO GUARD

We woke to rain. A drilling woodpecker led us through the dribbling forest and out into an opening where an old man wearing a rain jacket and flat hat turned the soil of his rather incongruous vegetable patch amongst the trees. We exchanged nods, and then continued on to the deserted town of Gellink where we bought a brioche, for its size and low price, before reuniting with the Albertkanaal.

After a couple of kilometres, the channel reached Belgium's eastern border where it was repelled southwards with a huge, sweeping bend. It had taken us just over two weeks to walk the length of the country. On the other side of the canal, the Meuse River wound between the medieval walls and eighteenth-century fortifications of Maastricht. Its sprawl of infrastructure was the largest we had seen since Antwerp.

'So, there it is, Germany, our fifth country,' Jake called through the rain.

Whether we were delirious or just extremely unobservant, we had made the rather astounding error of misinterpreting an entire country: Maastricht is not a German city at all, but Dutch. The mass of land that had filled our easterly horizon, and which we had also presumed to be Germany, was instead a bulge of the Netherlands, protruding southwards like a giant pendant.

By now, our knowledge of which language we should be speaking had diminished to total confusion. We had just left Belgium at the boundary between Flanders (mostly Dutch speaking in which regional Flemish dialects occur) and the nation's southern region, Wallonia (largely French speaking). However, having bridged the canal, we now stood in the Netherlands (definitely Dutch speaking, yet a little different to the Flanders Dutch) but we thought we were in Germany. All things considered, English felt like the most suitable option – a thought confirmed, as we continued along between the Albertkanaal and the Meuse River, by a large fellow with smeared spectacles who greeted us with an 'Alreet?' in the thickest Geordie accent.

'Very friendly, aren't they, the Germans?' Jake declared as a second man, dressed head to toe in a mustard-green cagoule, sped towards us.

'*Compostelle?*' he called, barely breaking stride as he brushed by.

'No, the *GR5.*'

'*Ah, bon courage!*'

The well-waterproofed man, like a number of others over recent weeks, was referring to the *Camino de Santiago*, or the Way of St James. The *Camino,* a pilgrimage trodden by many thousands of people each year, winds through Europe towards the site of St James's remains in the north-west Spanish town of Santiago de Compostela. To some onlookers, Jake and I no doubt resembled quintessential pilgrims – trudging legs, fraying packs, and a permanent exhaustion embedded in our dirtied brows and dripping cheeks. More often than not, we would correct them – 'No, *GR5*' – but on other occasions we would let it slide, accepting their assumptions and wondering if the details of our final destination were, in the grand scheme of things, wholly irrelevant.

'It was a bit of a fox's wedding,' I told Claudia over the phone, my legs swinging from Visé's tourist information wall. With the rain easing off, the sun picked its way through the misted air. 'We've had squelching feet and pruned fingers all day, but the sun's out now. Jake's inside asking about a bed for the night.'

'Snail's wedding!' Claudia chirped.

'Sorry?'

'That's what they call it in Brazil when it is raining and sunny at the same time. A fox's wedding is Japanese, and a snail's wedding is Brazilian.'

'Oh.'

'And, in Sudan, a sunshower means that a donkey and monkey are getting married.'

'Wow, you really know your folklore.'

'That's not the worst of it,' she continued. 'In Liberia, they say that the devil is fighting with his wife over a chicken bone!'

'Ver L'Oie,' Jake muttered with his head in the map. 'It should be this way.' We retraced our steps through the bustling town centre and back over the mumbling Meuse River and its banks of grazing white geese. Somewhere between Maastricht and Visé, we had crossed from Flanders into Wallonia. The change from North to South Belgium couldn't have been starker. Blue, white and red tricolours fluttered above the river whilst French words and flamboyant accents adorned the road signs, shops and restaurants – Côté Cuisine, Visé Voyages and Le d'Artagnan. I tuned into the conversations of passing strangers, noticing that they too conversed in melodic, rolling and romantic French.

Even the air smelt different. Without formal recognition of the boundary crossing, it was odd to be slung so starkly from one culture to another and, as we marched purposefully down Avenue Franklin Roosevelt, I couldn't help but feel we had just disembarked from a flight to Île-de-France and were on the search for our first bed of the holiday.

It wasn't long before we were outside the Ver L'Oie *chambre d'hôtes*, little more than a narrow terraced house, where two pots of red and purple petunias sat timidly up against the red-brick front wall. Gheslaine, a petite lady of perhaps sixty, with short, rusty hair and a croaky throat, welcomed us in. A dog from upstairs began to bark as Gheslaine politely ordered us to take off our boots. She gave us a pair of slippers each, mine yellow and Jake's blue, comforting our toes up the wooden stairs past a clutter of umbrella stands, hanging coats and shoe racks.

Gheslaine's quick steps soon halted, with a clamping together of her feet, in a large, sunlit room with white tiled flooring. Reels of wool, bowls of heavily scented potpourri and candlesticks covered an extensive collection of cupboards which, I assumed, were crammed with pillowcases and quilts for the low standing double bed that stood in the centre of the room. The wallpaper, apparently modelled on some sort of crystalline igneous rock sample, was covered floor to ceiling in faded photographs of Gheslaine and her husband, and prints of Van Gogh's *The Starry Night*, *Irises* and *Wheatfield with Crows*. That is, I assumed they were prints. After all, this was the kind of place where to discover an original masterpiece, hidden in the corner and unbeknown to the world, wouldn't have surprised me.

Gheslaine informed us that the bath was out of bounds because running it would use up all of the hot water. She wheeled a mobile extractor fan into the bathroom to get rid of the steam from the shower. We were not allowed to put our packs on the bed, the television was to be switched off at the wall, and eating was not permitted in the room. There was no doubt, with this long list of rules, regulations and do-it-yourself tips, that we were in someone's home. Yet, in spite of Gheslaine's bossiness, I could hear care in her voice and see love in her eyes – I felt comfortable and at home.

She invited us down into a raised conservatory that looked out over her colourful garden where the flowers looked as glad as we were to see the afternoon sun. In the magnified heat, over a coffee and chocolate waffles, Gheslaine told us about Ver L'Oie.

'My mother died six years ago. The house empty, what can I do? Ah! I make a *chambre d'hôtes* – the house now full. I have Japanese girls who like taking photos, old Brazilian lady and Netherlands couple.' She pushed a plant pot filled with tiny flags stuck to toothpicks across the table towards us. 'All the countries that have stayed here!'

Gheslaine loved to talk, in both English and French (never Dutch). Conversation swiftly turned to *l'oie* which, after several vocal imitations and furious flaps, we gathered meant 'goose', an exceedingly important animal for the people of Visé.

In the middle of the fourteenth century, the inhabitants of the town agreed that Visé needed protecting, and what better animal to guard the people than a goose or, better still, a whole gaggle? The feathery defence failed, however, and, as a result, the poor old birds had to go. The best way to dispose of the several hundred geese was to throw them into a pot of simmering milk and chopped garlic. The recipe, predictably named *L'Oie de Visé*, turned out to be rather delicious – creamy, succulent and warming. It continues to be made all over the world.

Jake and I retired to our room as the clock struck nine, worn out by the fractured conversation but content. I turned on the extractor fan in the bathroom and then stepped into the shower. Two minutes later, I was out of the tub and just grabbing my towel as Gheslaine burst into the room.

'How was the shower? OK?' she croaked.

I checked my modesty and sheepishly replied, 'Yep. Good, thanks,' at which she wheeled the device out of the room with its electrical cord and plug trailing buoyantly in her wake.

RAIN AND ILLNESS

A brief session with the maps and our faithful piece of red thread suggested that, despite having crossed the country, we still had another week of walking remaining in the southern region of Wallonia. We were about to enter the Ardennes, a wide band of river valleys and forested canyons stretching from North France, across the southern Benelux nations of Belgium and Luxembourg, and into East Germany. The Ardennes, we had been told, were where the real hiking would begin, and for that we were excited.

We made our way through a sun-dappled meadow bursting with lush spring grass and bobbing balls of dandelion seeds. Pastel-coloured butterflies and warbling birds speckled the air, whilst slow-worms, deer, rabbits and the black and yellow print of a fire salamander turned our gaze to the ground. Beyond the fields, amongst the first few gentle hills of the Ardennes, sat the Germanic village of Dalhem, a bunch of staggered stone buildings known locally as the 'Place of Residence in the Valley'. Steep, cobbled streets took us beneath seventeenth-century archways and up stone stairwells that led onto a higher track and into a hummocky landscape of rounded knolls. The foothills of the Ardennes were quiet and peaceful, and it was the cat sleeping on the corrugated tin roof above the haystacked barn that, above all else, dictated the pace.

'Here we go again,' Jake sighed, tilting his head to the sky. Having enjoyed a morning of sun, Belgium once again returned to its apparent meteorological preference: rain. Statistically Belgium's driest month, May was seemingly set on rebelling against its norm: of the fourteen days that we had spent in the country, it had rained on twelve. 'I didn't mind it to start with, but the novelty is beginning to wear off,' Jake grumbled. 'Heads down and keep walking, I guess. I'm sure it'll pass.'

In spite of Jake's optimism, it didn't pass but continued for the next three days. In the company of a grieving sky, we traipsed over slippery tree roots and through muddy puddles. Having spent our first night camped beside the Kasteel van Wégimont in Soumagne, we pushed on deeper into the hills, stopping, as the daylight began to fade, in the Bois de la Picherotte, a wooded valley of beech and oak between the villages of Winamplache and Creppe.

Cold, wet and tired, we briskly got cooking. Screwing our pocket stove to the butane gas, I filled the saucepan with two cups of water, covered it with the lid, and waited for two minutes until the first few bubbles began to pop on the surface. To save on fuel, I turned off the stove, poured two packets of noodles and a sachet of soup powder into the pan, then covered it again. Waiting for the dinner to cook, I spotted a few shoots of wild garlic at my feet, picked a couple of leaves, and tore them into the broth. We both loved the spicy sweetness of the herb and often used it to liven up our dinners, altering the monotony of another evening of noodles or couscous.

Five minutes later, with our hands gripped around the plastic bowls, we held the soup to our cold faces and drank the heat with pleasure. But, unlike the garlic further north, the herb was bitter and harsh. After a few more seconds of intrigued chewing, the flavour had intensified, and I spat the leaves to the floor.

'Why did you do that?' Jake queried, taking his mouth away from the bowl.

'It's not garlic. It tastes like earwax!'

'Really?' Jake lifted his spoon and inspected a piece of greenery that swam on the surface.

'Don't eat it!' I yelled. I then grabbed another leaf from the ground, noticing a series of subtle lines running down the length of its body. 'It's definitely not garlic.'

'Should we still eat it?' Jake queried nervously.

'I'm going to. I'm starving,' I replied. 'It'll be fine. Just pick the leaves out.'

*

I opened my eyes to darkness. The tent poles rang with the falling rain. 'Uh oh,' I uttered, quickly pushing my sleeping bag away and scrambling out of the tent porch. There was barely enough time to grab the toilet roll, let alone get dressed, and before I knew it I was squatting down in the waterlogged forest, wearing nothing but my boxers. It was an odd moment, on the face of things totally undesirable, but as I cowered next to a tree, drenched, cold and hugging my cramping stomach, I decided that perhaps it was a moment to cherish. Looking up, I could see the glow of the moon trying to break through the cloud, whilst raindrops bent towards me. I should have felt demoralised by the precariousness of the human condition for being incapacitated so easily by a leaf. But I wasn't. Instead, I thought long and hard, still squatting, with the weather beating down on my shoulders. Eventually, I pulled up my boxers and returned to the tent with an adapted proverb swimming irrepressibly through my head: every cloud – including those filled with a seemingly infinite supply of rain – has a silver lining.

At the time, I found the incident of the mistaken plant identity to be mildly humorous, if a little uncomfortable. But later research – which unveiled the herb to be the inedible and highly toxic Lily of the Valley – suggested I was lucky to have escaped its consumption relatively unscathed. In response to the question 'So, I definitely shouldn't be eating it (Lily of the Valley) then?' Matt Soniak of Mental Floss wrote:

> *Not unless blurry vision, diarrhea, vomiting and nausea, disorientation, drowsiness, headaches, red skin rashes, excessive salivation, sudden alterations in your cardiac rhythm and possible death sound like your idea of fun.*

It took us two hours to walk the seven kilometres to Spa, where a winding road dotted with expensive-looking cottages took us down into a small town. Known locally as the 'Pearl of the Ardennes' or the 'Water Town', Spa sits in the heart of the Ardennes hills and is surrounded by a network of rivers and natural springs, a geographical blessing that has allowed the town to flourish through the centuries. Birthplace to the word 'spa', the town now claims to have the oldest resort in Europe. Indeed, during the seventeenth and eighteenth centuries, luminaries such as the writer Victor Hugo and King Leopold II of Belgium used to visit the relieving waters to bathe their tired hands and wash their long beards. Nowadays, the visitors are less prestigious, and the Thermes de Spa – fully equipped with pools, hot tubs and baths – attracts a more common breed.

'I'm not sure if we could even constitute ourselves as commoners,' I said, looking at Jake's dirty clothes and greasy hair. 'We're more like peasants, sleeping around the castles rather than in them, forced to eat toxic plant materials that almost kill us!'

'Bit dramatic, Dan. But I am looking forward to a wash.'

We must have passed the large white pillars and jetting fountains of the town's Casino seven or eight times as we scoured the streets for a place to stay. Eventually, after several hours of rejections – '*Pas de chambres*' and '*Désolé*' – we found La Tonnellerie au Chalet du Parc, a warm and friendly hotel which became the unfortunate recipient of two rucksacks full of muddy, fetid clothes, dripping camping gear, three slugs and one worm.

Whether it was the noxious plant or the twenty-four-hour absence of food in my gut, I felt dizzy and my head was throbbing. We did our usual chores of washing, drying and cleaning, and then lay on the double bed, emotionally and physically drained, sharing our last bag of scroggin and a lump of Edam cheese. I opened my diary and wrote:

> *A good long distance walking companion is someone who:*
> - *When just as cold and tired as you, offers you the towel and first shower;*
> - *Makes your bed (in the tent);*
> - *Laughs when times are good, and when they are bad;*
> - *Does not complain if you snore a little bit;*
> - *Washes the gusset of your three-day-old boxer shorts without any sign of disapproval;*
> - *Offers you the last fizzy cola bottle from the day's scroggin rations.*

LAND OF THE SPRINGS

In the early days of April 2013, not long before we left Bristol, we had gathered all our maps together and laid them on the floor in front of us. It had taken us several months to acquire the necessary charts, which included: eleven pink *Landranger Ordnance Survey* maps for England (1:50,000); twelve grey *Institut Géographique National (IGN)* maps and one overview map for Belgium (1:50,000 and 1:300,000 respectively); two orange *Le Gouvernement du Grand-Duché de Luxembourg* maps for Luxembourg (1:50,000); nine blue *IGNs* and nine green *IGNs* for France (1:25,000 and 1:100,000 respectively); plus a dozen low-quality printouts of 'bridging areas' between maps (we deemed buying charts for just a few kilometres of use to be a waste of money).

With the aid, or perhaps hindrance, of a particularly blurry bridging map, we left Spa beneath a silky blue sky, sweating as we climbed towards the Blue Ardennes or, as the hotel's tourist magazines referred to it, 'Land of the Springs'. For some unknown reason, we had chosen to print the region as a satellite image, thus meaning that the canopies of any forested areas, which were pretty much everywhere in the Ardennes, successfully camouflaged the large number of paths that ran between the gorges and over the spring-leaking hills. Nonetheless, despite the printing blunder, we trundled joyously into the trees, glad of the splats of red and white paint that confirmed our direction.

The forest of beech and birch was ablaze with filtering sunlight that striated the air with bands of drifting dust and seeds and gliding insects. We followed a small, clunking river, one of the Amblève's many tributaries, up the leafy valley, skipping from one dapple of fiery oranges and rusty reds to the next, whilst jays swooped and woodpeckers poked at decaying, fungi-stepped trees. The forest soon opened to a hilltop of grass and bracken, and then dropped down once more through the villages of Andrimont and Ruy, where dogs lazed on the roadside and chimneys smoked. After practising a little French with our pocket dictionary – '*champ, colline, arbre, rivière*' – we found a spot on the verge of a quiet country track and sat, each with a cheese-filled croissant that we had pocketed at breakfast, amongst dainty white Parnassus flowers and yellow dandelion heads.

After lunch, the path continued through pine, soon emerging into a clearing of trees stacked with sun-bleached, disfigured logs, like piles of forgotten bones. In our brief experience of the Ardennes, the mass graveyard of trees and branches was a somewhat anomalous sight. We *had* seen evidence of logging, but on a more selective scale with the use of workhorses – pre-industrial, muscular and discreet.

'We're a long way from the seaside, aren't we?' I said to Jake an hour later as we reached the outer buildings of Stavelot, a small town of no more than 7,000 people, encompassing the bold, coral-coloured brickwork of the Abbey of Stavelot.

'Yes, a *long* way!'

'Then why does Stavelot have one of those?' I said, pointing down the road. Overflowing with buckets, spades, flip flops, balls, beach towels, sun cream, straw hats and blow-up toys, of which the most extravagant was a man-sized, inflatable crocodile, was a beach shop. In Florida or the French Riviera, or even the cold, muddy waters of Weston-Super-Mare, this wouldn't have surprised me. But with no nearby lakes and over 250 kilometres separating Stavelot from the nearest beach, I couldn't help but feel that there was something a little sinister about the town.

'My God, what is that?' This time it was Jake's voice that wavered with alarm. Between two sash windows, extending from the wall above a second shop, was a head wrapped within a white wimple hanging from a chain. A closer inspection revealed that the face had blacked-out eyes, a gaping mouth, and a long carrot-like nose. 'That's horrible. What is it?' Jake questioned again, his mouth downturned in disgust.

'It looks like a cross between Pinocchio and a nun,' I retorted with equal revulsion. 'And look, there's another!' I pointed to a second gurning head further down the street, this time above a café window.

Apparently not the only passers-by to be disturbed by the looming figures, we were glad to learn a little more on the matter in the town's tourist office. Known as *'Blanc Moussis'*, the heads are part of a costume worn for the *'Laetare des Blancs-Moussis'*, a Walloon carnival celebrated on the fourth Sunday of Lent every year. I scanned several of the leaflets, peering closely at the photos. Hundreds of locals, dressed in white robes and hoods, and plastic masks with long red noses and hollow eyes, paraded down the town's main road. Confetti poured from the hands of beaming children in the upper windows of the street's houses, whilst the *Blanc Moussis* slapped the unfortunate onlookers with what looked like balloons but were in fact dried sheep bladders.

Needless to say, we left Stavelot at pace.

In a spacious forest of mature spruce, just north of Hinoûmont, we pitched Ted on a soft ground of moss and climbed into our sleeping bags as twilight fell. Keen to distract us from the *Blanc Moussis*, I asked Jake what colour he thought the wind would be if it was visible, to which he answered, 'Purple.' Then I showed him how quickly I could eat a salt and vinegar crisp, to which he didn't respond. We were asleep before 8pm.

GOODBYE BELGIUM

Waking suddenly from my sleep, I opened my eyes and saw Jake's silhouette sitting upright beside me.

'What was that?' I whispered.

'I dunno.'

Bang! Bang!

'Shit!' we hissed simultaneously. We had read signs leading into the forest the night before warning us of hunting in the area, yet, having seen no evidence on the track, decided we had nothing to worry about. But these were definitely shots, and they were close. So close, in fact, that whoever was firing the gun must have been able to see our tent. It was likely that the Vango Tempest 200 was of very little interest to the hunters, but having been woken up at 5am to the sound of a firing shotgun my mind was not operating rationally. It wasn't long before I had convinced myself that a white-hooded figure with no eyes and a vegetable for a nose was standing outside the tent swinging an inflated bladder in one hand and wielding a shotgun in the other.

'Shall we get out of here?' I urged, already rummaging in the darkness for my shorts.

We left the trees with haste, stepping over bundles of pine cones that coated the ground like a plague of giant grubs, only relaxing once we had rejoined the path. I adored this time of the day, just before daybreak, when only the tuneful trills of the blackbird sang and not a leaf moved.

Half an hour later, the robins, wrens, dunnocks and finches had joined the dawn chorus, just as the tips of the pines across the valley began to glow amber with the rising sun. Fields of frosted swords glistened below a thin blanket of mist, and beads of dew clung to the barbs of old ramshackle fences. It was a cold start, and the drip on the tip of my nose self-replenished as quickly as I wiped it away with my mittens. We stopped and boiled a pan of water for a hot drink, then pushed on south through the village of Logbiemme where the stillness was broken only by a slow trickle of water from an ornamental pump on the roadside.

It was a long day and, as our path wound lethargically through farmland and forest, morning turned placidly to afternoon, and afternoon to night. We filled our bottles in the Rivière Fagnes, where a swarm of determined mosquitoes bit our ankles and arms leaving our skin feeling like braille, then pushed on to Rüfensberg Forest, six kilometres short of the Luxembourg border.

4

The Luxembourg Border to Luxembourg City

1,040 to 1,168 kilometres from home

THE GRAND DUCHY

'A banana chip!' Jake said, holding a small dried disc in the air. 'It's a banana chip, all the way from England. I can't believe it! I mean, I guess if we're mixing old scroggin with the new scroggin then there's the chance of an old ingredient rolling over to the revamped scroggin, but this must be three weeks old, at least!'

'So, it's been three weeks then?'

'I know, right! I can't believe it's lasted that long.' Jake beamed.

'No, I mean it's taken us three weeks to get through Belgium. That's a week quicker than we thought. And we were a week faster than we predicted in England. At this rate, we'll be in Menton by September,' I calculated.

'Let's not get ahead of ourselves. We've got mountains to come yet,' Jake mumbled as he chewed on the dried fruit.

After a drizzly start to the day, we stopped beside the wall of a small, uneven cottage on a hilly street in Burg-Reuland. Surrounding an old stone castle, the tightly-packed village, with its hanging baskets and roadside oak trees, was a pleasant place. However, there was something inescapably unnerving about Burg-Reuland that we found difficult to ignore: its garden gnomes. A quick count confirmed that the colourful creatures outnumbered the human population by a staggering ratio of one human to every thirty gnomes: fat and thin, young and old, big ears and small ears, hatted and bald. Some were wielding signs, others fishing or cheekily revealing their terracotta bottoms, whilst one particularly chubby gnome stood in his vegetable patch, swinging a hula hoop about his exposed belly. Their astounding population, we agreed, was the result of monthly activities under the cover of a new moon, when the gnomes would meet behind a pile of plant pots at the back of the garden. Secretly multiplying, the brittle beings would return to their positions before dawn broke, unbeknown to the village people.

We spent the rest of the morning climbing around the bowl of a forested valley side patchworked with large oblongs of felled trees. A pair of mewing kites with wedged tails and fanned wingtips conspired side by side as they scanned their hunting grounds from the sky.

It was 11am by the time we arrived at a wooden bus shelter that sat on a junction between half a dozen country lanes. We had been climbing steeply for an hour, and our view from the rolling summit stretched out in all directions. We skulked inside the shelter to evade the wind, and opened the map. We were 505 metres above sea level and just a few kilometres from the Belgium-Germany-Luxembourg tripoint. A ripple of deciduous forest flowed south into the Oesling, Luxembourg's northernmost region, dragging the Ardennes with it and steaming with the promise of a new landscape.

For Jake and me, the Grand Duchy of Luxembourg was a country of mystery. We knew that Luxembourg City was the capital – enough of our friends had told us – but what about the footpaths, signposting, weather and terrain? And the laws on wild camping, the cuisine and resupply points? We were wildly ignorant, yet, for whatever reason, not anxious. To us, though it was unconfirmed, Luxembourg was safe, pristine, and steeped in serenity.

Our route would take us north to south along the Our, Sauer and Moselle Rivers, and with them Germany's western border. Cutting in from the east, we planned to gravitate towards the nation's capital, Luxembourg City, where we would pick up a valuable parcel of maps before moving south for two more days, eventually dropping into the Lorraine region of France. Our bisection of the country, based on our current daily average of twenty-five kilometres, was to take us no more than ten days.

A track to the south fell away from the bus shelter and then rose once more into dense woodland. We trod the gravel for a few minutes, weaving in and out of its milky-coffee puddles, their shores stained with yellow pine pollen, before arriving at a clearing on the western ridge of the Vallée de l'Our. A lead-coloured river swam 200 metres below through cattle-grazed fields stippled with hamlets – Welchenhausen, Oberhausen and Peterskirche.

The Our was smaller than I had imagined, with just four metres separating its west bank from its east. But the landscape it had created brought the change we craved after three weeks of Belgian pavements and fields. We were now amongst hills and valleys.

Reaching for the map to check our location, I realised we were just a centimetre or so from the edge of the paper. The Belgian charts had finally run their course. Having been initially sceptical about their practicality, we had become attached to the accuracy and detail of the charts and were sad to see them go. Instead, our navigation would now be dictated by two 1:50,000 topographic maps: *Luxembourg Nord* and *Luxembourg Sud*. 'These are amazing!' Jake had said back in England after we received the maps through the post. 'Bold colours, pretty symbols. They're like adventure maps!' A closer inspection, however, suggested that their practicality would struggle to match their aesthetic value.

We stopped at an ambiguous path junction in Junkersberg Forest. I pulled the map from inside the front of my jacket (its new, easy access location). The chart was ginormous, folding and flapping in the wind. I wrestled the chart under control and, with no help from the fuzzy print, realised that, whilst the map directed us left, the *GR* signpost said right.

We decided to stick with the waymarking that had served us well until now, turning right down a steep, jolting gorge path, sheathed with moon daisies that slouched over limestone rocks, and towards the sound of rolling water. The trail eventually spilt out into Ouren, a German speaking Belgian hamlet almost totally surrounded by Luxembourg and Germany, except for a thin band of territory that connects the enclave to 'mainland' Belgium. Beyond the shuttered windows and vine-covered walls of Ouren's riverside houses, our route along the road passed a large rock monument – the tripoint of the three countries. We crossed a small stone bridge, leaving Belgium for Luxembourg, and joined a riverside path.

To our left, the smell of the disturbed riverbed bubbled up with the chinking water. To our right, a stratified wall of dirt and stones, scoured out by floodwater, hung with exposed tree roots. Further up the valley, I noticed scores of toppled pines lying on the forest floor in untidy piles like an oversized game of pick-me-up – the result of a storm perhaps, or more likely felled for the fire.

'I haven't seen a *GR* sign for a while, have you?' Jake queried, a couple of kilometres downstream.

'No, I haven't.'

'And what are all these?' he said, pointing at a cluster of symbols that had been spray-painted onto a tree trunk beside the path. 'I keep seeing them. Blue arrows with yellow circles, white arrows with green triangles, swirls of green with '*NaturWanderPark*' scrawled across them.'

'Perhaps they don't have *GR* signs in Luxembourg?'

'Well, which one is ours then?'

Having never seen any of these signs before, or even heard about them, our attention returned to the cartoon map.

'How stupid!' Jake announced, shoving the chart into the side pocket of my bag. Unfortunately, the cartographers had deemed hang-gliding launch sites to be of such importance that they had overlaid a large, opaque glider silhouette onto the very junction we were now stood at. 'Let's give up on the map and signs, they're useless. We can follow the river instead.'

To our delight, the old-fashioned method worked wonderfully, and we soon found ourselves strolling down the road towards a campsite. Having spent the day being distracted by maps, we had managed to ignore the lack of food in our packs – a couple of Oxo cubes and some old salami – and were thus relieved to see a gas station just beyond the campsite.

Half of the store's shelves were occupied by coffee, and the other half were stacked with confectionery. It wasn't perfect, but it was food nonetheless. We spent eighteen euros almost exclusively on strawberry syrup-filled chocolates, and, after a decidedly muddled interaction with the cashier lady, learnt that the language in the area was now either German or Luxembourgish, with the acceptance of French, depending on who you met.

The Valleè d'Our campsite was deserted, so we erected Ted in the overgrown grass and accepted that payment for our pitch would be impossible.

'Wow!' Jake said, as we lay in the tent a few hours later recording the day's activities into our journals. 'With all that border crossing and gas station excitement, we managed to pass our 1,000-kilometre mark without even noticing it!'

Navigation was still proving to be an issue. We had woken the next morning and set out along a forest track, following the wavy lines of a green and brown symbol that appeared to correlate well with the *GR5* path marked on the map. However, soon the lines disappeared, and we were forced to join another route, painted with yellow circles, which seemed to take us at least vaguely south.

Within a couple of hundred metres, the track narrowed and the ground fell steeply away on either side. We tiptoed along the forested ridgeline, winding through birch and oak, their canopies dripping with soft light, as the luscious smell of pine resin drifted up from the warm valley. Tussocks of feathery grass brushed against our ankles whilst spider threads crossed the path, accentuating our solitude. As I waved the strands to the side, I noticed an intermittent string of small plants with jagged leaves lining the eastern side of the thin track – wild strawberries. Eager to taste their sugars, I knelt down to the ground and searched for the deep red fruit.

'Can we not stop so much?' Jake said as I got to my feet.

'I was just looking for strawberries,' I replied a little defensively.

'I feel funny. I think it's the vertigo. Can we just keep moving?'

'Yes, of course. I totally forgot,' I apologised.

Until recently, Jake had never been anxious about heights – quite the opposite, in fact. At a young age, we had both developed an interest in loftiness, jumping into the ocean off the highest rocks we could find, and scrambling along teetering garden walls above thickets of brambles and stinging nettles. On one occasion, when we were perhaps ten or eleven, Jake had fallen from a rope swing, landing upside down on his neck. He couldn't breathe for almost a minute, and his face turned a faded aubergine colour. But this didn't stop us. I remember one summer, in the dying days of August, announcing that we would climb all of the trees on Durdham Downs, a 400-acre grassland close to our house, scattered with giant horse chestnuts and a congregation of less appealing, rickety hawthorn trees. Having conquered a particularly difficult climb, I decided to celebrate by swinging from one of its sturdier-looking branches, only to hear it snap. I fell several metres and hit the ground with my back, eventually breaking into laughter once I knew I wasn't hurt.

Indeed, it wasn't until our early twenties, along the snowy slopes of the Kepler Track in the Fiordland National Park, New Zealand, that Jake first experienced the dizzying symptoms of vertigo. We had spent the night in a hut on Mount Luxmore, huddled next to two friends and an unproductive log burner. Intent on warming our muscles quickly the following morning, we left the shelter briskly, skirting the mountain's north-west flank towards Luxmore Saddle. Save for burning thighs and numb fingertips, we climbed 1,200 metres without incident until Jake suddenly froze midway up to the pass, declaring he couldn't go any further.

Initially, I thought that he was messing about, but as he hesitantly turned towards me, I was shocked to see sweat dripping from his terror-filled face. Until that point, I hadn't appreciated the potential danger of our situation: deep snow, frozen on its surface, covered the path to the saddle, and, with our thrift-inspired naivety not to have brought crampons, coupled with the forty-five degree slope, I too was suddenly struck by the peril we were facing.

Most sources will tell you that vertigo is caused by a disturbance of either the balance mechanism of the inner ear or of the brain. However, for Jake, it seemed clear that his vertigo was not the result of a physical disturbance but of his sudden recognition of danger. Whether he liked it or not, exposure to height made the ground spin beneath his feet, and with that came the fear that inevitably he would be dragged over the edge to his death.

In the years that followed our trip to New Zealand, he found ways to cope with the vertigo, and the spinning disorder was pushed to the back of his mind. But with our ambition to cross the Vosges, the Jura and the Alps to reach the Mediterranean Sea came a resurfacing of his anxieties. 'Before we go any further,' Jake had said, as preparation for our journey began to snowball, 'I think I need a test.'

To assess the strength of his mind, Dad took Jake up to Striding Edge in the Lake District National Park. Moulded by glaciers, the knife-blade crest ascends for almost two kilometres towards the 950-metre peak of Helvellyn. Renowned for its perilously poised path and extreme weather conditions, Striding Edge has taken a number of lives.

They both completed the walk without physical injury, but Jake's mental trauma was so great that he vowed never to put himself in that position again. 'But what about the Alps? You can't cross the bloody Alps without climbing something steep!' I had repeatedly exclaimed, to which he would inevitably respond, 'Well then, we might have to go around them.'

Although the highest hills along our Luxembourg section rarely exceeded 550 metres, and their paths were more often than not gentle and harmless, completing this first vertigo challenge was important for Jake.

'It wasn't too bad,' he said merrily as the ridgeline sank into the valley floor. 'I just can't talk, and I have to keep moving with my eyes straight ahead. Anyway, it's over now. What's that?' he questioned abruptly, ending the discussion.

I traced the line of his hand to a blue signpost further up the path. We had arrived at the *E2-E3* intersection: the meeting of two great paths. Whilst the *E2* (comprising the *GR5*) dissects Europe north to south, the *E3* moves east to west from Bulgaria and the Baltic Sea to the Spanish Atlantic coastline. Since leaving Bristol, we hadn't met another long-distance walker, let alone someone attempting one of the Continent's illustrious E-Routes. I wondered if there had ever been a time when two bodies, each on their own magnificent adventure, had met at this insignificant intersection. It seemed unlikely, but what a chance it would be.

We had spent two days in the shadows of the Oesling's dense oak and beech forests, and, though we loved the trees, it felt good to climb from their shade out into the open, where a blanket of arable hills edged into the distance.

It was midday, and with rumbling stomachs, we decided to stop for lunch on the brow of a farm lane. Surrounded by joyous yellow rapeseed fields, and with warmed cheeks, it felt like summer was on its way. Jake yanked a baguette from his pack, and we tore bits off, chewing boyishly as we gazed eastwards over to Germany.

I deemed our lunch stop to be an appropriate time for me to search my body for ticks. Once the exposed areas of my person had been given the all-clear, I worked my way up the inside of my thighs and a little beyond, justifying my search with the discovery of one of the little critters high in my groin. With the Vaseline and penknife buried deep inside Jake's pack, I decided a quick scratch with my finger would probably prove as effective, hearing Mum's voice in my head: 'Make sure you remove them properly, OK?'

After several attempts, the hardy tick came free, and I flicked it to the floor, where it no doubt waited patiently for the next short-shorted hiker to pass by.

Our first acknowledgment of Vianden came with the red, white and blue stripes of a drowsy-looking Luxembourg flag, which poked above a steep-sided meander of the Our. We rounded the bend and realised it belonged to the Château de Vianden, a magnificent complex of conical towers and arched windows, cushioned by a gathering of deciduous trees, their limbs tussling at the lower walls like a crowd of beseeching peasants. The château, with its origins dating back to the eleventh century, had been modified many times. Under its unusual blend of Romanesque, Gothic and Renaissance architecture, I couldn't rid myself of the feeling that we were standing in a romantic fairy tale.

However, Rapunzel didn't drop her hair, and we ambled down into Vianden's centre without mythical incident, albeit amongst enchanting streets of cobbles and steps, and unbalanced buildings, their jaunty windowsills iridescent with geraniums.

We crossed the Our over the arched town bridge and filtered down one or two streets until we reached Op dem Deiche, a campsite at the far end of the commune.

In spite of the summery skies, it was not yet June, and with only a few pitches taken, we found ourselves assembling Ted just metres from the verdant riverbank, with a view of the castle opposite.

Of the ten or so campers who were already pitched (parked is probably the more appropriate word), nine perceived Jake and me to be more interesting than their previous entertainment – a group of grazing ducks and an old man fishing a little further down the river. We were thus watched intently until our last peg entered the ground, at which point the attention of our spectators once again returned to the ducks.

It had been four days since our last wash. Stamping on my dirty clothes whilst scrubbing my armpits in the shower, I must have rinsed enough filth from my body to physically reduce both my height and weight. I also discovered two more ticks, one on my hip and the other under my watch.

With our chores done and a few hours of light still remaining, I left Jake in the company of two swans and their troop of imitating cygnets, and made for the town centre. I sat outside Hôtel Victor Hugo (apparently the writer not only enjoyed the thermal pools of Spa but the beer of Vianden too) and sipped on a bottle of Hoegaarden. Eavesdropping on conversations that I didn't understand, I watched old men congregate by the bridge for seemingly no other reason than to share their day's quandaries with those who would listen.

When I returned to the tent, Jake, wearing his white long johns and blue sandals, was taking photos of the castle, now lit with a saffron yellow glow. The cygnets, which had been pursuing the flicking tail of their mother all day, clambered clumsily on to her back and nestled themselves amongst a heap of feathers.

'It's been a magnificent day,' Jake whispered, so as not to disturb the sleeping birds. 'Perhaps the best yet.' Then we retired to our sleeping bags and nodded off with the utterings of night-time strollers behind our heads and the subtle rumbles of the Our's flow at our feet.

It was 11pm when I woke up with the same nausea I had experienced one week earlier after my toxic plant consumption. I opened the tent and rushed to the toilets, where a tremendous bout of vomiting was succeeded by an equally furious course of diarrhoea. We had not eaten any forest plants since the misidentification. Perhaps it was sunstroke, dehydration or food poisoning? With nothing left to expel, I gave up trying to figure out the cause and made my way back to the tent, apologising to Jake whilst I clambered back into bed.

But an hour later I was up again, only this time the toilets were a stretch too far, and I was forced to the ground just metres from the porch. Unable to sleep, I returned once more to the toilets and leant in front of the mirror, registering my colourless face and dozy eyes. Lifting my T-shirt, I suddenly realised the impact that six weeks of walking and a night of vomiting had inflicted on my body. I was horribly skinny.

A little discouraged by the whole affair, I stumbled back to the tent, the château aglow, and the starry sky enough to make me smile.

I opened my eyes to a blazing kaleidoscope of creases and folds on Ted's ceiling. My head was throbbing, and my stomach felt fragile. Jake helped me out of my sleeping bag and sat me on the grass in the sun before disappearing off into town. He returned some minutes later with a breakfast of fresh oranges, yoghurt and juice, along with a packet of rehydration tablets. After washing my socks and packing up the tent, he handed me the phone. 'We're staying here another night, in a hotel. Now, speak to Claudia, or Mum, or whoever. I'll sort the rest.'

I took advantage of Jake's offer and proceeded to call not only Mum and Claudia but Dad and Jessy too, each time receiving enough sympathy to give me the energy to phone the next unfortunate person.

During the days since our last conversation, Claudia had added to her already extensive collection of tattoos. 'I drew a bumblebee, and then decided that I wanted it tattooed on my arm,' she told me in that blasé tone that only someone with existing ink could achieve. 'Apparently, bumblebees shouldn't be able to fly because their wings are too small to carry the weight of their body. But they can fly!' she elated. 'It's a symbol of defying the impossible.'

I was encouraged by this theory, whether it was true or not, and helped Jake pack up the final few pieces of gear before mentally waving goodbye to our onlookers who, I was sure, had not moved from their plastic chairs since we arrived.

After what felt like thirty kilometres, but in reality wasn't even one, we squeezed through the front doors of the Hôtel Victor Hugo, and were shown to our room.

That afternoon, we watched clouds tumble into the valley through the bedroom window. A crack of thunder signalled the opening of a terrific downpour that made us grateful to be within four walls and under a roof.

A pool of sweat gathered on my chest in the night, and I dreamt about a giant Labrador dog waiting at a zebra crossing. By morning, the surface water on my body had all but evaporated, and the bilious symptoms from the day before had faded. I felt almost spritely.

However, Jake did not. Perhaps unsurprisingly, given our close living quarters, he appeared to have contracted the same ailment. He missed breakfast, and I returned to the room to find him still lying on the bed with darkened eyes and a pale face. 'I know I look bad, but I feel sort of alright. Perhaps somewhere awkwardly in between brilliant and horrendous. I'll give it a few more hours. Hopefully, the nausea will pass.'

With Jake resting, I had some time to kill. Gathering several things together – sponges, my handkerchief and the sewing kit – I sat on the bed and got to work. Still yet to use the hanky, I cut it in half and wrapped it around two sponges, each of which I stitched to the inside of Jake's hip belt. Much like the socks that Jake had tied around his strapping back in Belgium, theory suggested that the sponges would mimic an increase in his waist size, thus providing more purchase for the bag. With any hope, this would reduce the abrasion that he had been experiencing over recent weeks.

'Right, I can't sit still anymore,' Jake said after a couple of hours. 'We're going!'

TROTT-A DISASTER

Our exit out of Vianden was steep, slow and damp, no doubt exacerbated by our compromised immune systems. But we were happy to be back on our feet and took the fresh air with pleasure. Keen to stick with the Our River, we clung to the Luxembourg-Germany border, parting temporarily from the GR5 which ventured west towards Diekirch.

Instead, we kept our eyes wide open for a red triangular symbol which had replaced the yellow circles, and continued south, skipping from Longsdorf to Hoesdorf, and Hoesdorf to Reisdorf ('dorf' being the German word for village). We passed through a landscape awash with yellow – forests of broom, hills of rapeseed, and fields crammed with buttercups where no man, woman or child could hide their love of butter. With the Ardennes now behind us, we left the Oesling for the Mullerthal region – also known as 'Little Switzerland' – immediately passing a snail more reminiscent of an equatorial mollusc than something I would have expected to see in rural Luxembourg.

We ate a slice of bread beneath a bus shelter, and moved sluggishly through the drizzle into the Mullerthal Forest, where ivy climbed the rough, creaking pine trees towards birdsong high in the canopies, and star-shaped mushrooms, small and delicate, flecked the soil.

Stopping for a break at the Château de Beaufort, we watched the reflections of its walls and weathered towers ripple, like an impressionist's painting, through its moat. Boulders jutted from a noisy stream that meandered through beech and hornbeam before joining the slightly larger Haterbaach Rivière. The trail skipped across its course on mossy stone slabs as imposing limestone walls, the result of millions of years of fluvial erosion, staggered skywards all around us. Dimpled and grooved, the rock faces were home to hundreds of small birds that dipped and chirped across the steaming gorge.

After some time, we arrived at Sieweschloeff Labyrinth, a network of Jurassic precipices interwoven with chiselled stairwells and archways.

'Are you going to climb it?' a voice sounded. We craned our necks up towards a lofty cliff ledge across the gorge where a young girl and boy, and their smiling parents, looked down at us.

I followed the small girl's prompting finger to a vertical wall beside them, dusted here and there with chalk marks. 'No!' I shouted through a laugh, imagining two orange balls scaling the giant obstacle.

The family had travelled the short distance across from Germany into the Mullerthal. 'We come here every year. It's so beautiful,' the mother announced. 'But people in Germany don't get that. They think it's boring – just money and banks, and serious people. But we love it, especially here.' She looked pensively across the gorge. Moisture rose from the forest floor, feeding the cushions of moss that disguised trees as rocks, and stones as branches. 'We like to watch the climbers. That's why my little one asked you if you were going up.'

'I see,' I said. 'No, we're walkers. I'm afraid it wouldn't end well if we tried to climb that!'

We spoke to the family for a few minutes and then left them to their lunch. 'I hope you have your waterproofs for tomorrow. There is a big storm coming!' The mother's voice echoed across the gorge just before the rock maze took us out of sight. 'Good luck!'

'Great,' Jake muttered, summing up my thoughts. 'More bloody rain.'

According to the symbols on our map, Echternach, Luxembourg's oldest town, held much promise: museums, monuments, archaeological sites, picnic areas, water sports, camping, and, of course, the all-important provision of a hang-gliding launch site. In fact, the town was so well equipped, and the playful reference pictures so abundant, that we were once again forced to abandon the illegible map and find our own way into the centre.

As it turned out, the promise depicted on the map was entirely justified. Two violinists and a cellist bowed *Always on my Mind* in the stone-patched market square, bordered by buildings of cream, coral and white. The town centre was busy with German tourists, and our garish packs, both cumbersome and bullish, bounced from shoulder to shoulder through the crowded square – 'Sorry. *Désolé*. Sorry.'

At the southern end of town, in the quieter backstreets, we followed our noses into a dusty yet wildly fragrant corner shop stacked with baskets of garlic, onions, fruit and dried fish. Amongst the disorganised shelves, I found a bag of cherry tomatoes, whilst Jake discovered two tins of beans and meat, a wholesome meal for the night ahead.

Seventy-eight meandering kilometres from its source in Hautes Fagnes, south-eastern Belgium, the Our tributary unified with the Sauer River, alongside the grassy, duck-inhabited riverbanks of Rosport. I cracked open one of the tins we had bought back in Echternach and lumped it into our bowls. It had an odd bounce that I wouldn't usually have associated with food, and the meat dissolved curiously in my mouth. A little reluctantly, we cleaned our bowls, and then Jake opened the next can whilst I scanned the ingredients: '53% kidney beans, 15% pig's trotter, 9% pig's head'. Feeling a little repulsed, I watched as Jake struggled with the contents of the second tin with his spoon. A jellied trotter bounced out, followed by a large piece of wobbly skin covered with black bristles.

Jake and I rarely wasted food, but with both of us on the tapering end of a stomach bug, we gladly left our bowls full and our bellies empty. The title of my journal entry that night read: 'Thursday, 30 May, Trott-a Disaster'.

THE MOSELLE

As warned, rain came early the next day. I unzipped the tent to a dribbling sky and a misted river, watching a moorhen from the warmth of my sleeping bag whilst it foraged in the reeds on the opposite bank. We packed up hastily in the drizzle, leaving our bags oddly shaped with roll mats stuffed here and books wedged there, and left Rosport, stopping at a gas station where we bought a breakfast of waffles and sardines.

Having spent several days in the Mullerthal region, the path now took us into the hills of the Moselle, a landscape dominated by a deep history of vineyards and winemaking, and so named 'the birthplace of Luxembourg wines'.

We slipped and skidded up the well-watered paths and practically skied back down them, snatching and grappling at branches for last-second support to avoid the mudbath below. First vineyards and then orchards began to appear on the slopes through the trees. But, unlike the engineered and linear orchards of the modern farm, the crops were reminiscent of the days when land was abundant. Time had picked off the weak trees and left the strong. Breaking through the soil, the gnarled trunks were thick and scarred, and the branches, brittle and old, drooped with the weight of the late-spring blossom.

'Wow!' Jake said, diverting my attention from the ancient crops and pointing at a settlement on the map. 'Was there ever a more tastelessly named place than Dickweiler?'

Although a valid point, Jake's reference to the map was not brought about by his delight in crudely named places, but more pressingly by our whereabouts. We were back on the GR5 and assumed the abundance of red squares painted on a number of the flanking trees were now our waymarkers. However, the signs began to contradict the compass, and then proceeded to lead us into a vineyard where a dead end left us standing on a hillside a dozen metres above the busy N10 carriageway in Mertert. The rain had hardened, and our patience was diminishing so we decided to bushwhack through a steep, dense slope of brambles. Using Jake's walking poles as makeshift machetes, we eventually bumbled out onto the road below, where onlookers pointed through the windows of their cars, some clearly sympathetic and others openly sadistic.

With our hearts set on a night under a roof, we ditched the uncertainties of the GR5 and joined a path that ran alongside the river. 'Look!' I gesticulated towards the water. 'It's changed direction.'

Jake glanced at the flow around the corner of his hood. 'That's because we're on the Moselle now. The Our joins the Sauer, the Sauer joins the Moselle, and then the Moselle joins the Rhine, which is a south to north river. Actually, we will be seeing this river a lot more. Apparently, its source is somewhere in the Vosges Mountains.'

Having bled the Lorraine and Alsace regions of France for more than 300 kilometres, the Moselle was wide and ran with confidence and power. We walked south against its flow, passing a caterpillar of bank-holiday cyclists, each grazing the wheel of the one in front. Their heads down and bodies clad with disposable ponchos, I predicted that enjoyment was perhaps no longer their goal. I imagined muffles of self-motivational curses seeping from beneath their hoods: 'We've bloody well come on holiday, and I don't care if it's raining in June. We're going to have a good time anyway!'

For another two hours, we marched along the concrete pavement, never quite leaving the sprawl of houses that connected Mertert to its neighbouring settlement, Grevenmacher.

To our delight, the city's campsite offered us the rental of an apartment for the night. We were not expecting much for the price but were gifted relative luxury, with unlimited power supply points, two beds, a shower, a corner sofa and, most notably, a kitchen. With a rare opportunity to cook beyond boiling water, we rustled up a feast and then spent the rest of the evening taking advantage of the kitchen's diverse collection of glasses.

'Champagne flutes!' Jake declared after several hours of experimentation. 'Champagne flutes amplify sound better than all of the other glasses!'

I stood in front of the steamed bathroom mirror the next morning and wrote the words: 'A Walk to the Water, June 1 2013'. Watching the letters drip down the glass, I began to think about life back home.

Jake and I were into our third month of walking. I felt strong and wholly involved in our venture. Distractions from the outside world no longer felt like distractions, but were simply words and actions with little emotional attachment. This was a distressing thought in some ways. Of course, I still cared immensely for Claudia and my family, and I thought about them often, but the thoughts were numb, and whether I liked it or not, I had become detached.

We spent the first hour of daylight running a tube of superglue along the cracks of our worn-out boots in an attempt to re-establish their waterproofing, before climbing away from the houses and reuniting with the *GR5*. Passing a church on the hill, just as the sun pushed beyond its silver lining, we then skirted a terraced vineyard where vines hung over the shoulders of their supporting fences like ungainly drunkards. Indeed, all around us, the hillsides were blanketed with vineyards.

With the sound of a thousand whistling birds encouraging us on, we entered Houwald Forest only to discover that the chorus was not that of a bird colony but a gushing waterfall. I jumped over the rocks singing Joe Purdy's 'Skinny Dippin' Girl' whilst Jake experimented with the long-exposure settings on his camera.

Since entering Luxembourg, the clarity of the *GR5* had gradually diminished, our presence on the route being more down to coincidence than effective signposting. 'To be honest, I'll be glad to see the back of it for a few days,' Jake said as we veered westwards away from the *GR5* and towards the country's capital.

We were two days from Luxembourg City, a milestone that represented our only en route capital and, more significantly, our map resupply point. We had included the city because we deemed it the most secure location from which to collect the maps. 'The bigger the city, the safer the parcel,' we had both agreed before leaving Bristol. 'We'll send it by recorded delivery. That's the safest way.'

With thirty-five kilometres to cover before reaching the city, our pace slowed and we ambled through rolling fields of maize, studded with vacant farm towns, save for a swift here and a cat there.

In a field of tall grass, we rested in the sun next to a tier of flat-capped mushrooms, chewing on slices of rye bread smeared with chocolate spread. A twisting caterpillar sailed slowly on a thread of silk from a towering oak, and Jake alerted me to a pine marten on the rooted path ahead. Pulling Nicholas Crane from my bag, I sank into his adventure – a 10,000-kilometre mountain walk across Europe – as Jake picked ticks from his legs, both of us unperturbed by the astounding array of creepy-crawlies that busied themselves on our sunbathing bodies.

'Argh!' Jake shouted, jumping to his feet and slapping his shoulders.

'What is it?'

'Ants! Bloody red ants!' he blared.

After several minutes of frantic brushing and cursing, we abandoned the heat of the field for the cool, damp beech trees of Katebësch Forest, following a leaf-covered gully down towards a trickling stream. We pitched Ted on the opposite side, just up from the flow, hanging our water bladder on a tree and drying our shoes in the dappled sunlight.

Footfall woke us. Thankfully, it was not a drift of wild pigs but two roe deer stripping fresh shoots from beneath the leaf litter as they sniffed and hoofed at the ground. One wandered off, but the other paused in a streak of fiery light. I watched the deer intently through the beech, before the thunderous rumbles of a low-flying plane spooked it. Luxembourg City was close.

Within ten steps of setting off, I had soaked one foot right through, after failing to make the leap across the dark stream of water that we had successfully crossed the day before. 'Crap!' I blurted instinctively, before Jake consoled me with a reminder of the blue skies above us. It was a beautiful day and, as long as the sun was shining, a wet boot meant nothing but pruned toes.

We made our way along a small track of delicate dog-violets and starry white flowers, which linked Katebësch Forest with Schëtterhaard Forest. It was in this second extent of trees that we noticed a profusion of cobweb balls hanging from the branches, each containing a glowing amber spider, like a cluster of silky Chinese lanterns.

Uebersyren was much like Munsbach, and Munsbach was much like Sandweiler: quiet, clean and lined with houses that were neither offensive nor appealing. We stopped for an early lunch in one of Sandweiler's small parks and watched on with curiosity as a well-tanned man with muscles, waxed hair and sunglasses flew down the sleepy road in a pink VW Beetle Convertible.

'Well, we must be nearly there,' Jake said. 'We really must be. Look,' he continued, pointing at the map and then looking over to the west, 'we're only about four kilometres away, but I can't see a thing. Surely we should be able to see the buildings by now!'

115

Three kilometres later, we crossed a faint line on our map which suggested we had arrived in our fourth Luxembourgian region, Bon Pays (also referred to as the 'Good Country', the 'Luxembourg City Area', the 'Luxembourg Plateau', or simply 'Luxembourg City'). In spite of this information, the city was as elusive as it had been fifty kilometres earlier. We stopped beside half a dozen cottages, each fronted with red geraniums and backed by the vertical cream walls of the Alzette River gorge. White sheets billowed on a washing line outside the houses, pushing the smell of summer into the air.

'Well, this is confusing,' I said, reverting to the map for the umpteenth time. Sure of our location, we continued on, marvelling at the secluded nature of Luxembourg's capital.

After rounding a curved precipice and crossing a bridge, we were thrust without warning (aside from the evidence shown on the map) into an urban landscape of beeping horns, tinny car stereos, high-rise blocks and rattling train tracks, home to some 100,000 residents.

To say that Jake and I stood out – with our grubby skin, untamed hair and sizable packs – would be an understatement. The city felt wealthy, and as we traipsed down the Avenue de la Liberté, one of the most opulent shopping streets in the world, I sensed the stares.

Routine would have seen us stumble into the cheapest hotel, where we would then proceed to ask for the cheapest room. However, finding a budget room in the capital city of a country stated by the International Monetary Fund as having the second highest per capita gross domestic product in the world was a challenge that we had no interest in. Claudia had kindly booked us into the rather aptly named Hotel Bristol in the city's southern Garer Quarter, allowing us to focus on our priorities: send home unnecessary items and receive necessary maps.

A man with spiky brown hair and a tight pinstriped shirt undone to his hairy chest welcomed us off the shopping street into a narrow hallway. 'I don't speak English,' he retorted sharply after we greeted him in English, French and German. 'Only joking, I can, I can speak any language. Now, you are in room 312, up the stairs there.' He pointed without looking and in the same breath continued, 'And here are two free beer vouchers for the café next

116

door. And now the city!' He slapped the vouchers onto the desk and, scrawling on a map, circled the Hotel Bristol. 'Now, here and here,' he put two large crosses through the southern suburbs of Hollerich and Bonnevoie, 'they are nothing. Only four people sleep here, nothing! Passports?'

'Oh,' Jake said, waking suddenly from his voice-induced coma, 'yes, of course.'

'Bristol!' the man yelled excitedly. 'You are from Bristol? My hotel is Hotel Bristol!'

'Yes, we know, that's why we booked it,' I replied, enjoying his delight. 'So, why is it called Hotel Bristol?'

'No idea!' the man revealed after an uncharacteristic pause. 'I have worked in this hotel for many years, and I have no idea!'

'So,' I turned to Jake as we climbed the stairs to the room, 'we've been on the path for fifty days, yet we're still in Bristol?'

'Very clever, Dan,' he replied sarcastically.

It was a Sunday, and, with the post office closed, we decided to leave our chores for the following day. It felt strange to be walking without the weight of our packs, and even more unusual to blend in with the crowds, even if we were wearing knitted socks and sandals. Strolling down the Avenue de la Liberté, we stepped onto the Adolphe Bridge, crossing the Pétrusse River and its deep valley of trees just as the dropping sun pinched the city's iconic viaducts to the width of a shoestring.

From one square to the next, we ambled through the old town, along busy alleyways of ice cream-licking tourists and SLR cameras, stopping off at Quality Burger (a restaurant with a misleading title) before retiring to the hotel, where a game of handball on the television proved the catalyst for sleep.

'What the hell?' I heard Jake shout as he took his morning shower. 'There's a bloody tick on my...'

I showed no sympathy: 'That means I'm on six, and you're on eleven! Or does it count as double if you find it on your you-know-what?'

'This is not a good start to the day,' Jake replied. 'Let's hope it's not a sign of things to come.'

It was. After breakfast (which not only involved eating, but filling a plastic bag with sachets of Nutella and jam, apples, bread and yoghurts) we walked into the city and found the Bureau de Poste Luxembourg-Centre, our map pickup point.

'I am sorry, we have no such parcel under your name,' the pursed-lipped man behind the glass informed us with sickening predictability.

For the next four hours, we trudged from one building to the next – from the Bureau de Poste Luxembourg-Centre to the Bureau de Post Luxembourg-Gare, and then onto the information centre, back to the city post office, the internet café, the information centre again, for some reason the bank, and then back once more to the central office – all the while on the phone to Mum, who did well to calm our frustrations.

'But this is where your website told us to send it. It should've been here a week ago,' Jake urged as we grovelled through the glass in the central post office for the third time.

'That is not our address,' the man replied. 'That is the address of someone's personal box, and your name doesn't match theirs, so your parcel would have arrived and then been returned back to England.' But the parcel wasn't in England, and nor was it in Luxembourg. Somewhere vaguely between the two, our hopes of continuing on south were bouncing around in the back of a courier's van as the driver, I imagined, sang distortedly through a cigarette, with sunglasses on and the window down.

After hearing the news that the parcel could take up to thirty days to reappear, we called upon our last resort: to ditch the box and its £200-worth of maps, many of which were difficult to acquire given the uncommon nature of our route, and hope that we could reorder the charts from the suppliers we had initially used back in England.

'We still have to wait at least three days, even if our suppliers do have the maps,' Jake said as we sat in the smoky café next door to the hotel, making the most of our free beer vouchers. 'And who's to say that the same thing won't happen again?'

My largely alcohol-free diet over the past months had quickly rendered me drunk, and Jake's anxiety had trouble keeping up with my new optimism. 'Yes, that may be the case, but we have the Vosges in our sights. Well, not in our sights, but you know, it's soon. How exciting to think: mountains, Jake!'

*

Nicholas Crane, on his walk across Europe, certainly had his share of failed pickups. As did Chris Townsend, the first man to walk the length of the Canadian Rockies, who was forced to spend the best part of a week in Banff waiting for a vital parcel of gear. I had always found these accounts mildly amusing. Townsend was stuck in Banff, surrounded by outrageously stunning mountains. What was the big deal? But I now understood the addictions of walking and the compulsion to keep moving. Resting against one's will was by no means a chance to recuperate but an irritant for the itchiest of feet.

Unable to focus on anything but the parcel, we decided that we would check the post office every day until the end of the week, and if it still hadn't arrived by then, we would have no other option than to continue on, acquiring local maps along the way. But this was an unreliable method of travel, and something that appealed to us less than a tin of pig's trotters and jellied skin.

It was a Tuesday, and as the pursed-lipped man from the day before rejected our queries yet again – 'I am sorry, the *bureau de poste* does *not* have your parcel' – I began to feel that we had become a nuisance.

'*Arrêtes!* Stop!' a lady shouted as we turned for the door. We both spun around to see a woman clutching a shoebox-sized package with a smile on her face. 'Name please?' she ordered, reading the label on the box.

'Graham,' I answered, my heartbeat quickening.

'Then this is for you. It's your missing parcel.'

Thanking the lady and grabbing the package from her hands, we quickly found the nearest bench and unwrapped the box like excited children, unable to relax until we saw the contents inside. After identifying the package as our own, I felt a flood of jubilation surge through my body and looked up to see Jake, with glazed eyes, hugging the box like it was a long-lost relative.

Along with the maps, there were two guidebooks – one for the Vosges and Jura, and the other for the Alps – a couple of packets of migraine tablets for Jake, and a letter from Mum. She wrote:

Hello my wonderful sons,
I hope this parcel reaches you in one piece – you will literally be lost without it – ha ha!

Just want to say that you're in my thoughts every waking moment. I know how hard it must be at times for you, but keep going – you'll be so proud of yourselves when you dip your poorly feet into the Med. I have still to put together a leaflet, but will do it to try and get you some more donations. Lack of activity doesn't mean people have forgotten you – people in the road ask how you are doing (Monica, Vivienne).

I can't say often enough how proud I am of my little family – the world is a better place with you all in it.

Paul and I went for a lovely bluebell walk in the Forest of Dean. I wish I had taken my camera, not for the bluebells but for the little group of seven boars that we came across. Someone we passed told us they were on the edge of the forest path further in front of us. We walked quite a way and thought we'd missed them, and then they appeared. So cute and not too afraid of us. I did wonder where the mummy and daddy boars were! Then later we came across them again and stood watching them for about ten minutes. It's the first time I've seen them in the forest, or anywhere.

Getting closer with the kitchen, but still haven't settled on the cupboards and the worktops, but the design is sorted. Lynne was a great help.

Hope Brenda manages to meet up with you as it will give you something to look forward to. I will ask Grandpa again if he intends on going out.

I haven't done one Tesco's shop since you've been gone – not eating very well! I have a week off work next week and hope to finalise the kitchen arrangements then.

Anyway, again, so proud of you both. Look after each other and check for ticks. If you get a rash or feel unwell, get yourself to the doctors. They carry very nasty diseases with long-term effects.

I know, I know, worry, worry, but that's what Mums do. Love you both so much, Mum xx

5

Luxembourg City to Jussy

1,168 to 1,304 kilometres from home

SNAPPING TOOTHBRUSHES

With the inclusion of our recent delivery, the weight of our packs had risen to over twenty kilograms, and we had still to buy food provisions for the coming days. Whilst it had been possible to move the bulk over the soft hills of the Ardennes and the Moselle, our challenge was about to become tougher, with rising temperatures and, more potently, the steepening climbs of the Vosges Mountains which lay just two weeks away. We needed to cut down.

Top of the cull list were the twenty-three maps that had got us this far. And then came the rest: string, lip balm, floss, plug adapter (we had two), sunglasses case, walking trousers (we were yet to wear them), boxers (now down to just two pairs each), Jake's walking pole attachments, half a sponge, eraser, pencil, spoon, French phrase book (we kept the pocket dictionary), small scissors, flashlight, a book, some notes, the tape measure (it was about time), and the lower half of our toothbrushes which we snapped in half to reduce weight.

The hip belt modifications that I had applied to Jake's pack in Vianden seemed to be doing the trick, but they had begun to fray a little. Keen not to waste any of our unwanted supplies, I cut into the boxers and used the material to patch up the padding. Also in need of repair was another of Jake's zip handles that had broken from his pack, so I braided a second tie to match the first one that I had made back in England. A few stitches here and there, in both socks and hats, completed the repairs, allowing attention to turn to our bodies.

'I shaved mine,' Jake said, as I peeled a strip of plaster from my foot. Both Jake and I had been experiencing a little abrasion between

121

our big toes and, after experimenting with a bit of strapping some weeks earlier, decided that it was an effective method for blister prevention. Amazingly, the plaster had sustained its adhesive qualities for almost two weeks, and judging by the pain of the removal, still had a lot to give.

'You shaved them?' I questioned through a grimace whilst inspecting the sticky side of the plaster, now covered in dirt and hair.

'Yep,' he confirmed, flashing his stubbly toes in my eyeline before handing me the razor.

For the first time in my life, with the aid of a little soap and water, I ran the blade over the top of one of my big toes and then moved calmly onto the next, one by one transforming the digits into something disturbingly unfamiliar. Hairless, soft and nude, I was unable to rid myself of the thought that my toes now resembled a mischief of naked mole rats. Before dwelling on the thought any further, I rewrapped my toes with plaster and joined Jake to pack up our final bits and pieces. With just three items unable to make it into the parcel bound for home, we left the room, placing a note next to my discarded walking trousers and, quite unnecessarily, the tail ends of our toothbrushes:

Bonjour monsieur/madame,
Merci pour la chambre, vous pouvez garder le pantalon et la brosse à dent.
Bonne Journée

Under blue skies and with lightened packs, we dropped our return parcel into the post office and then left the densely packed buildings of the city along the N3 highway, so thrilled with our updated maps that not even a mouthful of truck fumes could dampen our spirits.

Having seen the ease with which Jake had cruised up and down many of the recent hills, I decided it was about time I invested in some walking poles too. We hadn't passed an outdoors shop, large or small, since arriving on the Continent, and so considered ourselves a little lucky to stumble upon AS Adventure, an outdoors superstore in the city's suburbs.

'Those are for children!' a man said over my shoulder as I inspected the cheapest poles I could find. I turned to see a chap of perhaps thirty. One side of his head was shaved whilst the rest was heavily haired and brushed into a ponytail. A thick, French accent came from within a bushy yet well-tamed beard. 'I am Florian.'

'Danny, and this is my brother, Jake,' I replied, accidentally prodding Jake with a walking pole as I pointed his way.

I'm not entirely sure what questions we asked, but we were soon involved in an in-depth tutorial concerning AS Adventure's intricate past, which finally concluded with, 'Thankfully, despite the complicated history of the company, we are doing very well. Forty stores in Belgium, Luxembourg and France, with almost 2,000 employees. Last year, we generated 335 million euros in sales.' Florian must suddenly have realised that he had strayed off-piste and got back to the matter in hand. 'Anyway, we have these wonderful Leki poles – the Makalu Classic.' He held up a pair of black and gold poles, to which I nodded approvingly, not really sure what differentiated one pair from the next. 'They have an aluminium body, CorTec grip and industrial diamond tips. They're durable, light and comfortable.'

I paused, pretending to consider the range of options, before asking the only question that really mattered, 'And, are these the cheapest?'

'Yes, sixty-five euros.'

'I'll take 'em!'

I liked Florian a lot. He seemed appreciative of the right things and was as eager to advise us on our upcoming months as he was to try and make a sale. He agreed that Luxembourg was a friendly place, but France was more treacherous. 'I am from France, so I know that you must be careful there. There are strange and dangerous people,' he told us, to which I joked that we now had diamond-tipped poles to protect ourselves with. He laughed, but quickly reverted to a stern expression. 'But, seriously, you must stay safe.'

Jake needed the toilet and so agreed to meet me at the checkouts. Just as I was beginning to worry that the previous night's 'Quality' Burger dinner was showing its true colours, he appeared at the exit with a panicked look on his face. 'Let's go,' he said under his breath.

I followed Jake into the car park, joining him as he stopped to look nervously back towards AS Adventure. 'What's up with you, Jake?'

His alarmed expression transformed into a grin as he reached into a side pocket to reveal two packets of Compeed blister protection. 'Florian shoved these into my bag!'

'Really?'

'Yes! He stopped me as I was coming out of the toilets and asked if I had any spare pockets. I was a bit confused but said yes. Then he stuffed the Compeed into my bag and told me to walk out and "just keep smiling". He said it was a gift from him and AS Adventure, though I'm not sure AS Adventure was entirely aware of their kind deed.'

'No, I don't expect they were,' I agreed.

Quickly and quietly, we left the retail park. The dual carriageway dwindled to a single-lane road, then to a country track, and finally, with the hum of the city behind us, we joined an earthy path, the 'Sentier du Sud', which somewhat misleadingly took us west into the forested leisure complex of Kockelscheuer. It was late afternoon, and given the emotional fatigue of the day, we decided to stop for the night in Kockelscheuer's immaculate campground.

We lay in the tent with the porch doors open, gorging on our new set of maps and mountain guidebooks. It must have been dinnertime or thereabouts, because a string of grey-haired caravan goers, each laden with dirty bowls, plates and saucers, chugged slowly to the kitchen. An hour later, the dishes were done, and now the convoy carried towels and toiletries, ambling slowly towards the shower rooms that steamed and pattered with hot water. With the fading light so too came a lessening in activity. One or two night-time strollers chattered faintly, whilst a grandpa, boasting a pair of torn jeans and a striped navy sweater, demonstrated that age doesn't always imply dignity, with an unpleasant rumble of flatulence which crested audibly with each step like a motorcar going through the gears.

1,580 KILOMETRES TO NICE

In the middle of the nineteenth century, the iron-rich soils of Luxembourg's south saw much of the land subjected to quarrying. But, with time, the industry ran its course, and the scars of prosperity were healed by blushing flowers and buzzing bees. Veering from its westerly orientation, the Sentier du Sud now followed its implied passage, winding through woodland where terraces of terracotta rock stepped the land.

We had entered the Terras Rouge, the 'Land of the Red Rocks', the last and most southerly of the country's five regions. Despite its industrial past, I was taken by the tranquillity and diversity of the area. We stopped at an old quarry, which since the mining days had been flooded to create a recreational fishing lake, and ate a cupcake that we had found on the path a few minutes back. Red Admiral butterflies fluttered amongst the silver birch, each lichen-smattered trunk protruding gratefully from a cushioned floor of wildflowers, nettles and dock leaves. I closed my eyes, tasting vanilla sugar and a little dirt on my tongue. The sun had blessed our last five days on the path, and in the midst of my daydream I affirmed to Jake, 'I could get used to this.'

However, serenity rarely lasts, and it wasn't long before we were on the move again, thanks to the discovery of a tick in my belly button and a swarm of hungry mosquitoes about our heads. Even the scroggin was showing its nasty side, as the new mix made us heavily regret the inclusion of the most disgusting mint-flavoured jelly sweets ever to taint our taste buds.

The border, and with it France's famous Lorraine region, was close. Though we were still treading Grand Duchy soil, to our delight, a quick inspection of the *Hayange* map revealed that we had just crept onto its page. We were thus able to ditch the inaccuracies of Luxembourgian cartography and turn to the detail of the French 1:25,000 *IGNs*. This did present one problem: no longer were we able to blame bad navigation on the mapmaking abilities of others.

Whilst much of the quarrying in the Terras Rouge had ended, it was clear that the mineral-rich ground was still being exploited. We ascended through Rodenbusch Forest along the tracks of Weisskaul Quarry, feeling the ground rumble as loaded trucks hammered by, each transporting the earth's crust to its imminent furnace. Soon our hair and cheeks were tinted with fine red specks from the plumes of drifting dust.

By the time the sixth or seventh vehicle had thundered by, I decided that I didn't much like the drivers, who seemed to discount our presence altogether. However, beyond the settling dirt of yet another truck, a wonderful sight appeared through the cloud: the beautiful red and white flicks of the *Grande Randonnée*. We were back in France. Also marking the border crossing was a small sign nailed to a tree. It read: '*Le Sentier E2/GR. Holland-Mediterranee. Nice 1,580km*'.

We were not out of earshot of the trucks, but the dense beech trees of Rodenbusch and the completion of our twenty-eighth kilometre were more than enough to entice us into an early camp. Amongst a throng of close-growing trunks that typified the forest, we found a clearing just big enough to set up for the night.

The successive weeks of camping were beginning to take their toll on Ted, and with each pitch came the added routine of improvised fine-tuning. We had discovered long ago that the sleeping compartment was only just big enough to fit Jake and me, along with a few small valuables. Likewise, the porch area provided just enough space for our shoes and packs, which we enveloped with the waterproof bag covers. For a few weeks, this system kept us dry, aside from a little dampness where our bodies brushed the tent walls. However, often assembled at haste in the rain and then packed away wet in the morning, Ted had gradually begun to lose his shape. With dips here and fissures there, the outer fabric had become a haven for pooling water, and with that came leaks. Of all the tweaks perhaps the most successful was the use of two foot-long sticks that we wedged into the ground between the inner and outer skins. Not only did this ensure that the layers never touched, but it kept the tent taut, dimple-free, and thus relatively dry, although our recent good fortune with the weather had not yet allowed for a rigorous test.

Somewhere in the distance, the call for the *Maghrib* prayer rang out from a mosque, its waves catching the wind at one moment then fading the next. Whether it was the swaying *salat* or the closeness of the forest, I felt secure and comfortable. On occasions like this, our tent became more than just a shelter: it was our home. I fell asleep as my head hit my makeshift pillow and didn't wake until the morning.

Another melody woke us as day broke. However, a far cry from the pre-dawn *Fajr*, the sound appeared to be that of a novice clarinet player who finally completed a full version of 'When the Saints Go Marching In' just as we left the flattened ground of sticks and shoots where Ted had rested.

With our toothbrushes in our mouths and squinting through tired eyes, we broke out from the trees and onto the path, looking right and then left before continuing on the latter. 'One day we're going to give someone a shock doing that,' I mumbled, through the foam of my toothpaste.

'I know,' Jake agreed, swilling his mouth with water. 'That's what I thought, but then I figured…well, we hardly ever see people in the day, so what are the chances that someone will be here at 7.30 in the morning?'

He was right, of course. Our experiences in the Benelux had been predominantly ones of solitude. Even the Ardennes hills, seemingly renowned for their hiking trails, had not lived up to the hype, merely hosting the odd day walker or fearless mountain biker. This was not a bad thing – quite the opposite, in fact. We were glad to walk unhindered by fleeting social interactions which, until now (with the exception of a few), had largely consisted of warnings concerning our inadequate gear, our route ahead and the weather. But perhaps we were missing something. Perhaps we should have been listening to the wisdom of others, and letting unwanted comments go unheeded.

'I guess we'll have to start taking note of what people say a bit more when we get into the mountains. You know, weather warnings and path conditions and all that,' I said to Jake.

'I guess so.' He paused momentarily. 'I kind of find other walkers to be a bit like salt and pepper: a little is good, but too much can taint my palate, maybe even put me off my meal.'

'True. Sometimes too much salt can make me feel sick,' I agreed, before thinking that perhaps I had strayed a little from the analogy.

We emerged from the forest onto an expansive arable plateau where an artist's thumb had smudged fields of yellow rapeseed across the canvas. I looked across the vastness and realised I knew almost nothing about it. We had been raised so close to France, yet my knowledge of its geography was, at best, poor. I knew where Paris was and, having visited the northern coast on a school trip when I was eleven, I knew where Normandy and Le Havre were too.

'Well, now's our chance to learn,' Jake consoled as I mused.

We pushed on through farmland, from one cluster of houses to the next, passing grunting tractors and an endearing wealth of plant life. The small lilac wings of mazarine butterflies moved between hosts of tall sun-coloured mulleins and deep blue columbine petals that hung like bells from sprawling stems.

Gradually, the pastures began to fold, and we found ourselves on the side of a valley, moving along a woodland edge of hawthorn bushes and maple trees, with a scent of toilet plants and garlic leaves in the air. After a few moments, a house appeared in an undergrowth of tall grasses and untamed hedgerows. Unlike many of the well-rendered buildings we had seen in Benelux, the house was ramshackle, constructed from anything that the owner could find. Smoke wisped from its crocked brick chimney, and jasmine clawed the uneven walls, meshing the wooden shutters and reaching into the garden. Horses poked their heads from the adjoining makeshift stables into a mess of cane-supported tomato plants, brambles and garden tools that reminded me, quite blissfully, of my granddad.

The water we had collected earlier in the day from a village stream was running low. With no reliable sources for the next dozen kilometres and the imminent prospect of another night in the woods, Fontoy (according to our map, the only settlement within reasonable walking distance) was our only hope of rehydration. After following the directions of several misinformed locals, we finally stumbled upon Score, the town's inconspicuous, and thus oxymoronic, convenience store.

The shop was dimly lit, and the fridges were turned off. A dusky-skinned woman greeted us with a smile from behind the counter, and then returned to her conversation with an old man sitting on a stall beside her clutching a half drunk litre-bottle of beer. We lumped two armfuls of bananas, tomatoes, beans and drinks onto the counter and responded to the lady's intrigued expression by explaining our journey. Without hesitation, she glanced to her side, snatched two chocolate bars from a small wicker basket and thrust them into our hands.

'You know what?' Jake said, after desperately gulping down several mouthfuls of Fanta on a wall outside the shop. 'It's warm, and almost certainly out of date, but I think this is the best drink I have ever had! And with free chocolate, it doesn't get much better!'

Clank! Clank!

We had started the day early after being woken at 5am by a barking deer, and were well on our way by the time we passed an old chap splitting wood just north of Neufchef. He wore a woollen hat and flannel shirt despite the heat of the morning, and hammered down an iron wedge into a split in a round of wood. *Clank! Clank!*

He wasn't the only one set on spending Saturday morning in the sun making woodpiles: the forest appeared to be peppered with lumberjacks, each surrounded by shards of pine that baked sumptuously in the heat.

'*Ça va?*' a man with a faded cap and high white shorts called out to us as he trimmed his hedge in the quiet backstreets of Neufchef.

'*Oui, Monsieur, mais il fait chaud aujourd'hui, non?*'

'*Ah oui, très chaud,*' the man replied, lowering his shears in preparation for a full-blown conversation, in which Jake and I were woefully ill-equipped to partake. Within an instant, the middle-aged man was joined by his wife. She examined us excitedly between glasses and a blonde fringe, before our congregation expanded once more, with the addition of a moustached man and his dog.

It was the dog walker, clad head to toe in thick canvas clothing the colour of overcooked asparagus, who adopted the role of group mediator. He couldn't speak English, just as Monsieur and Madame Rene Ringenback couldn't, but was clearly proud of his ability to gesticulate, flinging his hands skywards to depict the weather, and then marching his fingers through the air to create two pairs of tiny walking legs.

It turned out that the Rene Ringenbacks had two sons living in England, and as they handed us a bottle of cold water, I felt that perhaps there was more to them stopping us than just politeness. '*Où allez-vous maintenant?*' Madame Rene Ringenback asked.

'*Le GR5,*' Jake replied, pointing at the map.

'*Ah!*' the dog walker cried, once more propelling his arms into the air, indicating that we must follow the road straight ahead before turning right. However, with experience so far suggesting that our route almost always contradicted that given to us by a local, we were not altogether surprised, having bade farewell to the trio, to reach the end of the road where both map and sign guided us left.

Jake gulped at the cold water and then handed the bottle to me. 'It's becoming an issue, isn't it? We didn't need water in Belgium with all the rain and cold. But the heat is a problem.' A quick assessment of the map revealed that we had just two opportunities to refill our bottles between here and our camp twenty kilometres south.

Soon, we came to the first of the two rivers trickling alongside a lonely gravel track leading into the township of Rosselange. No wider than a couple of metres and no deeper than twenty centimetres, the murky water was not suitable for drinking, even if treated with purification tablets. However, with four days of sweat and grime coating our bodies and clothes, we didn't want to miss the opportunity for a wash.

I saw half a dozen newts dart for cover as I lowered my naked body into the numbing stream, stirring the bed of mud below with each step. Jake threw down some clothes which we washed, wrung out and hung over my bag with the aid of a washing line made from the cord we had found back in Belgium.

Greatly refreshed, save for a rather large mosquito bite on my bottom, the GR5 directed us through Rosselange, where gardens bulged with early summer vegetables, and irises of every colour strove for the sun.

In Rombas, the next town along, we bought twenty stamps for our letter writing and set up camp several kilometres later amongst the ivy-clad beech trees of Côte de Drince, a verdant hilltop perched high above the Moselle Valley to the west.

Once settled, we left the tent and filtered through the trees to a rare pool of light in the otherwise shaded forest. I lay on my back across the trunk of the fallen tree that had created the clearing, and watched the clouds drift from east to west, transforming as they went – talon, bird, heart, dragon, angel. I felt uncharacteristically relaxed, a sensation only heightened as Jake drew my attention to a nearby tree shanked off at its waist. Like many of the dead beech trees we had seen, its decaying trunk was stepped with hoof fungus, a highly combustible fungus also known as tinder or iceman fungus. From the underbelly of the parasite's body, thousands of microscopic spores took to the forest, eddying and rotating with the delicate air currents, the sunlight making the hidden visible.

WITHOUT A MAP

On our way down from Côte de Drince, as I filled our bottles from one of the forest's few draining streams, I managed to drop the pedometer. I watched the numbers on the small screen slowly fade and then broke the bad news to Jake. Never had the cliché 'it's all relative' been more applicable. Until now, the device had been central to our walk, both in the day to clock our pace and at night to record our progress. We mourned the gadget like it was a dear friend. A little comfort came with the rediscovery of our piece of red thread which, although not entirely accurate, had served us well until now.

However, we had greater issues to contend with than our inability to measure footsteps. Having passed through the village of Bronvaux – where in a fine display of French stereotyping, we passed a bronze-skinned man, with an oily face, a shoe-brush moustache and three baguettes under his arm – we made our way up and over the A4 Autoroute (connecting Paris to Strasbourg) and, to our definite surprise, off the map.

'Why didn't we print off this section?' I asked Jake, already feeling a little anxious as we edged along the Sous Roche ridge into the unknown.

'I have no idea.'

Feeling vulnerable and hot under the glare of the sun, we took the opportunity to have a break in a worn-out orchard. A burst of poppies swung their delicate heads in front of the Moselle Valley to our east. I picked one of the flowers and pressed it between the pages of my notebook, imagining Claudia's reaction to the dried petals as they fell into her hands in the hallway of her house.

Although the apples were far from ready, I was excited to spot the glimmer of a cherry between the leaves of a pollinating tree a few rows down. I jumped to my feet, plucked a couple of the ripe fruits, and threw one into Jake's hands. Just as I was absorbing the taste of summer, a fly found its way into my mouth, no doubt to its own dismay as much as mine. I couldn't help but feel, after my theft, that the incident was deserved (for me, not the poor fly).

131

Cautiously, we waded from one field of long blonde grass to the next, grateful for the occasional splash of red and white paint on the verging hawthorns and decrepit gates that led us on through the early afternoon.

Relief finally came as we arrived at a stone *lavoir* centred amongst a small group of houses known as Fèves, which to our delight signalled our return onto the map. Originally built as a shared space for washing clothes, the public bath was no longer in use yet still remained full, courtesy of a dripping tap. With the midday heat sitting just below 30°C, we threw caution to the wind and ducked our heads into the pellucid water. I held my breath beneath the surface, anaesthetising momentarily away from our adventure – the strains, glories, smiles and tears – before pulling my body back towards the light, chilled water pouring down my shoulders.

Fèves was the first of many villages to fill our day. In Norroy-le-Veneur, locals hung bunting and carried long wooden benches towards the square in preparation for a festival. In the next village along, Plesnois, I glanced through an open window to see a silver-haired woman with slumped shoulders stirring a pot, whilst the smell of her hearty creation floated out, mixing with the scent of the wisteria that climbed the building's facade. In Villers, two young boys threw cups of water in the baking heat of the afternoon, and in Saulny, an intriguing vending machine outside a strawberry farm, filled with fruit and vegetables, allowed us to quench our thirst for vitamin C.

For the second time in a day, we were flung from the map, only on this occasion our return was less swift, and certainly less comfortable. For twelve kilometres, we made our way down streets and alleyways, each turn seeing the buildings grow in stature and the *GR* signs fade.

After an hour, we arrived at a huge girth of water – the Moselle River. With little else to guide us, and remembering that the source emanated from somewhere in the Vosges Mountains, we turned south against the flow and marched purposefully onwards. On the eastern bank, the parks and gardens of Metz, Lorraine's capital city, led our gaze to an urban horizon of tower blocks and church steeples. Distracted by the populous environment, it was some time before we realised that 160 kilometres back, alongside

Luxembourg's eastern border, we had already acquainted ourselves with these waters.

'Finally,' Jake said, some hours later, 'we're on the next map.'

By the looks of things, we had strayed a kilometre or so from the *GR5* and were now in Moulin-lès-Metz, a close neighbour to the stirring metropolis on the other side of the river. But this mattered little – we were back on the charts and we knew our location. To mark the occasion, we rewarded ourselves lavishly in the town's Casino supermarket.

After glugging down a litre of juice each and a tin of ravioli, I then proceeded to eat an entire round of Camembert. Unquestionably overfilled, I was sure I felt the cheese leaching through my skin in thick globules of sweat as we climbed away from the urban environment into a more familiar landscape of intermittent villages amongst rolling hills.

The map suggested that the next patch of forest was an hour's hike south. But we had been walking for forty-two kilometres already, and with the additional weight in our packs, we were ready to stop. We hobbled beyond the church at Sainte-Ruffine with sun-weathered eyes and sticky skin, and then passed lethargically through Jussy. Beyond the village, I spotted a man pushing a wheelbarrow above a terraced vineyard and decided to seize the opportunity.

'*Excusez-moi, Monsieur?*' I shouted. '*Bonjour!*'

The man grew closer to the path, his black vest sitting on broad shoulders and muscular arms. From a distance, he was a young man, but now that I could see the grey hair on his head and chin, his crooked teeth, and his folded brow, it was clear he was closer to fifty. '*Bonsoir, Monsieur. Nous sommes très fatigués. Vous avez une place pour la tente?*'

After a few seconds of consideration, he nodded, beckoning us over the field's stone wall.

Dominique's words were quick, but between us we were able to glean the key points: the horses were friendly, we could burn what we could find to stay warm, the best spot for camping was at the top of the hill and, finally, if we ventured into the vineyard, the owner, said to be the nastiest man in Jussy, would make us live to regret it.

'*Si vous avez des problèmes, ma sœur vous aidera. Elle*

s'appelle Eliane, et elle vit dans le village. Vous comprenez?' Dominique held his gaze, only relaxing once we had agreed that we understood: any problems and we were to walk back up to Jussy and find Eliane, his sister. She would help.

We pitched Ted on the crest of the hill beside a huddle of yellow and purple irises, and then joined the horses at their trough, washing our bodies and clothes in the cloudy water as they drank.

The iron fire basket, which Dominique had carried to the top of the field, lit quickly, and soon the dusk swifts were joined by licks of flames from the burning twigs. We smoked our socks beside the fire, to dispel their incurable odour as much as to dry them, and then watched the sky turn pink, silhouetting the poplar trees that lined the hills to the west.

THE WOES OF MANURE

If ever I needed a reason to dislike horse manure then our night in Dominique's field was it. We had pitched on the flattest ground we could find, assuming it would deliver the most comfort. However, although the gradient was favourable, the mounds of manure that lay beneath the tent were not. My exhaustion from the long day, along with the aromas of the fire, sent me into a dangerously deep sleep.

I woke to darkness. Some seconds passed before a flash of lightning illuminated Ted's interior, pursued quickly by a rumble of thunder that shook the ground and then rolled violently off into the distance. I tried to move, but couldn't. I was paralysed. And then the rain came.

I didn't like to wake Jake unless it was necessary, but as the shower intensified, my dread grew. 'Jake. Jake.'

'Mm,' he groaned, still half asleep.

'Jake. The tent's leaking,' I whispered loudly, 'and I can't move.'

'What's wrong?' he quickly returned.

'Those fucking mounds of horse shit beneath the tent, they've done me in. It's my back, it's seized up. I can't move.' By this time, I was becoming increasingly exasperated and spoke with panic in my voice. 'I can't move. We aren't going to be able to do this now! What are we going to do?'

'We'll be alright, Dan,' Jake said calmly as he sat up.

134

'I can't bloody move! And the fucking tent is leaking,' I shouted desperately. 'We won't be alright!'

I couldn't remember a time when I had felt so defeated. Failure to reach the Mediterranean had never crossed our minds, even when others had doubted us, and they had. Yet, as agonising pulses thumped up my spine, I began to wonder how we could possibly go on. My back had failed us, our shelter had failed us, and, worse, I had given up.

But what are travel companions for, if not to pick you up when you are down? And what are brothers for, if not to tell you what you need to hear in times when all else appears lost?

'I'll sort it, Dan, OK? You don't have to worry about anything. I'll sort it.' And that was enough, because I knew when Jake said he would take care of something then that is exactly what he would do. He handed me my earplugs. 'Try and sleep,' and then he scrambled out of the tent and into the rain to adjust the pegs and tighten the guy ropes.

When the light of day finally came, Jake left the tent once more, returning some minutes later with an expression of accomplishment beneath his sodden jacket hood. 'Come with me. Leave everything else here,' he said softly.

In the time that Jake had been gone, I had been able to roll onto my side and bend my knees. With my improved mobility, I edged gingerly and cautiously out of the front porch, at which point Jake took hold of my arm and guided me to the bottom of the field, back up the country lane and into Jussy.

We came to a halt outside a faded red door built into a tall garden wall, cloaked with lush wisteria. Jake pulled at a chain beside the tarnished wood, sending a rusty bell into song, and then disappeared back down the hill as the door swung open. A pair of warm eyes and a broad smile greeted me sympathetically through the falling rain. Eliane ushered me through the gateway and into a garden. I followed her pink dressing gown and greying hair, bound tightly in a bun, up a short flight of stairs, past a sleeping black Labrador and a rousing German shepherd, before entering an old stone house.

Eliane led me into her kitchen and offered me a chair beside a long table adorned with the kind of clutter that makes a room homely – candles, notepads, breadcrumbs. It was a kitchen that cooked. Blood from a bag of defrosting meat trickled into a white sink big enough to bathe in, whilst vegetables, herbs and spices were piled where space allowed on the work surfaces and rickety shelves. The walls held brass pots, ceramic jugs and sun-faded paintings, whilst the south-facing side of the room was paned with French doors that opened out into a conservatory overlooking a long garden of citrus trees, flowers and fruit bushes. Though the rain was still falling, light flooded the room.

Eliane grabbed a baguette and put it on the table, along with a pot of home-made red-berry jam and a shallow bowl of coffee. With these remedies, the pain in my back gradually eased. Added distraction came as I was beckoned to my feet and handed a bottle of warm milk. Its nozzle, to my surprise, was quickly latched onto by the mouth of an enthusiastic goat. No older than a few weeks, the creature then proceeded to jump up onto one of the chairs and yank the tablecloth to the floor, sending our breakfast into the air and plates crashing to the tiles below. Amongst the commotion, Eliane appeared entirely unfazed.

Unfortunately, my weak state meant that my French was even more disjointed than usual. But we continued nonetheless, and with a little help from Eliane's impressive sketching and a tacit mutual patience, I began to learn about Jussy's, and indeed Eliane's, dark, war-influenced history.

In May 1944, Jussy was bombed by American ammunition, an error by the United States which reduced eighty per cent of the buildings in the village to rubble, including a section of the family's seventeenth-century house. Amidst the bombing, a young girl who had sought refuge in the garden was hit. Eliane began to draw again, quite disturbingly revealing that, as the dust settled, the victim's legs were found in the apple tree, and one of her arms amongst the roses.

'*Un peu de bombe*,' she said with raised eyebrows, taking a lump of oxidised metal from the shelf and placing it in front of me. Apparently, since the war, the gravitational pull of the moon had dragged such fragments from their buried state to the surface of the garden. Each year, remnants of the bombs are discovered as the family turn the soil to plant their bulbs and dig their annual potato harvest.

We talked for some time about the war until a man in his early twenties walked through the door, stretching his arms and squinting as the daylight hit his face. '*Bonjour,*' he said, a little shocked at my presence, before exchanging a few quick words with Eliane.

'*C'est Pitau, mon fils.*' She smiled towards me, rushing to her feet and pouring another cup of coffee for her son. '*Pitau, c'est Danny. Il est Anglais et il a un mal de dos.*'

'Hello, Danny, I'm Pierre, but people call me Pitau.' He spoke kindly like his mother, had slight shoulders, short brown hair and a fair-skinned face, darkened with bristles on his chin and cheeks. 'So, you were able to speak with my mother,' he said with a grin. 'I'm impressed.'

'Yes,' I laughed. 'Well, the notepad came in handy!'

I apologised for imposing, to which I was told off by Eliane: '*C'est votre maison maintenant.*'

'She said this is your home. No apologising!' Pitau translated. 'She's right too. If you need anything, you ask. Ah,' he shouted as the hanging bell chimed, 'it sounds like your brother is here.'

Jake stepped timidly into the kitchen, as wet as the sky outside and with both bags hauled over his shoulders. He was whisked immediately off to the bathroom by Eliane as she muttered under her breath, '*Une douche, une douche,*' leaving Pitau and me to talk.

From wine to camping, and jobs to girlfriends ('I am seeing someone, but not really seeing them,' he told me with a wink), Pitau spoke for some minutes and reminded me of the joys of socialising. 'I'm not sure I've ever met anyone who's been paralysed by horse poo before,' he laughed after hearing how I had hurt my back.

I too was shown to the shower a few minutes later. Seemingly not content that I had taken enough care over my body, Eliane burst into the room as I was drying, wielding a tube of mysterious cream. She rubbed it into the small of my back with firm hands and then strapped my waist with a back support saying, '*C'est un cadeau* – it's for you.'

At the back of the house, I found Jake lying on a bed in a room with closed shutters, filled with eighteenth-century wardrobes and dresser tables. With the exception of a yucca and a Swiss cheese plant, the mild stagnancy of the room suggested that it was usually vacant. 'Eliane's taken all our clothes. She said they'll be ready by the morning,' he grinned up at me.

'The morning?'

'Yep, we're staying the night, and you're not to complain. There's no way you're walking today. In fact, Eliane said we can stay as long as we need to.'

'Attention! Attention! Faire attention à votre dos!' Eliane shouted from the window after we had accepted Pitau's offer of an afternoon tour of the village.

'Yes, yes, we will be careful, Mother,' her son replied. 'She wants you to go slowly, Danny, OK?'

As one of just three Jussy residents unaffected by greying hair, I had expected Pitau to show the kind of rebellion, or at least boredom, so often displayed by a young lad in a countryside village. But perhaps I was guilty of transferring my experience of rural England to France, because instead of pulling out a marker pen from his pocket and defacing a road sign, Pitau pointed out features of the village's extensive history – the seventeenth-century architecture, the scars of war, Jussy's *lavoir* and the village church.

'Uncle Dominique, the man you met last night, he was a mischievous child,' Pitau began as we looked up at the post-war church. 'One day, when he was young, he found the steeple door unlocked. He climbed the stairs all the way to the top and pulled the bells long and hard. It must have been very funny,' he grinned, 'but the locals didn't think so. No, they were not happy!'

I imagined Dominique with schoolboy shorts and knobbly knees swinging from the bell ropes and laughing with delight whilst disapproving listeners craned their necks towards the chaotic chimes.

'He was in a heavy metal band too, you know,' Pitau added after catching our smiles. 'Fisc, they were called. If you think that story about him dangling from the belfry is funny, you should see the photos of his band – perms, eyeliner, Spandex, they had everything!'

I thought about the burly leather-handed man that Jake and I had met a day ago pushing a wheelbarrow across his field. 'I guess they didn't make it to the big time?'

'You'd be surprised,' Pitau grinned. 'But, he likes the farm now, the peace and quiet. You know, the French call places like this *villes dormir*, a sleeping village. No people, no noise, everything is always quiet – everything except the animals!'

'The animals?' Jake queried.

'Yes, we have a lot of animals.'

We returned to the house and Pitau pushed the garden door open. He led us down beyond the apple trees towards a hubbub of squawks and bleats where goats, sheep, chickens, geese and an unruly turkey jostled for the handfuls of food he threw to the floor. 'My mother does not like to eat them. They are pets. We just eat the fruits and vegetables,' he continued, as a particularly eager goat jumped up at his thighs. 'That reminds me, follow me.'

Back at the top end of the garden, he eased open a door, weak at the hinges, taking us down below the house. The temperature dropped and the sunlight faded as we moved from one damp room to the next. Timber beams, hammered in when the war began to prevent the basement from collapsing, held the crumbling walls in place. In the dim light of two grubby light bulbs, we passed an old bread oven, inscribed with the date 1854, and then entered a final tunnel-shaped room at the back of the basement.

'The Germans built this,' Pitau began. 'They used our house as a place to stay in the war. Actually, my grandmother had to cook for them. And then the Americans dropped their bombs, but the basement survived.'

The tunnel was lined with shelves, each crammed close to breaking point with glass jars and bottles. Pitau grabbed a bottle of red wine, wiping a thick layer of dust from its surface. 'Lorraine wine, from the farm I work on. And these,' he pointed over my shoulder, 'these are pickles, jams and juice. My mother made 300 bottles of apple juice this year. Dominique says it is a laxative,' he laughed, 'but I like it.' Pitau piled half a dozen bottles of wine and spirits into our arms. 'We will try these later!'

We returned to the kitchen just as lunch was being served, joining Eliane's husband, Roland, a quiet man with a slender face, a bushy moustache and a pink shirt, and Dominique, who rolled his eyes at us as if to say, 'What have you English boys done to yourselves?' The table was brimming with beef skewers, *frites*, Arabian couscous, Lorraine tomato salad, fruit cake, and several bottles of wine.

'*Ça va?*' Eliane questioned, offering seconds and thirds, and then spooning food onto our plates before we could politely decline. We drank red wine with the meat and a Lorraine delicacy of white wine and peach juice with the dessert, both of which met my blood flow with astounding speed, blurring my vision, numbing my back, and improving my French.

Pitau was the only respectable linguist in the room, and for that he faced a constant barrage of questions and queries concerning all manner of conversations – television, tax, the Queen, Sarkozy, America, wine, fruit. I adored the family's love for discussion, though was glad to be a spectator when talk became heated, no doubt perceived by them as French passion.

Lunch seemed to merge smoothly into dinner which, I gathered, often occurred, and once Eliane had cleared the table she stocked the oven with a Lorraine classic of pastry and eggs. Whether it was the two months of taste bud deprivation, or more likely the love of the cooking, I knew that Eliane's Quiche Lorraine would be a taste I would never forget.

Come the evening, with our stomachs filled, bottles of home-brewed concoctions began to pop. First came the white wine and *cassis* (blackberry liqueur) which we drank with a spread of cheese, followed swiftly by an iced glass of *calvados* (apple brandy), its strength twice that of a normal spirit, yet tasting smooth and sweet. The third brew, *mirabelle*, was made by Pitau and his father. 'Make sure you are ready,' they warned me, leaning in with excitement like two curious chemists testing their latest invention as the liquid touched my lips. The spirit, made from the region's famous mirabelle plums, was clear and pungent, and evoked the reaction that Pitau and his father were no doubt looking for as my neck tensed and my lips tightened.

I went to bed that night with two overpowering thoughts: how thankful I was that people like Eliane and her family existed, and how, for the second day in a row, I had managed to consume an entire wheel of camembert in one sitting. As the anaesthetic of the alcohol began to wane, a third, more awful thought returned: that Jake and I may well have hiked our last day on the path and that our dream to walk to the Mediterranean was over.

6

Jussy to Belfort

1,304 to 1,812 kilometres from home

VULNERABLE TIMES AND BREAKFAST WITH A PEACOCK
Mussolini, Hitler, Geurre France and *L'Artillerie Française:* the
small, windowless room was a library of magazines, books and
pictures, each of which ensured that, in Eliane's house, a trip to
the toilet was an opportunity to learn as much as it was a place
to relieve oneself. And if I wasn't already sure of the family's
passion for the First and Second World Wars then the dozen or so
helmets – both French and German – encased in a range of glass
cabinets throughout the house surely sealed the thought.

The night of rest, in which Jake and I had been sandwiched
between a pile of quilts and the softest mattress ever to greet my
bottom, appeared to have done my back some good. But when
I rose several minutes later, I felt my shoulders tighten and my
lower back groan with pain.

Eliane greeted us good morning, and then summoned me into
the bathroom where she applied a handful of muscle-warming
cream to my back before putting the tube into my shorts pocket.
Unable to escape the 'necessity calculation' of use against weight,
I duly decided the cream *was* worth packing, and then made my
way into the kitchen where Jake was waiting with a cantaloupe
melon in one hand and a bottle of rosé in the other.

'It's a gift,' he said, correctly predicting my imminent
question. Given that the idea of tying my laces frightened me, the
thought of hoisting a pack weighed down by wine and melons
was unappealing. 'Don't worry,' he continued quickly, 'I've only
accepted the melon.'

'Well, you're carrying all the weight anyway,' I replied, having
agreed on Jake's terms that we would attempt to walk to the next

village on the one condition that he carried the bulk of the load.

'Of course, I'll take it. Now, are you sure you want to go today? We can stay here another night if you need it. Eliane wouldn't mind.'

'No, I want to walk. I'm already getting fidgety. It's almost ten. Let's go and pack.'

I gathered my belongings at a snail's pace, with each bend and stretch imagining a terrific twang as the damaged muscle in my back gave way. Jake's bag was already crammed full, with infectious-looking bulges spanning its length. In need of extra space, he unzipped the hood pocket of his pack, a compartment usually dedicated to the stowing away of shed clothing, and delved in to check for space.

'Argh!' he yelped, retracting his hand from the bag. To our mutual disgust, his fingers were coated with a layer of viscid black mucus, the unfortunate product of a fermenting slug.

Pitau walked us five metres down the lane and bade us farewell as the rest of the family waved from outside their house. In our drawn-out goodbye, we had offered Eliane twenty euros for her to spend on a bottle of wine to drink with the family. Offended by the idea of taking our money, she had pushed the note away, instead making an alternative request: 'Postcard, from Menton?'

'We will write!' Jake called out as their figures grew smaller and their waves slowed. 'Au revoir!'

Jussy had allowed me the opportunity to rest and, in spite of my pain, I had woken in the morning feeling ready to continue our journey. However, with shoulders held forwards and boots scuffing the ground, I could tell that Jake wasn't right.

After a little probing, I learnt that, whilst I had slept after dinner the previous day, Jake had been busy writing a letter to our mother. He handed me several sheets of paper from his pocket. 'I'm going to send this home. I think Mum should know.'

I opened the pages and, with careful steps, read on:

Mum,
Today was one of those days where everything can seem so awful one minute with no apparent way out, and the next minute there is hope and then resolve.
I was awoken by a worried looking Danny. It was still dark, but just light enough to see his expression. He first explained

that his back was hurting a lot, and he was really worried that walking would not be possible. There was an ominous but distant crack in the sky. Danny was unable to move, there was a huge thunderstorm on its way and we didn't know anyone or really where we were. It was a slightly sickening feeling that made me feel suddenly scared. I continually looked over to check on Danny just half a foot away from me. I can't describe what it's like to see him in pain and to feel so helpless. I wished we could have been anywhere else, and most of all I wished I could help. I thought about what you or Dad would do if you were in my position. Both of you seem to have this way of making everything seem OK. I tried to give Danny words of encouragement and positivity, barely believing them myself.

With my waterproofs on and the map in hand I headed up the road. It was deserted and I didn't hold out much hope. I rang the bell of the first house…No answer. I walked through the village in the rain and after five minutes saw a man. I tried asking if there was a place to stay nearby, but he didn't understand. I couldn't bear going back to the tent having not helped. I rang the bell of another house near the edge of the village. And that's when everything changed. After collecting Danny and introducing him to Dominique's sister I went and collected the rest of the gear.

I wanted to share this experience with you in some detail because I want you to know that at the times when we need help the most, there are people out there that care. Whatever happens to Danny's back tomorrow we have learnt an important lesson – to keep faith in people and to always have hope.

It was clear that Jake's anguish had mirrored my own. And that is when it hit me: Jake and I were not simply two beings stepping one behind the other, alone in thought and observation, but instead a single unit. The hardships of the path were not behind us. Indeed, with our feet still to feel the rubble of Western Europe's largest mountains, perhaps they were yet to truly begin. But it didn't matter, for rising through the jubilant highs and despairing lows that had studded our journey until now came one invaluable message: our happiness was shared, invariably and joyously, but so too was our pain.

'We're going to make it, you know?' Jake declared.

'I know,' I returned, looking over at my brother to see his eyes transfixed on the path ahead.

From Metz, the *GR5* adopted a convoluted route of footpaths, country lanes and roads, meandering through a profusion of small towns and villages. With each settlement came familiar features: cherry trees, *lavoirs*, and houses built without spirit levels, where terracotta roofs slumped and walls tilted. Our next notable settlement lay within the northern fringes of Nancy in the commune of Liverdun, also known as the 'Fortress on the Hill'. The town was three days' walk away, or four with the hindrance of a fragile body.

We began our first day back on the path moving with careful steps into dells of purple flowers, through tick-infested pastures, and along forestry tracks polka-dotted with puddles of floodwater. The storm at Jussy had taken the heat from the air, a relief only briefly enjoyed as we soon realised that the conditions were not only favourable to us but to the ravenous Lorraine mosquitoes, whose appetites made urinating a strategic nightmare.

The slippery ground was making life difficult too. Somewhere between the friendly town of Ars-sur-Moselle and Gorze, Jake stumbled back from a muddy verge into a thick puddle of chocolate-coloured sludge. He tried to correct his step with his second foot, but instead went skywards like a rag doll being tossed playfully into the air. He landed with a *splat* and didn't move for several seconds until his chest started to bounce with laughter. Thankfully, Jake's acrobatics didn't prove harmful, save for the substantial dirtying of his clothes, and we were able to sustain our steady plod onto Gorze without any further mishaps.

Eva, the owner of Le Petit Palais *chambre d'hôtes*, pushed aside her hooped brown hair to reveal an expression of exasperation. I got the impression that the elegant bed and breakfast usually catered for a slightly different clientele – perhaps an older couple with a car, money, an insufferable interest in history, clean clothes and mud-free hair. Unfortunately for Eva, we had none of these attributes.

To our delight, and no doubt to Eva's dismay, her idea to put us in 'The Loft', an outhouse at the end of the garden, backfired as the lights blew during her introductory tour, providing us with an unavoidable upgrade. We followed Eva back into the main house and up a sixteenth-century spiral staircase, where an extraordinary array of stuffed animals stared miserably from the curved walls.

'The "Colonial Suite",' Eva said begrudgingly as she introduced us to white wooden flooring, leopard-skin coated furniture (which I had no doubt was real) and yet more decapitated African wildlife. I began to wonder, remembering our dirty boots and Eva's apparent fury, whether we were about to find ourselves on the wrong side of a seething taxidermist.

Jake wrote letters as I washed in the en-suite's steaming bath, wondering whether the tub's four legs were a show of grandeur or an attempt to elicit envy upon the limbless wildlife that loomed above.

During breakfast the next morning, at which we were joined by a boar, a stag and a peacock, Eva informed us that she was an artist and her husband was a private pilot. This seemed to fit, and perhaps explained the décor. She then looked at her watch, stood up at pace, and told us that we must leave at once: *'J'ai un voyage en avion dans dix minutes!'*

With an hour and a half still remaining until our 10am checkout, we felt a little mistreated as we were ushered out of the house and onto the street before we had even a chance to put on our boots.

'Her husband owns the plane, and it only has two seats. I'm sure he could have delayed it by a few minutes if he needed to,' I grumbled as we left the babble of the town.

We walked for two more days without incident or injury, through Bayonville-sur-Mad and Onville, over the Rupt de Mad River, where a father and son fished in the stony waters, and onto Pagny-sur-Moselle and Prény. Just beyond Ste-Marie Farm, where a bunch of hairy cows flung tufted heads and strands of drool at their bodies to dissuade the flies, we clambered up a forested hill where we spent the night before moving on once more.

My back injury had demoted me to a man of little responsibility. As Jake waded down to the river to collect water, knee-high in brambles, or as he assessed the map, I was left standing on the path, picking Iced Gems from the scroggin in a daze. I was not even allowed to put my own bag on. Instead, like a four-year-old being dressed by his father for school, my job was to hold my arms in the air whilst Jake hoisted the red pack onto my shoulders. Alarmingly, my fragile state meant that I was only carrying about thirteen kilograms, leaving Jake with at least twenty-seven, an imbalance that I knew could not be sustained for many more days.

From one lonely farmhouse to the next, we traipsed slowly through the wheat fields of France's rural north-east. Gradually, my body strengthened and my confidence began to return.

But, the next day, as we rose gently towards the brow of a stony farm track with the sun still high in the sky, I was forced to an untimely stop as a sharp pain forked across the base of my back. Instinctively, I unclipped my bag and dropped it to the floor just as two more stabs throbbed up my spine. I tried to step forward but couldn't. 'No!' I shouted tearfully, slamming my poles to the ground. My disappointment was overwhelming, and not for the first time I found it difficult to accept my failure. I could see that Jake too was distraught, but he never uttered a negative word. Instead, he turned his head to a patch of forest beyond the sandy-green wheat fields just north of the track.

It took me some time to get to the trees as I followed Jake, who was now carrying both of our bags, between the crops. Adopting a chameleon-like crawl, I moved slowly into the vestibule of the tent he had put up, and collapsed onto my sleeping bag.

'You know,' Jake said as he prepared dinner outside, 'if I'm feeling down, I read a chapter of Crane.' He leant into the tent and placed *Clear Waters Rising* beside me. 'Because, whatever happens, it'll be likely that Nicholas Crane experienced the very same thing, or worse, and he finished his journey!'

This was an inspiring thought, and one that led me to open the book. Crane was in the Pyrenees, and after a hearty day of walking had decided to camp beneath the stars for the night. However, as Jake and I knew well, pleasant episodes on the path can often become unpleasant very quickly, and he was soon immersed in an atomic storm with nothing but his inadequate bivouac for protection.

I immediately felt better.

Sixty days;
Kindness, shopping, Compeed, quiche;
Closer to the waves.

Whether Claudia meant it or not, her poem, which we received in a text message sometime in the night, along with Jake's proposal to take yet more weight (this time the tent), was enough to get us back on our feet. We were thirty kilometres from Liverdun, quite a distance considering our situation. But, with the sun shining and the wildflowers blooming, we made reaching the Fortress on the Hill our goal for the day.

From a disused woodland lane, overgrown with purple bellflowers and meadow buttercups, we made our way through fields of maize, knocking puffs of pollen into the low morning light as we brushed their spearheads with our knees. The maize faded into huge fields of potatoes, the troughs barren and the rises green with bunches of shooting leaves. We saw lizards, a snake, and the battering ruby wings of a dozen small butterflies, before entering a cluster of haggard blackthorn trees, their white blossom dusting the ground beneath our feet.

Somewhere between the farming hamlets of Mamey and Saint-Jean, as Jake took a comfort stop, I spotted a stocky creature, like an overgrown fox with a chalky coat, ahead on the path. Suddenly, I remembered an article I had read back at Eliane's house about the reintroduction of lynx into the north-west of France following their regional extinction in the seventeenth century. As Jake returned from the trees, the animal slunk quietly back into the forest.

Just beyond Saint-Jean, where a man checked the oil of his Ute, and sparrows darted from barn to barn, we joined the Ruisseau d'Esch where reeds billowed in the fast moving water and emerald dragonflies the size of my thumb hovered and swooped. We stopped for lunch further down the course, chewing on sausage rind and rye bread, as a second azure species of dragonfly moved blissfully around the clinking river.

We pressed on through the afternoon beneath a sky of deep grey clouds that bumbled in from the west, threatening to jeopardise the warmth of the day, before stopping just north of Liverdun at a supermarket. Outside the shop, we loaded our bags with fruit for the evening and supplies for the coming days, only then noticing the Moselle River curving languidly around the town's medieval buildings at the base of the valley.

With great fortune, Ted's last peg skewered the ground of Les Boucles de la Moselle campsite just as the first drops of rain began to fall. We had pitched on a horseshoe bend of the river, with the Château de la Folie across the water and the town's old fortifications staggering up the hillside behind us. Preferring dinner under a sturdier shelter, we left Ted to the elements and found an empty room above the shower block, stacked high with tables and chairs and boxes of old children's games.

Halfway through my fourth nectarine, the door swung open and a large figure appeared in the doorway. Hooded and dripping wet, the man stamped his boots on the mat. '*Bonjour*,' he said, pulling back his hood to reveal a balding head and a kind smile.

'*Bonjour*,' we replied.

'You are not French!' The man hung his jacket over a chair. 'I'm Kareem, from Germany. I hear you are on a long trip,' he said, pausing briefly. 'Don't worry, I'm not a weirdo. The lady at reception told me.' Kareem, who was so tall that he had to duck beneath the door frame, was the kind of guy I imagined to be ironically nicknamed 'Little K'.

His voice was unexpectedly delicate. 'We are on a big walk too. We are walking for two years.'

'Two years! Where?' I replied eagerly, half choking on my nectarine.

'Well, we began in Cologne. Now we are here, and soon down through France and into Spain. We will walk back across Northern Africa, where it is possible, and finish in the Middle East.'

Jake and I had been starved of conversations with other long-distance walkers, and when Kareem and his brother – a younger man of perhaps twenty-four, smaller in build but more rugged in the face – sat down to join us for dinner, we found it difficult to contain our burning questions. It was clear that the excitement was mutual, and talk quickly settled on a rigorous and intriguing comparison of gear, diet, preparation and path experiences.

Whilst we had a pre-existing interest in hiking, the brothers admitted that neither of them had walked more than ten kilometres before the date of their departure. Nor had they saved money for the trip, but instead were relying on picking up odd jobs along the way. In fact, after being offered a painting job in exchange for free pitching by the campsite owner, they were going to be stopping in Liverdun until the beginning of the coming week.

Kareem had left Cologne with his bag weighing thirty-five kilograms – fifteen kilograms heavier than ours and packed full of supplies. This highlighted the extreme differences in our walking styles: they wore heavy-duty work trousers whilst we wore shorts; their tent was five times the weight of ours; they carried a laptop, GPS, phones, and two cameras; and they ate rice, which was heavy and required more gas to cook. To Jake and me, the repercussions were clear. They too had left in mid-April, but had only covered half the distance that we had, thanks to a steady pace of fifteen to twenty kilometres over a ten-hour day, with just one break from start to finish. An ankle injury and severe blisters had forced the brothers to spend an uncomfortable number of days off the path, which I knew for a walker was a trying experience.

But it soon became obvious that their motives were different to ours. 'We are on a pilgrimage,' Kareem told us as his brother leaned in like an apprentice, transfixed by his teacher. 'We are a Muslim family, and that is why we are walking. My brother has left his girlfriend behind, and both of us our family, but we are doing it for our religion.'

'And maybe a little bit for our future children,' the brother added with a grin. 'It will be a cool story to tell them!'

Amongst the wealth of differences in our respective journeys, there were a number of similarities that proved our ventures were not so unalike. They ate noodles, just like we did, and they too had developed a gag reflex with each mouthful. They had met strangers who had helped them in times of desperation, and they had discovered the protective qualities of Compeed, making it a staple in their first-aid kit. The brothers, like us, worked together, and they too felt at home in the forests at night.

'Ah, the barking deer!' I exclaimed, after learning that they had also been startled when they first heard the sound. 'We thought it was a farmer's dog, or a wild pig!'

'A pig?' Kareem began, a look of concern etched across his face. 'I'm glad it wasn't a pig. We were speaking to a guy close to the border who told us a story about his friend and wild pigs.'

Kareem's voice slowed. 'He was camping out in the woods one night when he heard some noise in the leaves around him. He had lived in the area a long time and knew it was a pig. They are very dangerous – strong and fast, with big tusks. He was not safe in the tent because he had food inside, so when the chance came he ran to the nearest tree and climbed to safety. But the pig followed him and waited at the bottom of the tree. Of course, the man thought that soon the animal would get tired and leave, which it did after a couple of hours. But, within seconds, a second pig had replaced the first. There was a whole group of them, and they were rotating guard!' Kareem laughed with wide eyes as he slapped his hands against his cheeks in shock. 'He was stuck in the tree all night! So, what I'm saying is, I really hope that none of us sees a pig, but they like the forest and they can smell food from far away, so we must be careful.'

Outside, the rain had downgraded to steady drizzle which fell from the cloud-blanketed sky, now pastel pink and arched with the elegant stoop of a double rainbow. We watched as the lamps of Liverdun blinked on, stepping the hillside like the candles of a menorah, before bidding goodnight to Kareem and his brother. Once again, they proved their walking paradigm was a far cry from ours as they spent the entire night, until the sun came up, watching fantasy dramas and updating their blog using their glut of electronic devices.

'I'm in charge of shopping next time,' Jake said on our way out of town the following day. 'This is ridiculous.'

Not for the first time, my involvement in a resupply had left us with an overabundance of food and drink. 'I can't help it,' I pleaded with a grin. 'It's all the things I crave when we're in the middle of nowhere. They call out to me from the shelves, "Buy me, buy me!"'

'Well, we have far too much food now, and it clearly isn't good for you to down two litres of orange juice before going to bed. You were up all bloody night!'

'I know, not the best idea, I must admit. Anyway,' I lowered my voice, 'this all seems a bit strange, doesn't it?' The houses of Liverdun had petered away and been replaced by a series of plots, each comprising a rundown caravan, a mess of scrap metal,

150

dismantled cars, and an abundance of seemingly rogue animals, including several barking dogs, a fluffy kitten, and a condemned chicken with its leg tied to a post by a piece of string. We thought about freeing the poor creature but, before we could act, we were chased up the lane by a yapping Jack Russell dog that snapped aggressively at our heels.

The weight was beginning to affect Jake, rubbing his hips profusely and digging into his shoulders. Feeling somewhat to blame, I took the one-kilogram tin of fruit salad, which had been so irresistible the previous day, from his pack and opened it in the sunlight at the mouth of a forest track.

After a gruelling ten minutes, I reluctantly gulped down the last mouthful, at which point something red in the undergrowth caught my attention. 'Wild strawberries,' I shouted with glee. From beneath a delicate white flower, I plucked two berries, handing one to Jake. In truth, the last thing I wanted was yet more fruit, but I had been waiting so long for my first wild strawberry of the season that anticipation overcame common sense. It was tart and then bitter, and I swallowed the tiny berry with a grimace on my face that suggested they were still not quite ripe.

We moved steadily through the morning and into the after-noon, drying our underwear on a pile of logged pine at lunch as a string of hard-working ants gathered breadcrumbs from about our feet before we were even aware we had dropped them. In the Bois de Faulx, beyond the Moselle River town of Custines, we began our search for a comfortable camping spot, rejecting a fly-infested pitch within a wall of brambles before settling even-tually beneath a canopy of sparse-growing beech and oak.

Ted, it seemed, was causing quite a stir with the local residents of the forest. Within minutes of his pitch, a host of animals had begun their exploration, crawling and sliding across the roof and abseiling from pole to pole, from the incandescence of a green huntsman spider to the spotted hind of a ladybird. My favourite of the lot had to be the tiny caterpillars that had a knack for finding their way between the inner and outer layers of the tent. Lying on my back, I watched the silhouetted larvae slink above me, moving in and out of focus with each step. My least favourite creatures were the slugs. They scratched along the walls (a sound I had never associated with slugs), leaving slime trails behind them, and found refuge inside our footwear, as Jake found out with a yelp during a trip to the toilet.

'Nancy must be close,' Jake said after returning to the tent and unfolding the maps. We had spent the day walking east and were aware that, for the next week, our path would continue along this trajectory as we navigated towards the Vosges Mountains and the town of Schirmeck, one of the most significant milestones on our journey. Schirmeck was the convergence point of the *GR5* and the *Grande Randonnée 53 (GR53)*, a variation of the main route, connecting the town to the French commune of Wissembourg, 180 kilometres to the north. The junction would signify our arrival into mountain country, a prospect that thrilled us. From Schirmeck onwards, the path was comparatively well documented, and to aid us south, we would have the added reassurance of two Cicerone guidebooks: *Trekking in the Vosges and Jura*, and *The GR5 Trail: Through the French Alps: Lake Geneva to Nice*. We also saw Schirmeck as a valuable resupply point, where not only would we be able to buy food but replace gear and clothing too. After all, there are only so many times you can sew a holey sock.

'Bloody hell!' Jake said, after a few minutes of quiet calculation. 'Tomorrow, we'll be halfway!'

'What? Really?'

'Yes, well, assuming my arithmetic is anywhere near accurate and we don't get lost, we're about eight kilometres from our halfway point.' He returned to the map and ran the red thread from our camp several centimetres to the east. 'Fleur Fontaine,' he read. 'So that's halfway, Fleur Fontaine.'

I went to sleep that night with a whirl of thoughts bouncing from ear to ear. What did halfway mean? Would the psychological boost of being on the 'return leg' make things easier, or would the mountains slow us down and exacerbate our weaknesses? What if Jake's calculation was wrong? Did it really matter whether we were halfway or not? The woodpecker in the tall oak beside the tent finally hushed, and the caterpillars returned to the forest's detritus. I terminated my mind-wandering with a final thought, and one that made all my other concerns feel suddenly redundant: how lucky we were to be marking the middle of our venture in a place which, to Englishmen like us, had the most angelic of names: Flower Fountain.

Beginnings: Kennet and Avon Canal, England

Sand under foot: Calais, France

Flatlands: Leopoldkannal, Belgium   *Reflection: Bruges, Belgium*

Aglow: Chateau Vianden, Luxembourg

Wild camping: Belgium/ Luxembourg border

Diary writing: Northern France

Trail Angels: Eliane's house, Jussy, France

Off the beaten track: Lorraine, France

Half way: Fleur Fontaine, France

Lavoir washing: Alsace, France

Misty morning:
Vosges Mountains, France

Poppies: Belfort Gap, France

Enlightenment:
Doubs River, France

Sun through the trees:
Jura Mountains, France

Fondue Family: Doubs, France

Taking a break: Saint-Cergue,
Switzerland (left, Jake; right, Danny)

Marmot: Alpine grasslands, France   *Alpage camping: Alps, France*

Col cresting: Parc National de la Vanoise, France

Scree slopes: Alps, France

Grandeur: Tête à l'Âne, Réserve Naturelle de Passy, France

*Through snow and ice:
Alps, France*

*Chamois: Le Brévent ridgeline,
Chamonix, France*

*Mont Blanc in our sights: Col du Brévent, Chamonix, France
(left, Jake; right, Danny)*

*Ascending: Le Brévent,
Chamonix, France*

*Jagged horizons: Mont Blanc
Circuit, France*

*In the company of Phil:
Lanslevillard, France*

After the rain: Parc Naturel Regional du Queyras, France

Towards the Italian border: Mercantour National Park, France

Mountains in our wake: Col Girardin, France

The final descent: Menton and the Mediterranean Sea

We nodded towards an old lady in a large straw hat as she tended to her vegetable patch, and then passed a young girl in a grubby white dress pedalling slowly down the hill on a rattling pushbike.

'Well, this is it: Fleur Fontaine,' Jake said, raising his head from within the map.

We dropped our bags on the verge of the quiet road, beside three large silos – rusted and abandoned – and ate a jam sandwich each before constructing a 'halfway' message in the dirt with stones.

Our midway point felt decidedly anticlimactic, a theme that seemed to suit the remainder of the day for a sock wash in the Étang de Brin proved, a little bleakly, to be the highlight. We had hoped to wild camp but were driven from the woodlands by mosquitoes and forced into Vic-sur-Seille, a town built on the banks of the Seille and once home to the seventeenth-century Baroque painter, Georges de la Tour.

Two ladies pointed us gladly through the village square to the southern end of town where we set up for the night in Camping la Tuilerie. The rather out-of-place holiday park offered us little in the way of rest, however: children screamed, fireworks popped, and a group of alcohol-fuelled bikers sang through the night until their lungs collapsed.

Thankfully, Sunday morning in Vic-sur-Seille didn't prolong the boisterousness of the night before. We found the village square just as the church bells were clanging, and the warmth of the day awoke. No different from any other French commune, there appeared to be an unsustainable number of *boulangeries*, each packed to its doors with bread-loving locals. We joined the longest queue, assuming that this implied the best produce, and bought an armful of baguettes and pastries, eating half on the spot. To our surprise, the *chasseur de pommes* bore little resemblance to an apple tart, but instead contained chicken and potato. The pastry was warm and crisp, and stuck to my beard.

Two more days of easterly steps saw our horizon gradually swell from a gentle serration to a range of rolling peaks. I found it difficult to take more than a dozen paces without lifting my head to admire the rising Vosges Mountains. The sight boosted our spirits, despite the mounting temperatures (now well above

30°C), which had turned Jake's blue T-shirt transparent with sweat.

At times, the path grew vague, leaving us with little option but to point the compass to the east and wade through meadows of shoulder-high grass, jump fences, and traverse the plough lines of crops and poppy-stained hillsides. On days like these, fruit became a delicacy, and as we passed a tree laden with cherries, we pulled at the branches and filled our pockets. Returning to the path, we ate the crimson fruits with great pleasure, launching the stones from our mouths to see who could spit the furthest.

Hoping to cool off in one of the many lakes within the East Region of the Parc Naturel Règional de Lorraine, we were disappointed to discover that the bodies of water were banked with thickets of impenetrable aquatic grass and bulrush. In need of shade, we skirted the Étang de Lindre, eventually finding sanctuary beneath the trees of a nearby forest.

'Imagine if we had swum,' I said to Jake as a swarm of mosquitoes helped us to achieve our quickest tent assembly yet. 'I'm wearing clothes, and they've managed to get me eight times on my arse! Imagine if I was naked.'

'I'd rather not,' he replied, leaping head first into the tent as soon as the guy ropes were in.

'I'm too hot and bothered to get in.' I felt the lumps on my rear. 'I'll be back later.'

Down by the water, the biting subsided. I found a fallen tree angled into the shallows of the lake, forming a natural jetty, and sat on it until the light began to fade. The day ended with a magnificent crack of thunder, followed shortly by a downpour that fell steadily through the night.

We overslept the 5.15am alarm, but were woken five minutes later by a foraging deer. Sunrise over the lake was still possible. 'Come on!' I urged Jake. 'We'll miss it if you don't hurry.'

Pushing aside the slugs and midges, I sprang from the tent and ran towards the streaks of deep orange light irradiating through the pines. Skipping over logs and batting branches from my face, I burst through the forest's edge and slowed to a walk. I was in a field of hay bales bathed in the light of the sunrise. The grass flowed unhurriedly down to the lake where it met a natural bank of common reed erupting with yellow iris petals. I climbed onto a bale close to the water, absorbing its sweet scent after the night of rain, and waited for Jake.

Moorhens and their impressionable young paddled in the shallows, and sparrows shoaled in the colouring sky. At the far end of the lake, three white storks, an icon of the Vosges, stood proudly in the reeds. All around the lake, splashes of water broke the surface, like tossed coins in candlelight, glinting and ringing in the rising sun. By the time Jake had joined me, I realised that the creatures responsible were dozens of feeding catfish. With their whiskers stuck into the air and their mouths open, the fish skimmed the water's surface, hoping to come across a sleepy juvenile carp or an unsuspecting water boatman.

We ate breakfast on a hill above the Étang de Lindre and then, a few kilometres on, stripped to our skins and showered in the overflow of its neighbouring lake just metres below the walking track. I counterproductively pulled on my sweaty shirt as pea-sized frogs tiptoed over the surrounding rocks and pond skaters skimmed the stagnant pools, leaving cat paw shadows on the bed below.

Not content with settling anywhere other than on the southernmost lakes of the East Region, we pushed on through the day with the glare of the sun seldom retiring from our necks, jeered on by the croaking frogs shaded below water-lily parasols and awnings of duckweed.

Relief from the heat came late in the afternoon. Sighting the rooftops and steeples of Gondrexange across the region's south-tapering lake, Le Petit Étang, we undressed for the second time that day and leapt from the dam wall into the water, dispersing shoals of tiny fish as we landed. The combination of sun, water and mild heatstroke laid a holiday atmosphere upon the afternoon, which followed us into town where we ate an 800-gram tin of apple purée on the grass of Les Mouettes campsite whilst sweat pooled in our belly buttons.

'And I thought our shorts were small,' Jake murmured through closed teeth, nodding to a cluster of caravans down by the water, amongst which several bodies had congregated. I was astounded by the shear diversity of French men in such a small space – from the abdominally well-endowed with stunted legs, to the tall, skinny and coppery-skinned – all of whom appeared to be enjoying rural Lorraine's climate as much as we were.

Whilst the men fell into three groups – the 'Small-Talkers', the 'Bathers', and the 'Shaders' – all flaunted one common feature: staggeringly undersized and wildly revealing Speedos. The Small-Talkers strolled leisurely from one camper van to another, propping an arm on a vacant windowsill, kicking their left leg behind the right, before releasing deep, lethargic sighs. Postures set, it was time for the well-rehearsed small talk to begin: 'Hot today, isn't it?' 'What are the chances it'll be raining tomorrow?' 'So, what's for dinner?' 'Red or white tonight?' And, finally, nodding towards the camper van, 'How many kilometres has she done?' Once conversation had run dry, the Small-Talkers would lightly slap the side of the van, return to the stability of two legs, and move coolly onto the next camper van for another inoffensive exchange.

The Bathers, generally speaking, were bronzed, oily and overweight, and spent their day lying flat out on specially designed beds in the sweltering heat. Of the three groups, the Bathers possessed the smallest Speedos, forcing them to engage in a number of rearranging activities involving impressive dexterity and muscle-clenching exercises. Every half-hour, almost on the dot, the dripping bodies would rise from their horizontal state, as slowly as possible so as to avoid fainting, and then, like large joints of roast beef lashed precariously about the midriff with a small piece of string, they would make their way to the nearest hose, splashing themselves with cooling water like a shower gel advert gone horribly wrong.

The most mysterious of the campers were the Shaders. Hidden beneath their awnings, expressions were hard to read. Of course, they still wore trunks – everyone did. But unlike the sun-damaged Speedos of the Small-Talkers and Bathers, theirs were black, lustrous and irrefutably suave. The Shaders were the James Bonds of Gondrexange, an image only slightly tainted by their milky skins and bright blue Crocs.

THE VOSGES MOUNTAINS

Over the past few days, we had learnt a lot about walking in Lorraine, concluding that hiking was not a common pastime in the region. Paths were long abandoned or absent altogether so we had been forced to forge our own, often subjecting our legs to an undergrowth of creepy-crawlies. At one point, we were so deep in maize that we spooked a roe deer in a midday slumber, sending its ears and white rump hurtling through the crops towards the safety of the bordering woods.

'I've never inspected my groin so intently,' I said to Jake on our way out of town. 'Forty-six ticks I've had to claw from my skin now, and you're on seventy-three!'

By 8.30am, I was glistening with sweat, and my mouth was parched.

'The guy at Les Mouettes told me that there was a heatwave spreading across Europe,' Jake said as we continued east with the bulging Vosges Mountains before us. 'Even my shins are sweating.'

We were carrying just four litres of water between us and were aware, from previous experience, that a river on the map did not always ensure a river on the path; and even if there *was* a river, it wouldn't necessarily be safe to drink from.

Fortunately, La Sarre Blanche Rivière, at the commune of Niderhoff, was a good size, and we were able to rehydrate on the village bridge whilst blue damsel flies flickered about our heads.

Niderhoff was a pleasant place – neat gardens, tiled houses, sunbathing cats – but, for us, it also represented a stark change in cartographical aid. Replacing the detail of the blue 1:25,000 *IGNs* were France's 1:100,000 green *IGNs*. The new maps were undoubtedly better suited to a traveller with wheels than with boots. But with our bank balances in mind, along with the added comfort of the guidebooks, we had hoped they would suffice.

Half an hour down the road, I stopped to assess the new map (*112, Strasbourg-Forbach*). We had barely left the edge of the page. In fact, the coverage of the chart was so great that it stretched beyond France's eastern border and into Germany, some 150 kilometres away. I began to feel anxious. The guidebooks had colourful photographs and interesting facts, along with rough path descriptions and sketched maps, but if we were to stray from these aids then the green *IGNs* were our only means of navigation. We had used thirty-four maps to get us from Bristol to Fleur Fontaine, losing our way on a number of occasions. With just eight maps remaining between us and the Mediterranean, perhaps we were tempting trouble.

*

'You must eat your bag empty,' Annika told us as Dick packed their old canvas tent onto the back of his motorbike. We had spent the night in Abreschviller's Le Camping de Moulin, a municipal campsite where the overnight lodging cost us less than a pint of beer. Looking to lose a little more weight from our packs, we had taken a wad of painkillers over to our neighbours to see if they were interested in a free handout. Presumably accepting the offer more out of politeness than necessity, we soon struck up a conversation. 'Yes, eat your bag empty,' Annika continued. 'If you have food in your bag, you have too much weight. Eat, eat, eat! As much as you can, and your bag will get lighter.'

Ordinarily, I would have argued against this strategy for reducing pack weight, and with good reason, for surely having no food would lead to starvation? But Annika and Dick, on a motorbiking tour of Switzerland, France and Luxembourg, were long-distance specialists. Not only had they biked around Europe, but they had also hiked the *Camino de Santiago* no fewer than five times, giving them a breadth of experience that made it difficult to discount their advice.

'On our fifth *Camino*, we arrived into Santiago de Compostela on day 100. It was very special. But like the first time we finished, and the second, we said, "Never again, this is our last," but we have done it five times now.'

Annika was the talker, and Dick, it transpired, the affirmer. His only skin-covering garment was a pair of three-quarter length canvas trousers. His shoulders were tanned, his chest spun with silver curls, his hair white, and his bushy eyebrows dark. Dick was perhaps the most content-looking man I had ever met. As Annika spoke, he looked at her endearingly with agreeing nods and glowing simpers. Annika was the female version of Dick, but she had more to say. I could have spoken to the couple for hours, absorbing the wisdom they had gathered from years on the path. 'You can only walk with one whom you love,' Annika said, before going on to tell us that Dick used to write letters home to his family on used maps.

'It's funny,' Dick said, as we lifted our packs onto our shoulders, 'when we bike and we see walkers traipsing along the bitumen, we're jealous. But when we walk and see bikers cruising the roads, we are also jealous. The grass is always greener, I guess.'

We made our way east beneath a chalked sky, dotted here and there with the feathery prongs of a hawk's wings. The parched paths were cracked from the heat, and sweat spilt from our foreheads as the ground began to rise, stinging our eyes. Reference to the map told us that there would be no water sources between Abreschviller and the 1,009-metre peak of Le Donon, our proposed camping spot for the night, and the highest point of our walk so far. We were carrying six litres of water, a substantial weight, but nonetheless an inadequate supply on an ascent that would see us climb for more than 700 metres.

Through boulder-filled conifer forests and banks of ferns, we zigzagged up to Belle Roche where the smoky-grey wings of a dozen wood white butterflies led us to a gap in the trees. The land dropped away at our feet, presenting a ridge of meringue-shaped mountains, deep green with pine, which continued on to the east, where the stiff peaks of Haut Rognol, Tête du Noll and Hunerstkopf shot up from the Sarre Rouge River valley.

Remembering that the combination of heat and hills was a recipe for painful blisters, we pulled off our boots and socks and put them in the sun to dry, before covering our vulnerable feet in a patchwork of Compeed. We had been fortunate, at least until now, to have experienced an extremely limited number of blisters, so often the bane of a walker's life. I had been suffering, albeit moderately, with a heel sore acquired two months earlier back in England. But, following its eruption not long after passing through Antwerp, it had turned into a rather unpleasant, yet almost entirely painless, mass of calluses and flaking skin. Meanwhile, Jake was yet to get a blister, proving that either his boots, or indeed his feet, were a fine example of perfect design.

Unwilling to invest all our trust in the promise of a mountain spring, said by our map to be close to a shelter not far from the Le Donon summit, we decided to preserve the water as much as we could, leaving enough for a second day of walking. Sweat poured from my brow, and my lips became sticky with dehydration. Somewhat cruelly, Jake was leading the way, and I was left to follow the three-litre water bladder attached to the outside of his pack as it sloshed and glimmered like a bag of transparent nectar. When we eventually stopped to take a precious liquid break, the water was hot from the heat of the sun and did little to quench our miserable thirsts.

With three wooden walls and a bench, the shelter – known locally as an *abri* – was basic but perfect for our needs, not least because of the signpost nailed to its frame: '*Source d'eau – 100m*'.

Within seconds, we had found the small water source trickling over the side of the path, and with each desperate mouthful, our worries of desiccation abated. In fact, not so far away, in the small Vosges town of Vittel, water of the same quality was being bottled, packed and readied for departure, soon to find itself sitting on a supermarket shelf in London. 'There's nothing like getting something for free!' I gasped between gulps of the cool spring water.

More comfortable with the prospect of a night under the stars, we decided to pitch beside the *abri* rather than under it. Jake cooked a pot of couscous with soup powder, proudly naming it 'walkers' risotto', whilst I wrote a letter to Claudia, inspired by our conversation with Dick and Annika some hours earlier, on the back of one of our used maps.

An hour before dusk, as the earth-boring dung beetles ceased their rolling and the birdsong heightened, I left the tent and followed a series of red rectangles under fallen trees and tumbled boulders. Without the weight of my pack, I drifted up the mountainside gaining 200 metres in fifteen minutes until I reached the crest of Le Donon, one of the highest points in the Northern Vosges. Once a place of Celtic and Roman worship, and more recently of strategic wartime importance, the flat summit was studded with relics from the past, most notably a nineteenth-century Roman-style temple, its pillars silhouetted in the haze of the setting sun. My eyes drifted to the surrounding slopes, each bulge of the land wrapped in a thick blanket of trees, their interiors unknown and their paths disguised. An engulfing shadow spread slowly over the hills. I was thrilled. Finally, we had reached the land of massifs and crags, outcrops and *arêtes*.

The Vosges Mountains, set in the far east of France, comprise 140 kilometres of relatively low-level mountains, peaking at Le Grand Ballon (1,424 metres) midway down the range. Falling largely in the Alsace region of France, the GR5 would take us along a convoluted path, dropping into the Rhine River Valley to the east – its waters dividing France from Germany – before ascending back into the hills. As the first of three mountain ranges, the Vosges (succeeded by the sub-alpine Jura Mountains and the Alps) presented us with an opportunity to begin our mountain acclimatisation.

I left the viewpoint and descended back to the tent, feeling my thighs tighten and my knees creak.

With our Casios set for 4am, we should have known that our sixty-eighth day on the path was going to be a long one. I unzipped the tent and poked my hand out into the night. No rain. Encouraged by the dry air, I clambered over the bags, waking Jake who had once again slept through the alarms.

Ever since the second day of our journey, we had roused each morning with agonisingly sensitive feet, too sore to walk on. Adopting a rather unusual technique, we soon learnt that it was far less painful to take our first few steps with our toes bent underneath our soles. Once upright, and with our feet gradually remembering their duties for the day, it was possible to return our clenched toes to their customary position, at which point the pain would subside.

The morning dew was still an hour away, and we were yet to hear the bark of a deer or the fluted chirrups of a blackbird. I looked above my head to see the pulse of a dull star. 'Sunrise is on,' I whispered to Jake.

We packed in the darkness without the aid of our head torches, letting routine lead the way: clothes first, sleeping gear second, food, and then tent.

After half an hour of climbing, a thick swell of dawn-lit mist rose from below us, reducing visibility to a couple of metres. Gaining what moisture they could before daylight came, we passed scores of croaking frogs which leapt from the path as our heavy feet vibrated towards them. Jake, who had dropped behind me, took the camera from his pocket, held it above his head, and then began to mutter voice-over narrative.

A few moments later, I heard a quiet thud and a rustling of leaves. I turned around to see that Jake had disappeared from view. Retracing my steps, I found him on his back in a ditch beside the path – apparently the result of slippery rocks, low visibility and the instinctive protection of a Fujifilm camera.

I helped Jake from the thorny shrub, and a few minutes later we were on the summit. Gusts of mist swept across the rounded peak and between the archways of the temple. We sheltered behind the pillars as wet air dampened our packs and condensed on the heather that grew between the mountain's sandstone slabs.

We waited for an hour and a half before conceding to the cloud, leaving Le Donon down the southern flank by hundreds of stone piles, no doubt the work of summertime tourists. Though the temperature had fallen, the day was still warm and the bowling slate-coloured clouds moving in from the east suggested that a thunderstorm was close.

As luck would have it, we timed our arrival into Schirmeck just as the lightning forked and the first drops of rain began to fall. Schirmeck was not a large place, and unlike the vivid image of a walker's mecca that we had conjured in our minds, it appeared no different to any of the other settlements we had passed. Jake did, however, manage to find some cheap socks in the local supermarket, which he doubled up to imitate the thickness of a hiking sock, hoping that his feet would be fooled.

The flash storm ceased as quickly as it came, leaving strands of cloud dragged across the washed heavens and puddles of stirred silt on the forest paths. By midday, the sun was shining through the trees, and we found ourselves climbing a steep trail towards the top of a hill in the Bois de Russ, from which the unfamiliar sound of prattling crowds rang down. We had arrived at the remains of Struthof Concentration Camp.

On 21 April 1941, the site, initially built as a forced labour camp, was opened, and the first deportees began to arrive. Struthof was the only concentration camp to be built in France, and though it began as a site for the forced quarrying of granite, its detainees were soon subjected to medical experiments and exterminations, making it one of the most deadly camps in Europe.

We walked along the southern fence of the site, looking down at the camp as lamenting visitors stepped slowly from one elongated building to the next under the looming structures of the Nazi watchtowers, built from timber poles and lashed with barbed wire. We dropped our bags beside the Monument to the Departed – a white stone memorial dedicated to the victims of the camp – and walked between the hundreds of white crosses that meshed the hillside.

Unavoidably, we left the camp talking about war and our ancestors' involvement. I remember taking my great granddad's oil lamp into school when I was ten for a 'show and tell' session. Of course, it meant little to me then, and my observations strayed no further than its beaten fuel container, cobwebbed bulb and a twistable knob jutting from its side, which I proudly spun in front of my admiring (or disinterested) classmates. That lamp meant more to me now.

Ferns, moon daisies, foxgloves and piles of silky grass twinkled in the dappled light of the beech forest. The path soon rounded to a flat crest at Grand Rosskopf (1,032 metres). From the acme, we peered south down the spine of the Vosges, where somewhere on the horizon Le Grand Ballon was waiting.

Progress for the time being was not southerly. For one week, we had been following the *GR5*'s easterly inclinations across Lorraine and into the Vosges, a trajectory that would continue until we dropped over the other side of the range and into Barr on the western fringes of the Rhine Valley and the Alsace Plain.

'*Cascade d'Andlau – 2km*' read a signpost, before the path descended into a wood of mountain ash, its creamy blossom snowing down on us as we skipped over scores of fresh springs, exposed rocks and wandering tree roots.

'You know what?' Jake said, through a mouthful of trail mix. 'This could be the best scroggin yet. I'm serious,' he continued, seeing my expression of disbelief. 'Toffees, sherbets, nuts, raisins, banana chips, Werther's Originals and jelly sweets.'

I took a handful and examined the contents. 'You may be right,' I agreed, unwrapping a grenadine-flavoured sherbet and putting it into my mouth with a crunch.

'What are you doing?' Jake swivelled to face me.

'Sorry?'

'Did you just bite that Sherbet Grenadine?'

'Well yeah, I guess so,' I replied, a little taken aback by Jake's accusations.

He shook his head disapprovingly. 'I can't believe you bit it. It's the best of the lot,' he said, lowering his voice as he turned on down the track. 'You know, something's wrong with the world when people are biting Sherbet Grenadines.'

We didn't speak for ten minutes.

Realistically, I don't think this heated exchange of words counted as an argument, but it was the closest we had got to one since leaving Bristol, a rather impressive feat considering we had spent the last 1,680 hours in each other's company.

We soon arrived at the upper reaches of the cascade d'Andlau, where a noisy torrent of water, just a kilometre from its source, rolled powerfully over a rock ledge into a plunge pool below.

In his eagerness to capture the scene by camera, Jake unclipped his rucksack and shrugged it from his shoulders. But, instead of rushing down to the water, he froze.

'I've done it too,' he said, with an awful look of disappointment.

'What's wrong?'

'It's my back. It's gone.'

Mirroring the distress I had experienced a week and a half earlier, Jake quickly became despondent. Just as he had done for me, I unloaded half of his gear into my pack and gave him my back support belt. Scrapping our plan to sleep by the falls, we cautiously made our way through the Forêt de la Ville de Strasbourg, arriving two kilometres later at a campground in the nearby hill town of Le Hohwald. We had been walking for fifteen hours.

As yet another storm thundered across the sky, I tried, unsuccessfully, to bash the tent pegs into unyielding ground with a rock salvaged from beneath a nearby caravan. Dissatisfied with Ted's sturdiness, but cold from the rain, I abandoned the outdoors and ran towards the shelter of the nearby ablutions block to join Jake.

After discovering that every room in the building was locked, we sat in the hallway, opened a tin of herring, and waited for the rain to pass.

INTO THE ALSACE

'No walking today,' I told Jake, leaving him in the tent before striding purposefully into the village centre, where signs of Alsatian living began to appear with half-timbered building fronts and steeply-pitched roofs.

I rattled optimistically on the door of the rundown-looking Pavillon de Chasse before noticing the '*fermé*' sign in the window. Le Hôtel Marchal was just as fruitless. '*Je suis désolé, pas de chambres,*' the receptionist told me as the tantalising smell of their buffet breakfast found my nose. My third enquiry, at the opulent-looking Le Grand Hotel, also brought failure. '*La chambre la moins chère est à 135 euros,*' the lady at the reception desk told me after I asked the price of their cheapest room.

In a final attempt to find a bed for Jake, I paced up the only street left in Le Hohwald and stopped outside Tilly's *chambre d'hôtes.* The large coral-coloured house, with white window frames and black sills, had an iron balcony leading to a staircase that reached the ground at my feet. The house was surrounded by potted plants and piles of drying logs, whilst a white Alsace stork, hand-painted onto the coral, flew clumsily below the rooftop guttering. I had a good feeling about this place, and one that was only heightened as I approached the front door to be welcomed by an array of Christmas decorations and fairy lights.

Christiana was a large woman and wore baggy clothes with a purple bandana tied around her greying hair. A thick brush of lavender eye shadow ran from lashes to brows and her bright red lipstick, presumably applied by the same heavy hand, strayed somewhat from its intended destination.

Before I could decide whether Christiana worked in the bed and breakfast or was a long forgotten guest, I was being led across the road to a small row of terraced bungalows, where a key with a teddy bear attached to it opened a door.

Pink. Everything was pink. The double bed in the middle of the room, with its swirly headboard and pink canopy, was covered in pink blankets and pink cushions. The throw over the wicker chair, the towels, curtains, lampshades, dressers and ornaments were pink. Even the chocolates on the pink pillowcases were pink.

'*Oui, c'est bien,*' I said to Christiana, to which she handed me the teddy bear and was gone.

'Wow,' Jake gasped an hour later as the door swung open and he hobbled into the room. 'You were right. I do love it!'

Jake had managed the short distance down the hill and into Le Hohwald without incident. Eager to take advantage of the facilities, I cranked the radiators up to full, draped them with washed clothes, and then hung Ted from the wardrobe to dry.

'Look!' Jake said, beckoning me over to the other side of the room. 'I don't believe it. It's Menton!'

Sure enough, hanging on the wall between two pink-framed paintings was a photograph of Menton. Taken from the sea, the shot captured the south-eastern French town at dusk. Smudged across the foreground like a pastel sketch, the town's amber streetlights shimmered and danced, whilst staggering up the slopes of the coastal mountains were the rainbow hues of Menton's emblematic Old Town buildings.

'Amazing!' I beamed at Jake. 'What are the chances?'

Ten minutes must have passed as we stared at the photograph – transfixed and silent – before the odorous humidity of the room became unbearable and, slipping on our sandals, we made for the centre of town to find food.

With little more than the nutrition of the complimentary chocolates sitting in our stomachs, we were disappointed to find that the bakery was closed and the restaurants too. 'It's Friday,' the lady at the tourist information office informed us. 'It's a holiday for the businesses. They are not here for the weekend.' Having delivered the bad news that we would be unable to buy food until we reached Barr the following day, she then added to our misery with a local weather warning: 'Storms in the Vosges are frequent and dangerous. Be careful.'

Driven by hunger, we decided that our only remaining option was to beg. Christiana was lying on a deckchair in the sun outside her house. Apparently a lady of diversity, she had replenished her lipstick, or should I say 'face-stick', with a more vibrant cerise tone. *'Bonjour Christiana! Je suis désolé, mais avez vous un peu de pain pour moi et mon frère? Les magasins sont fermés!'* I said with a puppy-dog face to exaggerate our pitiful state.

'Bread?' she replied, happily dismissing my attempts at French. 'Yes! One or two baguettes?'

Tilly, it turned out, was Christiana's mother. She had passed away some years back and left her daughters with the bed and breakfast business. They ran the place together, mostly catering for the large number of motorcyclists that passed through the area. Incidentally, it was a Vietnamese biker who had painted the stork on the wall.

'Do you like Cliff Richard?' Christiana interrupted as I began to query the colour choice of the house.

'Oh, well...he's...' The question felt a little out of context, but her wide eyes and light smirk told me that I should answer or else the offer of a baguette, which she now held firmly in her grip, would be withdrawn. 'Yep, yes, I do. I like him. *We* like him. And our mother likes him too.'

It must have been the right response, for the baguette swiftly changed hands and we were bade goodnight.

PETER AND BARB

We left Le Hohwald with the dripping letters of 'Summer Solstice' meandering down Tilly's bathroom mirror. Lizards basked in the sunshine, bumblebees hummed around pink foxgloves, and fruiting cherry trees bowed resplendently over the path.

The strapping on Jake's pack, usually home to our daily supply of liquid, now held an empty water bladder, reducing the weight on his back by three kilograms. With each step that Jake took, the bladder would flap flimsily against his pack: *Clap! Clap! Clap!*

Replacing our usual means of hydration was the ritual of me stooping down to each and every stream, no matter how big or small, to scoop a few mouthfuls of water into one of our plastic bottles. Crudely checking its clarity in the sunlight, we then gulped it down as if it was the last oasis for a hundred miles.

From one red rectangle to the next, we gradually became used to the new signage; its connotations running far deeper than a simple alteration of pattern and colour. Indeed, our route through the Vosges comprised just 330 of the massif's 7,000 kilometres of footpaths, many of which existed long before the GRs' designation by the Fédération Française de la Randonnée in the 1940s. From the iron hobnails of the Romans' caligae, to the pilgrims, traders and modern-day hikers, I suddenly felt we were no longer alone.

In fact, we *were* no longer alone. It was midday, and a short diversion took us away from the forested track and up to the sandstone outcrop of Mont Sainte-Odile. Built magnificently into the 760-metre peak was the Hohenbourg Monastery, an elaborate structure of archways and stone balconies that buzzed with crowds of people.

Legend tells that Saint Odile, born blind at the end of the seventh century AD but regaining her sight at baptism, founded a convent on the cliff edge of the mount. For a long time a site of fluctuation – from its destruction and turmoil in the Middle Ages to intermittent eras of prosperity – the monastery finally became a place of harmony.

We approached the outer walls of the convent, seemingly a precarious continuation of the vertical cliff that fell 100 metres to the trees below, and found a bench on the eastern terrace. After five days in the Vosges Mountains, it was our first clear view of the Alsace Plain. The land stretched like a vast arable rug, threaded with small towns and villages, to the subtle contours of the Rhine Valley. Beyond the snaking river, the hazy outline of the Black Forest tumbled down Germany's south-west border and into Switzerland.

I pulled the food bag from my rucksack and opened it to find half a dozen slices of bread which we had bought two weeks back, and the end of a cured sausage. The meat had adopted a greyish tinge and smelt worse than our feet, so we tossed it into the bin beside the bench and were left to chew dispassionately on the dry bread.

Throngs of bodies moved unhurriedly across our view – nuns, pilgrims, hotel guests (the convent was clearly broadening its appeal), Americans, Germans and, most prominently, several coachloads of chattering, grey-haired Japanese tourists. We people-watched for some time, and then, with our sights set on the plains, dropped into a deep forest and made for Barr.

On our descent into the town, it became clear that Barr was not just another collection of houses with a bakery but a town dedicated to the production, selling and consumption of wine. Convoys of wine tour buses helter-skeltered down the zigzagging roads, from Pinot Noir to Gewurztraminer, and Riesling to Muscat d'Alsace.

We were therefore not altogether surprised, as we stepped into the tourist office in the town centre, to find ourselves in the company of a highly inebriated Englishman. '*De rien*, that means "of nothing", doesn't it?' the man slurred to the information assistant behind the counter, with one hand in the pocket of his cream trousers and the other adjusting the straw hat on his head. 'Yes, *de rien*. Off I go now,' he continued as he turned around and made for the door, using the leaflet stand to steady himself.

'The internet is free,' said the young lady as she spotted us eyeing up the computer in the corner of the room. 'You can use it as long as you haven't had as much wine as him.' She nodded to the door where the intoxicated Englishman was trying to summon the courage to make the single step down onto the street.

It had been some time since we had last checked our e-mail accounts, a fact that made 'You have three unread messages' a little disheartening. However, amongst the excitement of my latest online bank statement and an e-mail about career prospects, I spotted a message entitled 'Guess what...?' from Brenda, instantly lifting my mood.

As a child I had spent hours on our grandparents' living room carpet flicking tirelessly through *Discovering the Wonders of the World*, and *The Atlas of Natural Wonders* – mesmerised by photos of the Great Barrier Reef, New Zealand's Mt Cook, Iguazu Falls, the Pantanal and Machu Picchu.

At seventeen, I landed a job as a shelf-stacker. I worked my scuffed shoes and poorly ironed shirt into the ground until, after a year of graft, I had enough money to leave England. With adulthood on my side, pay cheques in my back pocket, and a willing friend as keen as I was, we set off around the world to fulfil the childhood dream.

After four months in Asia and Australasia, we flew to Sao Paulo and caught the bus up to Rio. And that is when I happened upon Brenda, a wild, spontaneous and altogether outlandish Australian who I knew would remain in my life thereafter.

We met up in New Zealand a few years later, camping in the passes of the Southern Alps, and cooking mussels picked from the rocks of Marlborough Sound, and again a year after that in Brenda's home city, Brisbane, where we climbed Mount Tibrogargan, an iconic spire of the Glass House Mountains, and explored the cave-dwelling glow-worms of Queensland's Gold Coast.

I opened the e-mail expectantly:

I'm landing in Paris on 8 July. Then I'll catch the train and bus to find the town ahead of you and meet you pair on the roadside if that suits. If not, I'll find a pub and eat snails 'til I'm sober. How's the walking? 'Ave you got flattened feet yet?

Please let me know if I can bring any supplies for you. I can pick them up in Strasbourg, or bring stuff from Australia

169

or Malaysia: water purifying tablets, shoes, jackets, hats,
sunscreen, mosquito repellent...anything.
    I will be coming from the jungles of Borneo.
See you high on a hill!

'That's not too long away,' Jake said as we wobbled through the backstreets of Barr, passed window boxes of geraniums, bunches of dried corn and timber-infused walls, until eventually we reached a campsite on the western side of town. 'And Nan and Gramps are going to visit us when we reach Lake Geneva, which will be a week or so after Brenda leaves.'

The thought of visiting friends and relatives thrilled both of us, and it was difficult to hide our smiles as we threaded the poles and pegged the guy ropes in the sun next to a garden spilling with vegetables at Camping St Martin.

'*Vous aimez la salade verte?*' Ms Pierrette, the camp owner, asked with a look of compassion on her face before bringing us a bowl of lettuce leaves, onions and French dressing without charge.

There must have been something about the way we looked, or perhaps Jake's tentative movements, that was pulling on the sympathy strings of those we passed, for the next morning, as we were leaving the fuchsias and fountains of Andlau, Barr's neighbouring town some five kilometres south, we were subject to another act of unprovoked kindness.

'*Excusez-moi! Excusez-moi!*' a man's voice called out, stopping us in our tracks in the shadows of the Sainte Richarde Abbey, its lower walls surrounded by the stalls and guitar strums of the town's Sunday market. A man with a silver beard was running down the street towards us, his glasses catching the glare of sun with each clumsy step. In one hand, he held a fastened black umbrella and in the other his flat cap, which he threw loosely back onto his head as he came to a halt beside us.

'*Bonjour,*' Jake said, reciprocating the broad grin of the man.

'Ah, we thought you were French hill walkers!' he replied eagerly, with an English intonation running clean through his voice. The sun shone through his notable ears, and long eyelashes flittered behind the round spectacles now shaded beneath his cap.

'We're looking for a short walk in the hills and thought you'd be able to help. I'm Peter, by the way, from Canada. Well, not

170

originally. I was born in the north of England,' he said with a Yorkshire inflection before turning to welcome a slightly out of breath lady with pink lipstick, short blonde hair and a blue bonnet not too dissimilar to the one sitting on the grey of Peter's head. 'And this is Barb, my wife.'

'No, we're English walkers,' Jake said, still revelling in the thought that our skin was now tanned enough to disguise us as French locals, 'but we are going back into the mountains and know the tracks a little.' He opened the map and pointed out the paths.

Peter and Barb were fascinated with our adventure, bombarding us with a photo shoot and a long list of questions, overheard by two local children who giggled whenever Peter spoke. 'My son will love to hear about this, he really will. In fact, I have an idea! Are you in any rush?' he said, continuing on before we had time to reply. 'Because there is supposed to be this outstanding *pâtisserie* in the square. I don't remember the name, but I've heard it's the best in France! It's on us if you're interested?'

The queue outside the Pâtisserie Salon de Thé Rietsch was long, but the mousse cake delicious. Peter, a semi-retired lecturer of the French language and ex-marathon runner, and Barb, who hinted at being an actress, bounced from one subject to the next, slurping at their coffees and treating us to a second cake.

'I mean, I had brain surgery six months ago,' Peter admitted, after detailing his and Barb's most exhilarating Scrabble encounters, 'and I'm pretty sure the surgeons inserted a Scrabble chip into my skull, because I managed four consecutive "bingos" in my first game back from injury. I used all seven letters in one go, four times in a row! Brilliant!'

Barb's look of displeasure, as Peter rumbled out a brawny laugh, told me that their games were competitive and rarely friendly. 'Well, we've won pretty much an equal amount,' she said, reducing her husband's guffaws to a light splutter.

I liked Peter and Barb a lot, and after hearing that they enjoyed letter writing, added them to our expanding postcard list. 'We will let you know how we get on,' Jake said, waving them goodbye as we continued up the road we had started two hours earlier.

After passing a man scything in his tree-banked meadow, we began to climb back into the hills, eventually cresting at the Col de l'Ungersberg. On the crossroads of a dozen forestry tracks, where the pines creaked and mushrooms clumped like a spillage of Scotch pancakes amongst heaps of felled logs, we rested and ate the last of Peter and Barb's pastries. It was a changeable day, one minute sunny and fresh, and the next overcast and unsettled.

'I smell like coleslaw,' I admitted to Jake, who moments earlier had diagnosed his scent as that of a mild curry. 'Perhaps the longer we go without a wash the smell of coleslaw replaces the smell of curry?' I suggested, wondering whether I should be either concerned or glad that my two favourite dishes were at the wrong end of our body odour spectrum.

For the next two days, as we marched on to the Alsace tourist town of Ribeauvillé, the *GR5* seldom strayed from the low-lying eastern hills of the Vosges range. Though we were largely under the cover of trees, we caught glimpses of history through the canopies – the white stone remnants of the Château d'Andlau, Landsberg, and finally Bernstein, one of the oldest castles in the Alsace, its walls rooted with climbing trees and eiderdowns of ivy.

Determined to spend the night in the company of Alsatian ramparts, we aimed for a cluster of three castles printed on the map, hoping that one would provide us with enough solitude to pitch the tent.

To our delight, on a rounded ledge vegetated with young oak, hawthorn and creeping honeysuckle, we found a splendid view overlooking the Château d'Ortenbourg.

We waited with a tin of puréed peas as the last few tourists left the relics, and then pitched Ted as the first signs of dusk brought a nip to the air. The pentagonal keep of Ortenbourg, designed to deflect the projectiles of oncoming attackers, loomed imposingly over the Alsace Plain to the east, its height accentuated by the silent kestrels that hovered around its upper reaches.

We left the tent and made our way down a rubble-strewn path to the castle, spooking a black squirrel which darted along the side of the wall and into the bushes at our feet. Like children, we scrambled from one viewpoint to the next, never content with our spot for the worry that the next might be better still.

I found an arrow slit and peered through it. The force of the channelled wind glazed my eyes with tears, diluting the hues of the setting sun into a whirlwind of purples and pinks. Exploring further, I found an arched window that framed the Rhine Valley and the Black Forest beyond, and then finally settled on the south-east-facing wall where I sat on a heap of crumbled granite.

Gradually, the lights of the distant villages flickered on, their luminance distorted to a twinkle – trillions of particles, the catalyst for magic. Amber dots glided slowly through the darkness of the countryside. A bat swooped. Then the full moon rose from within the eastern clouds, taking charge of the sky and spilling silver onto the treetops of the Vosges. 'Take me someplace else and it would disappoint. If only you could see this.' I pushed my notepad back into my pocket and stood to find Jake waiting quietly at the bottom of the path. As we began up the hill to the tent, a small white moth fluttered across my vision and over Jake's shoulder, its wings flashing in the moonshine.

SNOW

'OK, this is what we're getting rid of,' I said to Jake on the steps of the *bureau de poste* in Châtenois. 'A pair of boxers each, a vest, a T-shirt, all the blue *IGN* maps and the MP3 player that Claudia made us. Oh, and we're throwing the pedometer away. It doesn't even work.'

With just over a kilogram less on our backs, we bounced through Châtenois, beneath the old town gateway – its terracotta tiles stained with the guano of two storks dozing in an enormous nest of sticks and mud on the apex of the roof – and up a steep woodland path towards a castle high on the hill.

The Châteaux du Haut-Koenigsbourg, one of the most symbolic castles of the Alsace, required an entry fee. At eight euros a head, a viewing of the inner walls would have cost us the same as three or four days of food. Naturally, we abstained and, instead, leant against the car-park wall, surrounded by binoculars and cameras, and gazed out over the Rhine Valley. The rain had come and gone several times on our climb up to the castle, and now that we had a vantage point, we could see why. From our pew to the Black Forest some forty kilometres to the east, bands of slanting rain showers fell, irregularly dousing the land like the chutes of a dozen watering cans, soaking one crop of villages but avoiding the next. It was an incredible display of localised weather, and one that soon drove us away from the bustling castle walls as the peripheral drops of a particularly aggressive-looking downpour began to patter on our sun hats.

'Walking habits?' Jake said as we moved efficiently through the afternoon along a forest trail and towards Trois Châteaux, where the remains of three more castles embossed the hillside. 'What habits do you think we have when we walk?'

'Well, we have lots,' I replied.

'For example? I want to write them down in my journal tonight. Like, whenever you take your pack off, you always face it outwards, twisting Hemingway's head to give him the best view possible.'

'Do I?'

'Yeah.'

'Well, it's what he'd want, I guess. OK, I put the map under my arm strap,' I announced, grabbing the case from my side. The map was the one item that had never quite settled. First, it was slung around Jake's neck, but soon began to chafe, and then it was shoved between the cords on the outside of my pack, but proved too difficult to access. In Belgium, I slotted it inside the zip of my jacket, but then the temperature increased and our coats had less use. The latest discovery, and one that was working well, was a gap between my waist and the strap that ran under my arm. 'Yes, that's a habit. And your snotting, of course,' I continued, remembering Jake's enviable ability to clear his airways by shooting a ball of mucus from his nose. Incidentally, I had been practising, but my lack of confidence meant that, more often than not, the snot would end neither on the floor nor in my nose but somewhere unfortunately in between.

'Daydreaming!' Jake added. 'We do that a lot. And food, we talk about food all the time! Oh, and when you hold your poles out to the side, sort of like you think you're rowing, that means you're happy.'

We slipped steeply between the Trois Châteaux, alongside collapsed walls and under archways. Soon the trees gave way to vines, which in turn parted as the flat roof tiles and half-timbered houses of Ribeauvillé came into view.

We turned back into the mountains the following morning, and for two days climbed from one Alsace town to the next – Ribeauvillé to Aubure, and Fréland to Le Bonhomme.

'Do you think we'll wear shorts all the way to the Mediterranean?' I asked Jake as he threw stones into a deep pool of water an hour south of Le Bonhomme. The surface lay green with algae, and as each pebble landed with a *plop*, a dark patch of water would appear, only to close again moments later.

'Huh?' Jake responded, awakening from a daze.

'I was just thinking, we've worn shorts every day so far. Do you think we'll wear them to the end?'

'Well, you left your walking trousers in Luxembourg, remember? And mine don't even fit me anymore. I'd be wearing them around my ankles if I put them on. Yep,' Jake sighed, putting a flat palm on his stomach, 'I've lost a lot of weight from this belly, that's for sure.' In truth, Jake was slim when we left Bristol, and I was even slimmer. But we were both burning more energy than we could take in, and with that came weight loss. 'But there will be snow in the Alps, and storms too. We'll have to see.'

It was a claustrophobic sort of day where the cloud sat low over the crests, obscuring our view, save for a few metres about our feet where the starry white flowers of sweet woodruff and emerging stems of spruce saplings greeted our eyes.

Jake's comments about our decreasing weight had got me thinking, and for the first time in a while, I began to feel a perspective of time. Jake had lost inches from his waist, and his hair, shaved at the beginning of our journey, had grown into a mess of short knotted curls. My beard, sporadic and straggly though it was, had developed enough for me to see it from the corner of my eye, and the tan lines on our necks and arms were dark and definite. Even the pink nail varnish, which Claudia had painted on my little toenail two and a half months back, had grown completely out.

Rusted wire and metal prongs jutted painfully from the orchid-filled tussocks of Tête des Faux, a 1,208-metre peak not far from the Lorraine border. As if remembering the sorrow of those who had fought, a huddle of spruce trees looked down upon the wartime relics, white sap dripping like tears from their scarred bark.

Also known as the '*Panorama des Alpes*', the summit of Tête des Faux was a poignant peak on our route through the Vosges, not only for its reminder of conflicts gone by but for its vast views over the surrounding lands. We rushed to the southern side of the mount, tripping on coils of barbed wire and fencing, before clambering onto a boulder and squinting towards the horizon.

'It's too hazy,' Jake said dejectedly. 'Still, it's exciting to think they *are* there. On another day, we would be able to see Mont Blanc!'

We hadn't seen another walker since heading back into the mountains. Yet if we had felt starved of human interaction over the past day or two then our emergence into the Réserve Naturelle du Tanet-Gazon du Faing – an all-you-can-eat social buffet – was certainly sufficient remedy. From the northern end of the reserve, we looked south along a broad, exposed bluff. A string of colourful dots lined the path, some edging towards us and some away. The trail, worn deep into the ground, led us from one headland to the next, through peat bogs and banks of woody heather. A little to the east of the path, half submerged in moorland and cranberry shrub, stood a series of eroded boundary stones which, for over forty years, from the Franco-Prussian War in 1871 to the end of the First World War, had divided France from Germany.

After several kilometres of stepping politely aside for the succession of onrushing walkers, we stopped at a sign where one arrow pointed left and the other to the right.

'This is the shorter route,' a French lady interjected, pointing down the path to our right, 'but *this* way is more beautiful.' She smiled with raised eyebrows, looking admiringly at the cliff edge path to her left. Far below the ridgeline, set deep into the valley's glacial cirques, lay the dark teal waters of Lac Noir and Lac Blanc. It was a magnificent view, and perhaps we should have felt a little more guilt as we thanked the lady and then proceeded to take the shorter track to the right, both agreeing a few moments later that our path was already long enough.

Intermittent social exchanges were the theme of the day. *'C'est lourd?'* a woman with a large twig protruding from a purple rinse called out, eyeing up our rucksacks beside a meadow of ringing cowbells at the southern end of the reserve. And then a little further along the track, as we approached the summit of Le Hohneck, a teacher and his class of shivering students greeted us: *'Bonjour,'* and *'Il fait froid, non?'*

Since arriving in Europe, we had learnt that a comprehensive French vocabulary was unnecessary, and at any rate impossible for

Jake and me who appeared to be linguistically inept. Instead, we had learnt a far more effective method of communication. Given that the majority of our conversations took place on the path, or were at least related to the path, we decided to forget all that we had learnt in school ('I have one hamster and three fish'; 'My bedroom is blue and my kitchen is yellow'; 'I hate learning French'). Instead, we concentrated on the things around us: the hills, trees, fields, rain and sun. In fact, our walking vocabulary was so accomplished that we could now specify the exact surface that we were treading on, be it a *chemin, route, sentier, promenade* or *piste*.

'Snow!' Jake shouted with delight, pointing towards a lower slope to the south of Le Hohneck. 'Our first snow sighting!'

My eyes fell upon a vertical white band that stretched lazily down a scree-filled gully. It felt unusual to be seeing snow so late in the year. But our progress through the Alsace meant that we were now in the Hautes-Vosges, the southernmost section of the Vosges Mountains and home to the highest peaks of the massif – Le Grand Ballon, Storckenkopf, Le Hohneck – and with that came weather.

Inspired by our snow sighting, we agreed that a night beside one of the glacial lakes on the southern toes of the mountain would round off a spectacular day. We dropped into woodland along a stony, zigzagging path, which bruised our soles and sent our ankles twisting, before finally spilling out onto the shores of Lac de Fischboedle.

I craned my neck upwards towards the radiance of the sun, which had just dropped behind the lake's towering cliff walls to the west. Water tumbled through the glow, falling fifty metres before being swallowed by an opportunistic gathering of trees rooted in the steep ground between the precipices and the lake. On the eastern flank, a colossal landslide of car-sized boulders swooped into the water, its upper reaches still heated by the warmth of the sun.

I unclipped my pack and clambered around the lake's verging debris towards the rockfall, grappling at handholds as I climbed energetically from one boulder to the next. After a few minutes, I came to a halt and sat with my legs hanging over a round of granite.

'You've barely made a dent!' Jake's voice echoed across the narrow cirque.

At the foot of the falls, amongst the trees and a bed of large aster leaves, we found a flat patch of ground. Lying hazardously between the trickling braids of the fragmented waterfall, we looked at each other for confirmation.

'It'll have to do,' Jake said decisively. 'There's nowhere else. Let's just hope it doesn't rain.'

LE GRAND BALLON

Falling leaves and singing birds,
A woodpecker beats his drum.
A beetle patters,
A doe leg clatters,
And the caterpillar taps its tune.

This journal entry could have been applied to any one of our daybreaks in the tent and, apart from my torrid awakening back in Jussy, we were both yet to rouse without an appreciation for the beauty of the wildlife that surrounded us.

Leaving Jake to ready his pack, I clambered from the tent and found a flat slab of granite jutting out across the lake. Save for the gliding swifts that skimmed their beaks across the surface, the water was still and the day quiet. Clouds were already beginning to form in the small patch of sky between the valley walls, suggesting that rain was merely a matter of time.

The path down to Mittlach was short but steep. Rounded stones set into the dirt, like nature's own cobbled streets, led us from worn wooden bridges and on to slopes of scree, peppered with giant daisies.

Knowing that the village was close, we finished the last of our food supplies (a bruised banana with flesh the texture of jelly, and a handful of wild strawberries from the path side), and then discussed the positives and negatives of a hypothetical genetic mutation that would leave snails with the ability to move as fast as mice, and mice as slow as snails.

We reached Mittlach's main street, if indeed you could call it that, to discover there was no shop.

'*Excusez-moi,*' I pleaded, running up the road towards a couple packing bags into a car. '*Excusez-moi, y a-t-il une boulangerie ou une pâtisserie près d'ici, s'il vous plaît?*'

I couldn't speak a lot of French, but of the few phrases I did know, this was my favourite. It felt smooth and comfortable and rolled from my tongue like half a dozen glass marbles. I had known this line for ten years. In school, it was the question I resorted to when all else failed, and trust me it did, and it was the line I delivered in social gatherings to show off my bilingual abilities. On occasions, I would even find myself singing it as I walked down the street. So why, I thought, sincerely perplexed, were the couple staring at me as if I was mad?

'I did try and tell you that it was right behind you,' Jake said defensively as we stepped into the bakery, sending the bell above the door into a frenzied ring.

'I was on the bloody doorstep!' I exclaimed, thankful that the smell of proving loaves and baking pastries quickly displaced my embarrassment.

We needed enough food to get us to Thann, two days' walk away. However, having stripped the *boulangerie* of five baguettes, one loaf, eight *pains au chocolat*, two *bichon au citron*, something with apple in it, and several croissants, we probably had enough carbohydrate to get us to the Alps.

Rain started to drip from the clouds, inducing hurried steps out of the town and into a sparse forest of trees, landslides and narrow, slippery paths. After 600 metres of climbing, we stopped at a clearing and looked back over the Mittlach-le-haut valley. Our ascent had reduced the town to little more than a peppering of chimneys and tiles, settled in the bed of the wooded valley.

'We've got to get a photo of all this bread,' Jake said, shedding his pack and running over towards a viewpoint.

Standing on a rock with the hill dropping sharply away behind him, Jake clutched the baguettes in his arms like a baby, looked up at the camera, and smiled. But before I could take the picture, something back on the path distracted me. I turned towards our bags, which we had left on a bench by the trail, and watched as mine rolled nonchalantly from its pew, onto the ground and down the hill.

'Shit!' I yelped, flinging the camera to the floor before darting over the lip of the slope in pursuit of the runaway rucksack. Down the wet and craterous hillside, I slipped and stumbled, every second or two glimpsing the bright orange rain cover of my bag as it bounced a few metres further on. With my pack nearing a particularly sheer-looking drop – which may well have taken it back down to Mittlach – I quickened my clumsy steps, quite foolishly leaping upon its bouncing body just metres from the ledge.

Sodden and muddy, yet glad to find all my limbs still intact, I hauled the pack onto my back, crawled back up the slope, and took a photo of Jake who was still standing on the rock nursing the baguettes.

We ascended again, reaching the open pastures of the Col du Herrenberg, where yellow orchids and clumps of toilet brush-shaped pink bistort blew bravely in the wind and rain. I turned my back to the weather and pencilled a few words of displeasure into my notepad: 'Cold. Sniffles. Wet nose. Mittens desired, but laziness prevailing. Wet feet.' But we could hardly complain. The Vosgienne cattle, black on their sides and white on their backs and bellies, were here for the entire season, rain or shine. How must they have felt? And, at any rate, if we were really that cold, why not give up our ridiculous short-wearing attire and buy some trousers?

A little disorientated by the low cloud and sheets of rain, it wasn't until we skirted the mount of Le Hundskopf that we saw the zenith of the Vosges Mountains, Le Grand Ballon, rearing up across the valley.

By the time we reached the radar dome on top of the 1,424-metre summit, the rainfall had ceased, and sunlight began to leak through the fraying, overcast sky. A quick scan of the information board told us not for the first time that, weather permitting, the Alps could be viewed to the south. But it was far from a clear day and, though there were rays of sunshine on the faraway hills, deep shadows cast by the aubergine sky began to swamp our surroundings. For some minutes, we watched vortexes of low cloud shift through the valley in front of us before the next downpour hit.

We joined a succession of fleeing sightseers who rushed down the hill to the refuge of an intriguing shop of honeys and jams, where I am sure we were not the only ones to take advantage of the free taster table. The changeability of the weather was stark, and within minutes the sky was dry again, tempting us back outside and onto the path.

180

Fifty metres from the apex of the Vosges, we unloaded our bags onto the floor of a small wedge of pine forest between criss-crossing ski runs, snowless for the summer.

Thunder rumbled, but it didn't rain.

MORT POUR LA FRANCE

Hidden within the weather, it wasn't until we rose the next morning, packed up our gear and broke free from the forest that we realised the splendour of our location. From a grassy hillock high on the southern aspect of Le Grand Ballon, we looked across a vast swamp of amber-tinted cloud, submerging the farmland and villages of the Alsace Plain. And crowning the horizon, subtle yet monumental, were the zeniths of the European Alps – a distant mainland in a sea of gaseous waves. This was the greatest spectacle of our journey yet: the dragon-back serrations of the Dents du Midi and the Dents Blanches; the rounded crest of Dôme du Goûter; and, to our immediate south, Mont Blanc – the 'White Mountain' – pyramidal and strong.

There were three weeks between our feet and Mont Blanc, from the summit of the Vosges Mountains to the highest peak in the French Alps. My body flooded with pride. We had walked from our home, *our* front door, to within sight of this incredible mountain. Jake marked the occasion with a howl that rang out down the grassy pistes and into the streaks of neighbouring forest, before turning to me with watering eyes and a smile as true as any I had ever seen.

An hour must have passed before we eventually left the lookout. 'We don't even need to reach the Mediterranean,' Jake said merrily. 'I could happily end the walk right here!'

With the aid of our thirty-fifth map, we descended Le Grand Ballon through meadows of basking wildflowers – red, white, yellow, purple and pink – as bees pollinated and the tail of a shrew disappeared beneath the undergrowth. A shepherd led his goats with a whistle down the tourist road, and the long ears of a brown hare twitched in the path's verging grass.

The morning sun was well received, and though we soon dropped into a forest of shading hazel and banks of ferns, its warmth remained. Having spent the last three days in the heart of the massif, the *GR5* was returning to the flat ground of the Rhine

Valley, taking one final gasp of air before diving back into the Vosges for the last time.

We lost height, as if contouring a giant jelly mould meandering from one forested outcrop to the next, arriving by late morning at the Col du Silberloch and the entrance to Hartmannswillerkopf (or Vieil Armand to the French). A set of steps led up the side of a large single-storey structure built from white stone, where the sun glared from the surface, obscuring our vision. It was only when we reached the centre of the roof that we realised what we were standing on. The mass crypt beneath our feet held the remains of 12,000 unknown soldiers – Hartmannswillerkopf was a First World War battlefield.

As the war began to spread across Europe, the Col du Silberloch was swiftly recognised as a valuable vantage point for French and Germans alike, with wide views over the Belfort Gap – an area of low-lying land to the south-east – and the Alsace Plain to the north-east. In 1915, Hartmannswillerkopf repeatedly changed hands, for several weeks guarded by the Central Powers before being taken back by the Allies. Thousands died with each attack. The exchanges eventually stagnated, with the last major assault for the summit coming in January 1916. Both sides held their positions until the end of the war, but the cost was dear: some 30,000 soldiers lost their lives.

A cemetery lay beyond the crypt. I walked between the white crosses, each labelled with the same words – 'Mort pour la France en 1915/02/27', 'Mort pour la France en 1915/04/26', 'Mort pour la France en 1915/04/24' – then made my way back up the steps.

Jake was talking to a man with a navy jacket and clip-on sunglasses and a woman with a shiny blue gilet and short auburn hair, who I presumed to be the man's wife. Christine and Urbain were from Bruges, and, after hearing that we had passed through there a couple of months back, were excited to tell us, albeit in Dutch, about the guidebook they were using on their historical tour of the Alsace: Hauben's At War.

In March 2012, the Belgian director, Arnout Hauben, and his two-man crew, Mikhael Cops (cameraman) and Jonas Van Thielen (actor), strapped on their boots and left the coastline of Belgium on foot, tracing the front line of the First World War through Europe to the Gallipoli battlefields in the north-west of Turkey. The men walked 1,500 kilometres over eighty days, from Flanders to the Somme, through the Italian Alps and across the Adriatic, where they met the front line at Greece, and continued on to the site of the Gallipoli Campaign, a battlefield that took over 100,000 lives. A documentary and guidebook portraying the journey were released several months later. It depicted the logistics of the hike and the emotional challenge of passing through, to quote Hauben, 'the biggest cemetery on earth'.

We stood in a closed circle leaning over the book as Christine and Urbain flicked through the pages, pausing every now and then on a poignant photograph or map. I found it hard to understand their words, but could hear the empathy and sorrow in their voices. Our time in Alsace, and indeed Lorraine, had been spent immersed in wartime memorials, graveyards and battlefields, and with each site came an overriding feeling of sadness, of which Hartmannswillerkopf was the most powerful yet.

We were not far from Thann and so decided to switch on our phone. The electricity we had drawn from Tilly's bed and breakfast a week earlier in Le Hohwald still remained, with the signal bar sitting boastfully one notch above the half-full mark.

Amongst a crowd of sweaty, unwashed bodies, somewhere between the tents and stages of Glastonbury Festival in south-west England, Claudia found a spot to talk.

'I've written a poem,' she said after twenty minutes of reacquaintance. 'Would you like to hear it?'

'Of course!'

'OK, it's about our experiences today, yours and mine, but mixed together:'

> *Seventy-seven days walking,*
> *Three days drinking.*
> *The Alps in sight,*
> *The Park stage in view.*
> *Dynamic and volatile,*
> *Rain and mud.*
> *Pain au chocolat and bread,*
> *Croissant and orange juice.*

We eased open the heavy door of Saint-Thiébaut church in the centre of Thann. Stone drapes pillared from the intricate flooring, climbing beyond the twelve apostles, the Virgin Mary and Saint-Ubald towards the light of the fifteenth-century stained glass where Jesus bore the cross. Jake moved slowly down the central aisle through the choir, and whether or not it was intended (for we were the only visitors in the building), with each step the pipes blew louder, eventually ending the crescendo as Jake stopped beneath Christ. If indeed the organ player meant it, it was a valiant effort to convert. However, with hungry stomachs and sore feet, we had more trivial matters to attend to.

'Hotel?' I said to Jake once he had completed his loop of the church.

'You read my mind!'

We checked into the unimaginatively named Hôtel de France, grabbing a handful of complimentary sweets from the reception desk on our way through. To our delight, the room had 'the big three': a hot shower, radiator and television. Our window looked out over the main street, where the tables and chairs of Restaurant Demi Lune and the flowers of Vetter Fleuristes occupied the pavement, beneath awnings and shutters blue, brown and green. I pushed open the window, filling the room with luscious scents carried up on the warmth of a faint breeze.

'What do you think about a rest day?' Jake asked, inhaling the heavenly air.

I nodded with a grin.

We had been on the path for seventy-seven days. Six of them had been static. However, they were not moments of rest, but of recovery and organisation, days to allow a damaged back to heal or sickness to pass, or days spent collecting provisions and fixing gear. On this occasion, we weren't injured or ill and, aside from a few errands, had little to do.

'The sole purpose of this rest day is to rest,' Jake exclaimed, lying on his back across the bed, hands behind his head.

Although the theory behind a respite day was good, it lacked achievement. Highlights of the two-night stopover were few and far between. I took pleasure in watching the car headlamps on our bedroom wall through the night, and the moment I stood back from the bathroom mirror after a hot shower to see the words: 'Alps sighting, day 77'. I perhaps even enjoyed removing the two-week-old strapping from my toes to unveil a mess of flaking skin and dirt. But these were all minor moments of joy compared to what we were used to. We missed the birds' morning chorus, the burn of a hill, and the weather on our faces. Perhaps we even missed the barking deer and slugs in our boots. A day of rest, it seemed, was a day wasted.

'I would've preferred a pile of clothes as a pillow, like we have in the tent,' I told Jake after waking the next morning with a sore neck.

The thirty-six hours of rest upset our rhythm. Jake's soles had softened from the shower, and the new strapping on my feet had already welded to my socks, pulling uncomfortably at the hairs on my toes which I had forgotten to shave. After an entire box of Chocolat Noisettes cereal, one kilogram of natural yoghurt and a tin of peach slices, our stomachs were heavy and bloated, and the bruising on our hips had ripened.

We were heading north-west towards the Ballon d'Alsace, and began the day plodding up a gentle hill and into the forested lowlands of the Hautes-Vosges.

It took us longer than it should have to reach the Col du Rossberg, where the trees thinned and small islands of isolated beech strung out into a sea of high pasture brimming with wildflowers: the violet-blue of meadow cranesbill, the white bloomers of bladder campion, the tufted yellow spikes of common toadflax, and the wild pansy's deep purple veins on blue-slate petals.

It was a Sunday, and the skies were pleasant. As a result, the path was busy, and groups of walkers rested by the *refuge* shelters and the *fermes auberges* that appeared every now and then on the cols. We nodded politely as we passed each crowd: them quietly assessing us, we quietly observing them.

Of all the groups, the couples were the most interesting. There was a pattern to their walking, we decided, that was absent in families, dog walkers and retired ramblers. The man, it seemed, was the navigator. And, as navigator, he always walked in front, five or ten paces perhaps, and depending on experience level (presumably correlating strongly with duration of marriage), the distance between the two would increase. Indeed, there was one particular couple who had worked up a staggering twenty-metre gap, suggesting a marriage of similar years, or more. The man's final action was to deny his wife the chance to rest. He would stop from time to time and turn to face her, panting heavily and glimmering with sweat, until she was close. And, just as reacquaintance was imminent, something would trigger an alert in his mind – 'Wife close, time to move' – at which he would ruthlessly swivel and continue on up the hill.

By lunchtime, we were above 1,000 metres, and saw Vogelstein, a rocky outcrop on the southern aspect of the Rossberg ridge, as a perfect spot for a jam baguette. Beyond our sandwiches and dangling feet, the ground fell south into the Vallée de la Doller, where the rooftop deposits of Masevaux, Lauw and Sentheim sat between its distant walls. The surrounding, low-lying hills began to lose height, eventually dropping onto a jigsaw plateau of urban development and woodland. In two days' time, the Vosges Mountains would be in our wake.

Wild mint grew with strawberries, and strands of old man's beard hung from the ancient branches of the birch. There was a muffled sound of nearby cowbells. We skirted the glacial waters of Lac des Perches – pastel and turquoise – along a hazardous path of scree slopes, metal girder bridges and hand ropes. Pollinators and sun-basking lizards filled the intermittent meadows before we were swallowed by a steep forest of beech and ferns, boulders and moss.

In spite of our best efforts to fatten up in Thann, my waist had returned to its default state of skin and bones, which brought annoyance. I could cope with the bruising on my hips, but was becoming increasingly irritated by the way my bag slumped onto my bottom. Noting the relative success of the hip-belt modifications made to Jake's rucksack back in Belgium, I decided, after setting up camp beside an old stone wall in the forest, that it was time to work on mine.

'Do you think she will mind?' I asked Jake, scissors in one hand and his birthday present from our Auntie Les, a Craghoppers fleece, in the other.

'I'm sure she'll understand,' he replied, swatting flies away from his face as he prepared dinner. 'Why are all these bloody flies around me and not you?'

'I'm just worried she'll be offended. Do you think it was expensive?'

'I'm not even using it. Really, don't worry, Dan.' By this point, Jake had stood up and was circling the tent in an attempt to lose the insects.

I held the material between the scissor blades, hovering for several seconds before backing out moments later. 'It just feels wrong. I know you don't wear it, but it's a good fleece.'

'Argh, these bloody flies are driving me crazy!'

'Right, here goes,' I said, ignoring Jake's frustrations.

The swarm was becoming frenzied, taunting Jake with daredevil twists and turns, remarkably avoiding his swatting hands. 'Right, I can't take it anymore. I'm going inside.'

An hour later, my adjustments were fitted, and all that remained of the fleece were a few patches of material. Dusk was settling so I crawled into the tent and joined Jake who was busy analysing the maps.

'All done?' he asked calmly, suggesting his frustration had subsided.

'Yep, all done.' I pulled my sleeping bag over my shoulders before rolling to face him. 'Jake?'

'Yeah?'

'Do you know that you have jam on your nose?'

THE JURA IN OUR SIGHTS

We ate a cereal bar atop the Ballon d'Alsace (1,247 metres) just as the sun was rising through a haze above the Black Forest to the east. Losing height through the ski fields, our path took us beyond thousands of yellow gentians, tall and robust, and along hillsides of buttercups and daisies. Alsace and Lorraine were now behind us, and we took our first few steps into Franche-Comté, one of France's easternmost regions.

The temperature rose gradually through the day, peaking at just over 30°C by mid-afternoon as we dropped our packs on a bench at the ramparts of Fort du Salbert, one of many fortifications surrounding the city of Belfort 200 metres below.

In the late-nineteenth and early-twentieth century, the strategic importance of Belfort – built on the plateau between the southern tip of the Vosges and the northern hills of the Jura Mountains –

led to advancements in the protection of the city. I squinted down at the sprawl of houses and high-rise apartment blocks, spotting a fort to the south and another to the east. At some point, over centuries gone by, these buildings would have commanded power and respect, like many of the castles we had passed through the Vosges. But times had changed. Grass grew plentifully between cracks in the concrete, and graffiti covered the walls. With the exception of two information boards at either end of the structure, the fort felt forgotten and unappreciated. But perhaps I was being hasty in my judgement, for spears of wall barley, sycamore and elder leaves softened the angles of the barracks and the afflictions of war. This, I concluded, *was* better.

T-shirts sodden with sweat and cheeks rosy, we turned into the Forêt du Salbert where the shade cooled our skin, and unrolled Ted onto a patch of dry leaves, kicking the blackberry tendrils to one side. Flies and mosquitoes circled our bodies. But, instead of irritating us, they kept their distance, seemingly content with catching the light of the sun before dispersing it explosively, like tiny supernovas, through the chitin of their wings.

I watched a spider for some minutes fixing its web – five legs harnessed to the line for stability, three to thread. Move. Four legs to harness, three to thread, and one leg hanging free. Move. Once the spider had finished its chores, it made its way back to the centre of the web, and I turned to a tuft of soft grass at my side, plucking a shoot from the ground and spinning it between my thumb and index. It twirled like a ballerina, back arched and eyes to the sky, wheeling flecks of seed into the surrounding air.

7

Belfort to Doubs

1,812 to 2,018 kilometres from home

WET

It was one of those nights when the morning couldn't come sooner. We had pitched on a slope. Instead of sleeping, I had spent much of the night gradually migrating to the lower end of the tent and then wriggling back up to my pillow when, just as I was about to drift off, I would begin to slide once more.

But when day did eventually break, I felt cosy in my sleeping bag, and with the shadows of the flittering leaves on the ceiling of the tent, we treated ourselves to a breakfast of *pains au chocolat* in bed.

We checked our shoes for slugs and found an inch-long ground beetle at the toe of Jake's left boot, then packed up silently in the sun with the alert ears of a roe deer close by.

We moved east through fields of shoulder-high daisies, our shadows stretched out behind us, before veering south onto the lowlands of the Belfort Gap. To our left, water gravitated eastwards towards the Rhine, and to our right towards the Rhône, 200 kilometres towards the setting sun. We were, it seemed, walking the Rhône-Rhine drainage divide.

With the mountains petering out behind us, we found ourselves skipping from one village to the next. From Châlonvillars – a collection of small houses, and rustic gardens spilling with redcurrants, raspberries and cherries – to the toasted streets of Échenans-sous-Mont-Vaudois, where our feet left prints on the melted tarmac of the quiet roads. In Banvillars, we drank from the village *lavoir* as school children prattled and giggled along the pavement, their oversized bags for a moment allowing Jake and me to blend in, before pushing on to the next town.

By lunchtime, we had reached Châtenois-les-Forges, and whilst Jake went to look for a bakery, I cooled my feet in the bubbling waters of the town's fountains. He returned a few minutes later, and we settled down by the splashing water, where first a lady with flowers in her hands warned us that the heat had reached its peak and rain would soon fall, and then a young boy with dark skin and a stick in his hand beckoned us across the street to inspect a dead hedgehog he had found on the roadside.

The woman's warning of a thunderstorm inflicted paranoia upon us. Each wisp of cloud became a suspect for rain, and we couldn't walk twenty metres without checking their progress: dissipation or escalation? On one overhead inspection, I noticed that a small patch of sky was slicked with the sun's spectrum, like a spill of oil across a thin curl of cirrus cloud. The iridescence eventually disappeared, no doubt spooked by the vaporous atmosphere appearing on the horizon.

We filled our bottles at the Savoureuse Rivière, and then entered a region of lakes just north of Montbéliard, where a series of well-maintained gravel tracks guided us systematically alongside tree-banked waters. A light breeze had picked up, and a drift of feathery white seeds began to float towards us. I caught one in my hand, and remembering my childhood told myself to make a wish. But before I could muster anything worthy, I noticed the falling seeds thicken. We stopped beneath a gathering of cottonwood trees in the epicentre of the storm, mesmerised by the millions of sleeting flakes that whirled in air currents around us.

'It's snowing!' Jake shouted. 'But it's sunny!'

On closer inspection, the cottonwood spores reminded me of snagged sheep's wool. The white clumps settled on our shoulders and bags, and clung to my beard. In fact, the profusion of falling seeds was so great that they soon began to find their way into our gawping mouths, forcing us away from the trees to where breathable air prevailed.

'That was amazing,' I said as we continued along the water's edge, the dispersing seeds dwindling behind us. 'I've never seen anything like it!'

'If you thought that was startling...' Jake pointed towards a bend in the track before us, 'take a look at that!'

It appeared that we were not the only ones enjoying the weather.

Ahead on the path, the gravel transitioned to sand, pushing away from the trees and onto an artificial beach that boomeranged the southern lake shores of the Étang du Pâquis.

After passing a game of volleyball in which each contestant was bronzed, glistening and, perhaps unsurprisingly, squeezed into a pair of astoundingly tight Speedos, the path forced us onto the beach. With our clothed torsos, heavy footwear, hairy legs, white thighs and red cheeks, we couldn't have stood out more. Tentatively, we picked a course between a minefield of sandcastles and adjoining beach towels. The sand was bestrewn with half-naked bodies, from the unnervingly fat to remarkably thin, and, inadvertently, I found myself glimpsing parts of the human form that I had long forgotten existed.

'Did that just happen?' Jake queried several minutes later after returning to the familiar solitude of rural France.

'Unfortunately, I think it did,' I grimaced, considering the possibility that perhaps the hundreds of unclothed bathers that had just flashed before us were a rebellious yet highly vivid hallucination induced by our lack of water intake.

We joined the modest waters of the Canal de la Haute-Saône, where a heron hunched on a beached log, and white admiral butterflies sailed above tangles of brambles edging the towpath, before sinking into mixed woodland just beyond the village of Fesches-le-Châtel. We pitched Ted below a towering beech tree and a darkening sky, and rain fell through the night.

'We might need to replace Ted,' I shouted through the downpour the next morning as we trudged with saturated boots through the dripping forest. 'My pillow was wet when I woke up. I think he's losing his waterproofing.'

'You might be right. I'm definitely going to need new boots too. Let's get Nan and Gramps to bring us a pair when we meet them at Lake Geneva.'

We began the day feeling vibrant and fresh, engrossed by the puddles as they jumped and skipped, like a reel of old film, beneath the falling drops. A fox leapt from the tall grass of a field between two bands of forest – its body arched, paws poised and eyes focused – before falling back into the undergrowth. And, just a few minutes later, three deer cut across the path and then vanished into the trees. On our way out of Dasle, between allotments and farms, we filled our hands with cherries from drooping branches that hung over the path, gambling for a fruit that would taste sweet and sugary when the next might be as bitter as the rind of a grapefruit.

We peered intently through the steamed plastic of the map case in a bid to decipher our route. Meanwhile, as we stepped slowly through a right-hand bend, the red and white licks of the *GR*, slapped conspicuously onto a nearby tree, escaped our notice. If it hadn't been for the splendid irony of the mishap, we may have been a little more annoyed. But as it was, an hour and a half later we were back at the same tree, this time spotting the paint that led us into a well-watered landscape of limestone archways and crags, and onto the Jura Plateau.

Boot-engulfing forestry tracks, deeply grooved by the tread of heavy machinery, muddied our boots and the backs of our legs. Eventually released from the sludge, we climbed up through a steep gorge filled with tropical-looking ferns and vines, and the song of rain-enduring birds, until the path flattened beside a weathered stone.

'Switzerland!' Jake beamed, running his hands across the worn engravings on either side of the boundary marker. 'France on this side...' he continued, pointing at the 'F' on the stone's western face before stepping to the eastern side where an equilateral cross, the Swiss emblem, indented the marker, 'and Switzerland on this side.'

We had arrived at the north-west border of Switzerland, and more specifically the Canton of Jura, one of the nation's twenty-six regions.

For a couple of kilometres, we followed the border along a ridgeline, catching glimpses of Swiss pasture through the trees and rain. Border stones, each a foot in height, lined the muddy path. With the opportunity to walk in our seventh country, we gravitated towards the left of the ridge – the Swiss side – noting that, apart from a slight increase in puddles, it felt much the same as the right.

With the rain pattering hypnotically on the Gore-Tex of my hood, I soon forgot my numbing fingers, my squelching feet, and the presence of my brother. *Thud*! I stumbled backwards onto a rock as my poles clattered to the ground. Squinting up through wavering vision, I realised I had just walked head on into the trunk of a pine tree that had been felled across the path.

This was to be the theme for the next few days: an obstacle course of forestry tracks and muddy, frictionless footpaths breached by fallen trees, providing us with an unforgiving dilemma – over or under?

Hurdling was the preference, though this could only be done with relatively low-lying trunks, perhaps a metre in height at the most. If the obstacle was any greater then we ran the risk of getting stranded midway across, one leg dangling to the left and the other to the right, trapped awkwardly between the weight of our packs and the rough bark of the pine. Having both had the uncomfortable misfortune of being marooned, we discovered that ducking under the logs was a safer passage. However, a far cry from a swift, seamless movement, it would often take up to a minute for us to crawl beneath the trees, blaspheming beneath the strain of the bags and the jousting pine needles that scratched our faces, before emerging onto the other side covered in dirt. We never considered removing our rucksacks.

We were ecstatic to find a hotel in Saint-Hippolyte – a small town of hanging baskets and balconies built on a meander of the Doubs River valley – where we poured rainwater from our boots and attempted, with little success, to dry forty kilograms of wet gear.

It was raining the next day, despite the weather forecast predicting 20°C and clear skies, and whatever items *had* dried overnight were immediately soaked through as we followed the Doubs upstream to the east.

I walked behind Jake, guided by the rhythmic squelch of his boots and the sound of frogs as they leapt from the path to the safety of the nearby puddles – *plop!* On an otherwise drab day, I was thankful for the wildflowers that struck colour into the sap-green landscape – the crimson red pincushion head of a musk thistle sitting forlornly above a stem of defensive thorns, and the reliable foxglove, tall and strong – and for the moments when our limbs brushed against the tall grass, sending lines of shining synchronised water droplets to the saturated ground.

No doubt a product of the many hundreds of kilometres of roads, pavements and cycle paths that we had traversed back in

Belgium, we had developed a surprisingly stimulating pastime known as 'stone kicking'. The aim of the pursuit was to kick a piece of debris, usually a small stone, as far as possible along the road without it jumping over the edge. Stones that mounted the verge and then returned to the road were tolerated, though frowned upon, whilst repeated kicks of the same stone, which required both skill and endurance, were highly praised.

Feeling the tedium of the day, Jake scuffed his boot through a pile of rubble on the roadside, sending one or two pieces into his path before putting his foot to the largest of the stones. It shot out in front of him, nearing the edge of the track before curling back up the camber.

'Wow! That was a good one.' I applauded, prompting Jake into a smile.

He maintained composure. Biting his bottom lip with concentration, he belted the stone for a second time. 'Crap!' he hollered as the pebble disappeared over the side of the road.

'Unlucky,' I consoled, quickly forgetting Jake's misfortune at the sight of a conveniently placed piece of rubble ahead. The pebble bounced off my boot and up the track. But just as it began to roll towards the verge, the stone collided with a pine cone that had fallen from one of the bordering conifers. The pebble jumped gleefully into the air, skidded back across the tarmac, and came to a halt in the centre of the roadway. Jake and I looked at each other in amazement and then exploded into uncontrollable laughter. Utterly euphoric and with cramping sides, we were forced to stop for several minutes to compose ourselves.

It was still early in the day and, in spite of our recent elation, we felt fatigued and worn out. 'You know, we could stay in a *gîte* tonight, Jake. The book says there's one around the bend. We've not tried it. It might not be as bad as we think.'

In addition to the wild camps, campsites, hostels, *chambres d'hôtes* and hotels that we were already familiar with, France also had *abris*, *refuges* and *gîtes* (*d'etapes*). The *abris* were the most alluring of the lot – basic shelters or huts, most three-sided and free of charge, whilst the *refuges* – seemingly catering for large groups at a high price – were the least. The *gîtes*, in our ill-determined opinion, sat somewhere between the *abris* and the *refuges* – dormitory rooms designed specifically for walkers and other outdoor enthusiasts, that appeared to be neither cheap nor expensive.

The problem was we didn't want to exchange pleasantries, we didn't want to make conversation, and we didn't want to be surrounded by an orchestra of snores and grunts as we tried to slumber. We liked the tranquillity of the forests, and on the odd occasion when we did stay in a cheap hotel, we enjoyed vegetating on the mattress whilst gormlessly watching the French version of *You've Been Framed*. We were not so much misanthropists with a vendetta against the human race but introverts keen for an early and undisturbed night's sleep. But our opinion of the *gîtes* was preconceived, and who was to say it was the right one?

'But what about all the snorers?' Jake protested. 'I'm not sure, Dan.'

'Let's take a chance, yeah? We can't very well judge it until we've tried.'

'OK,' Jake conceded. 'But we'd better be able to sleep.'

We rounded the corner to a large white-stone building set between two dozen other houses.

'Anyway,' I said as we made our way up the road to the *gîte*, 'I thought you said I snored!'

FOREIGN UNDERPANTS

Pink hollyhocks and the purple tips of garden lupins stood high alongside the *gîte*'s garden path, leading neatly around the stone walls of the house, past windowsills of geraniums and tall, dark wood shutters. Skirting the perimeter of the building, we peeped in through the windows before reaching the back of the house where a long lawn fell away to a woodshed at the bottom of the garden. The rain had finally stopped and a small patch of blue sky appeared above us. '*Randonneurs, installez vous*', read a sign on the back door.

A hunched old lady with an apron and scuffing sandals welcomed us in. She understood neither our English nor our French, so we paid the sixteen euros, gave up on conversing, and then got on with our chores.

Filling the bathroom sink with soapy hot water, Jake laundered the dirt from our socks as I unrolled our sleeping bags onto the wall-to-wall bunk bed in the vacant dormitory.

'I'll be in the kitchen,' I called to Jake as I made my way through the building into a brightly lit room bordered with large windows. I washed the bowls, spoons and Shammy cloth at the shallow marble sink, looking out through the glass at clearing skies, and then laid our remaining food across the large timber table that dominated the room. Deep shelves built into the surrounding cupboards were brimming with bags of half-eaten noodles and rice, tins of beans, sachets of soup powder and, quite curiously, several kilograms of cornflour, all left behind by previous lodgers.

Feeling my stomach rumble, I abandoned my duties and grabbed a bag of cornflour from the shelf. Putting a handful into a bowl, along with a few tablespoons of water, I began to knead the mixture with my fingertips. This simple recipe – cheap and effortless – was one I had used many times over my previous years of travel, yet, unlike the other occasions, the dough wasn't binding as I remembered. Growing impatient, I threw the glob of ingredients into a hot pan and watched it fizzle and bubble in the oil. Effusing an aroma not too dissimilar to that of burning plastic, I pulled the pan from the flame, turned the flatbread onto the table, and picked cautiously at the burnt fringes. Tasting worse than it both looked and smelt, I took my notepad from my pocket and wrote: 'Normal flour and cornflour are not the same thing. Remember this.'

We had passed two French walkers earlier in the day and half expected that we would see them again, especially after checking into the *gîte*. It was therefore not a surprise, as we wrote our journals in the kitchen, to hear the deep tones of the men's voices an hour later as they pushed the door open and stepped into the room.

Gabrielle and Yannick could have been twins. Both were balding, with short tufts of silver hair clinging to the backs of their heads, and both smiled as if showing off their well-cleaned teeth to the dentist. They were college friends from Brittany, and following their recent retirement had decided to undertake an eighteen-day hike through the Jura Mountains. The *E2*, and indeed the *GR5*, made up the middle section of their journey, after which they planned to unite with the *E4*, Europe's longest hiking trail (10,450 kilometres), finishing somewhere close to the Franche-Comtè-Rhône-Alpes border. The friends were not lifelong hikers, but had both enjoyed previous trips through the Pyrenees and, most recently, the Tour de Mont Blanc.

'*Oui, c'est magnifique,*' Gabrielle kept saying whenever Mont Blanc was mentioned. Glancing over at Jake, I saw a glint in his hazel eyes, guessing that he too had come to the same deliberation as me: 'Perhaps we should incorporate a circumnavigation of Mont Blanc into our route?'

Yannick sang as he finished his soup with his finger, whilst Gabrielle calculated their distance for the day. Then, just as Jake and I were ready to make an excuse and turn in for the night, the men stood up and bade us good evening. '*Neuf heures,*' said Yannick as he opened the door to the bedroom, smiling through a yawn. '*C'est le minuit du marcheurs!*'

A few minutes later, having flicked through several pages of our French dictionary, I looked up at Jake. 'Walkers' midnight. That's what he meant. Nine o'clock is walkers' midnight!'

We plucked our drying socks from the washing line the next morning, noting that they had been joined by two very miniscule pairs of underpants, and then left the *gîte* through the mist.

Beaded spider webs billowed lightly on the Rue de Fromagerie road sign whilst car headlamps struggled through the fog.

We climbed for a while beyond the translucence and into the sunlight, stopping outside a farmhouse to eat bread and Nutella. We were now amongst the forested hills and gorges of the Jura, a range of mountains sweeping from Franche-Comté across the northern border of Switzerland and into Germany. Beyond the sun-dashing tails of the cows that grazed the fields to our east, the land stooped into a network of valleys bursting with cloud.

Gabrielle and Yannick passed us as we ate, and then an hour later after sinking back into the fog, we passed them as they checked their map. The track grew steeper and we began to hairpin through pine forest, dropping lower into the Doubs Valley with each turn. Dung beetles, like the popped buttons of a jacket, dotted the rooted track, and jays tussled in the branches overhead. Then suddenly, in a moment of pure bliss, the sun split through the trees, spreading streaks of light and shade through the fog and across our path.

When we met Gabrielle and Yannick for the third time in the small convenience store of Goumois, we didn't even bother exchanging words, partly because there seemed to be an unsaid mutual agreement that this wouldn't be our last rendezvous, and partly because Jake and I had exhausted all the French we knew. We simply had nothing left to say, perhaps other than some brazen comment about the comfort of their foreign underwear.

THE DOUBS

We had first seen the Doubs River two days earlier through the pouring rain at Saint-Hippolyte, at which point it still had 280 kilometres of course to run before reaching the Saône, and many hundreds more before mixing with the waters of the mighty Rhône. However, we were walking upstream and, having rejoined the river at Goumois, were six days from the Source du Doubs.

We met the course at the northern end of the Gorges du Doubs – a deep limestone ravine winding for fifty kilometres along the Swiss-Franco border towards the town of Villers-le-Lac. With two days' worth of food in our packs and midday fast approaching, we pressed on alongside the zealous river as the walls around us narrowed, eclipsing the sun.

Ivy wrapped the bowing trees, and thick shredded vines hung like bell ropes into the turbulent flow. The path undulated merrily, bathing the soles of our boots in the lapping shores of the Doubs before climbing precariously through a labyrinth of limestone gullies hammered with iron ladders, worryingly named 'Les Échelles de la Mort' (The Stairs of Death). We wound between boulders the size of houses, roofed with velvet moss and chimneys of hardy beech, and passed gatherings of fallen trees, bunched like flowers in the bottlenecks of the river. 'Do not camp by the river. It is very dangerous,' a plant worker warned as we passed a hydroelectric dam built arrestingly into the Swiss side of the river. 'The flash floods from the dam often inundate the path. We have had deaths.'

Though the gorge walls remained imposing, the river gradually slowed and began to widen at its banks before bulging, like the belly of a snake after a successful hunt, into a placid and unhurried lake. Yellow irises and saucers of lilies were met at the riverside by broadleaf plantains and the glossy fronds of hart's tongue ferns, whilst moss clung like settled snow around the angles of ancient trees and rocks. With their heads together, this could have been the setting for a Kenneth Grahame and JRR Tolkien collaboration: earthy, enchanting, mysterious and infused with adventure.

'I'm worried, Dan,' Jake said as the day began to grow late.

'It'll be alright,' I reassured him, assuming that he was concerned about pitching Ted so close to the river.

'How do you know?' He clasped his bottom with both hands, making me think that perhaps I had guessed wrong. Had he drunk something he shouldn't have? Or maybe it was the plastic cornflour bread that I had made the night before…?

I quickly caught up. 'What's wrong, Jake?'

He was clearly upset, so I gave him some time to compose his words. 'It's my bum,' he eventually voiced.

'What d'you mean?'

'My bum is losing its shape. It's saggy. It never used to be saggy, but now it is. I think my pack is pushing it to the floor. I have the bottom of an eighty-year-old!' Unable to give a reassuring reply, I was thankful to see Jake's angst quickly subside after spotting a signpost: '*Abri de Perches, 1km*'.

Although Jake's shrinking bottom was, of course, a concern, it was just one of many changes that our bodies had undergone since leaving Bristol. Our fingernails were growing at a greater rate than we were used to, and so too was our hair. Indeed, I had cut mine twice already. Our shoulders were permanently red and our hips contused brown. Our legs were getting thinner, and the insides of our thighs were bald from abrasion. The soles of our feet were bruised and our toes rife with calluses, though Jake, quite incredibly, was still yet to get a blister. Our fingers were peeling, our skin spotted with mosquito bites, nettle stings and tick burrows, our backs twingeing, our body odour evolving, and our tan lines grotesquely vivid.

No bigger than a caravan and topped with a piece of corrugated iron, the wooden hut was raised from the river and stood timidly at the foot of a sheer limestone precipice. Aside from a bench, a log burner and a small axe, the *abri* was empty and we quickly settled in. I split some wood, and Jake got to work on the fire, which in minutes had turned the room into a sauna.

We hung our clothes above the rising smoke of the burner and then lay on the wooden floor, listening to the sound of rocks dislodge from the gorge walls and clunk into the river.

A kingfisher swept along the Doubs and disappeared towards a meander further upstream. The sun had burnt through much of the morning mist and now warmed the backs of the mayflies as they span above the shimmering surface. I ducked beneath the icy river water, feeling my temples numb and my feet ache. It wasn't quite the idyllic swim that we had hoped for, and we climbed awkwardly from the river with freezing bones and retracted body parts.

Incidentally, it was on one of these body parts, as we lunched overlooking the Barrage du Châtelot, that Jake recorded his one hundredth tick. It was a poignant moment, comparable to our border crossings, our phone calls home, and our first sighting of the Alps.

The river was as good as any map and, without the strain of navigation, the gorge walls soon gave way to flat-crested hills and the sprawling new builds of Villers-le-Lac.

Foolishly, we made the mistake of raiding the shelves of the local supermarket before discovering that the town campsite marked on our map was in fact a children's playground. The hotels were all out of our budget, and the last two beds at the Gîte des Clos Rondot had been taken two minutes before we arrived, quite appropriately, by Yannick and Gabrielle. Suddenly our dinner of tinned ravioli (two kilograms), couscous salad (one kilogram) and juice (four litres) seemed a lavish choice, and had we known we still had three hours of walking before eventually finding a suitable forest to camp in, we may have felt a little more regret over our casual food splurge.

A lady hanging out her washing in the garden of an *auberge* in Sur la Roche pointed us down an unused track, overgrown with buttercups: '*Vous pouvez camper là.*'

The smell of smoke wafted from the clothes that we had dried above the fire the previous night, drifting around the tent as we lay on our backs eating sweets. I held a fizzy cola bottle up to the light and examined the shiny crystals of sugar covering its surface. Just as I was about to draw Jake's attention to the object, one of the sugar grains fell from the cola bottle into my admiring eye. The pain was significant yet, given the strain of the last three hours, it seemed like a suitable way to end the day, and I fell asleep some minutes later with sweet tears weeping from the corner of my closed eye.

It was 7 July. In a day's time, we would be meeting Brenda who, in typical style, had set our rendezvous point as 'somewhere on the roadside'. All that we had to do was make sure our phone was switched on. To make things a little easier for Brenda, in spite of her love of a challenge, we decided to aim for the Château de Joux and the small surrounding town of La Cluse-et-Mijoux, a day and a half south.

Our path through the midriff of the Jura range was pleasantly torpid. A chorus of birds sang us along a crumbling wall cushioned with feather moss and the violet petals of Jacob's ladder, guiding us out of the trees and into a waking valley of barking dogs, cowbells and revving tractors.

During recent days, we had begun to notice an evolving landscape. Bands of conifer forest became more frequent, replacing the mixed woodland and broadleaf forests of Central Europe. Pine scattered across the billowing hills of brown and white cattle, whilst yellow gentians smiled at the sun. The hamlets of Les Cernoniers, Le Nid du Fol and Les Seignes were sleepy and small, comprising little more than one or two timber farmsteads adorned with rusty tools and machinery from days gone by – a two-man crosscut saw and a blunt scythe. We were walking between biomes, temperate to the north, and alpine to the south. Things had begun to feel undoubtedly Swiss.

Either side of a night amongst the trees in Les Bois de Vaux on the Swiss border, we saw chamois. Not too dissimilar to a mountain goat, we first spotted one through the trees not far from our camp, and then for the second time early the next morning in a drying lea, where a pair kicked noisily through the golden grass leaving a trail of settling seed in their wake.

'So, they are real,' I whispered quietly, trying to glimpse them again through the crops. 'I was beginning to think that the French had made them up to get more tourists over here!'

'If you wanted to get tourists over, I doubt very much that you'd create a mysterious mythical creature that looked like a goat,' Jake objected. 'Who would fly to France to see a goat?'

Since meeting Gabrielle and Yannick, we had rarely gone more than a few hours without bumping into them, or at least evidence of them being nearby. It was therefore not altogether surprising to drop into the hamlet of Les Alliés, before its residents had risen, and spot two pairs of stunted underwear, which were now worryingly familiar, hanging from a washing line outside the local *gîte*. 'They really are small, aren't they?' I said with a grimace.

'Very,' Jake agreed. 'How do they...? Surely it must...?'

'I know, they would really...' I added, unnecessarily rearranging my own underwear with some sort of twisted empathy.

A hot breeze saw us along a succession of quiet country roads, watering my eyes and tiring my mind. Through the haze, I smelt the sweetness of the freshly rolled hay that lay in the fields beside the road. Magpies bounced from one bale to the next, pulling tangled insects from the dry grass.

Taking advantage of the parched air, and in preparation for Brenda's arrival, we found a stream and washed a few clothes, hanging them on our packs before pushing on until lunchtime.

It wasn't until we stopped three hours later that I realised my shirt was no longer on my bag. 'It's gone!' I fretted. Exasperation took over, and I frantically rifled through the inside of my rucksack to make sure that I hadn't made a mistake. But my efforts came to nothing. 'Shit!'

Of course, it would have been easy to pick up another top in the next town. It may not have been the same but it would have served its purpose. However, my disappointment lay deeper than that. Jake and I had just over a hundred items between us: from everyday clothing, like socks, underwear, sun hats, boots, leg supports, to important equipment, which included a compass, distance thread, map case, pen, bottles, bowls and walking poles. There were also the items that we rarely used, but carried as a precaution, such as waterproof trousers, Vaseline, gloves and painkillers. Gathered into a pile and shoved into a bag, fifty possessions each equated to very little, and, because of that, each item became highly treasured. So much so, in fact, that to say goodbye to a long-serving plastic bag pulled on our heartstrings perhaps far more than it should have, and the thought of losing one of our Sporks – a spoon and fork hybrid – made us feel positively sick. Each item was a vital cog to which we had become practically and emotionally attached. How would I cope without my navy blue walking top?

'Wait here,' Jake said, leaving me to sulk on the side of the path as he unclipped his bag and ran off back down the hill.

I threw stones for a few minutes, got bored, and then went to talk to a horse in the field opposite. But soon the horse got bored of me and wandered off to shade itself beneath an oak.

I threw some more stones.

Jake had been gone for half an hour, and assuming that he would run for no more than a kilometre or two, I guessed that he would be back any minute, so I went to talk to the horse again.

After an hour or so, Jake had still not returned, and there were no more stones left on the path. I had begun to play mind games with the horse, which was now conversing with a fellow steed on the other side of the field. Where was Jake?

'OK, a few more minutes,' I muttered, alleviating my concern with a bag of scroggin. Where was he?

I looked at my Casio. Jake had been gone an hour and a half. I picked up our bags and took them to a cluster of trees a little down the track, hiding them within the undergrowth. Then, just as I was about to begin a search for Jake's body, his head bobbed into view over the rise of the hill. He was glistening with sweat and red in the cheeks and, of course, he had my top in his hand.

'Where the hell were you?' I blurted, trying to act angry.

'You're welcome,' he panted, smiling as he tossed the garment into my arms.

'Where was it?'

'Hooked on a piece of barbed wire at that farm just after Les Alliés.'

'Les Alliés? That's miles back!'

'Yep, twelve kilometres in all,' he announced proudly.

It was 2pm by the time we arrived in La Cluse-et-Mijoux, which was quite the contrary to the quaint village at the foot of a castle that we had expected. La Cluse was a congested and exhaust-fumed thoroughfare, built into La Cluse de Pontarlier, a river-carved notch in a tapering ridgeline of the Jura's eastern mountains. The road was hot and dry, and the houses were featureless and clad with the dusty throwback of the passing trucks. The Château de Joux overlooked the bedlam, half wrapped in scaffolding and plastic, and wondering, I imagined, where it had all gone wrong.

Hoping for a relaxing afternoon, I left Jake to rest on a small patch of shaded grass beside a busy roundabout, and went to find a hotel on the assumption that Brenda wouldn't much appreciate a night in the forest after a thirteen-hour flight and a seven-hour train journey. However, the one-star hotel was closed, and after a further eight kilometres of searching without fruition, I firmly labelled La Cluse a place I would never voluntarily return to.

'I've just picked up the car,' Brenda said excitedly down the phone.

'The car?'

'Yeah, I got the train from Paris to Strasbourg a few hours ago and since then have been looking for a hire car. Wasn't bloody easy, but I've got one now! Anyway, long story short, I'm on my way. Where am I meeting you?'

'Malbuisson,' I shouted to Brenda as another truck rumbled by. 'It's the next town on from La Cluse, twelve kilometres to the south.'

'Perfect, see you there!'

I returned to the roundabout to see Jake talking to a middle-aged man with a thick dark beard, and a faded sun hat.

Mark was Dutch, though his immaculate English implied otherwise, and he smiled softly between sentences. 'Can I walk with you to Malbuisson? I would like the company, if you don't mind?'

We followed a steep path around the mount of the Château de Joux, climbing a hundred metres before reaching the outer walls. A few moments passed as we stood awkwardly outside the entrance of the castle, waiting for someone to make a move.

Jake and I were used to our ways. We lived at the same pace, we were simultaneous in our hunger and thirst, and, more often than not, we shared the same feelings towards features on the path, where raising both eyebrows and smiling subtly suggested that we were interested, whilst a curling of the upper lip and squint of one eye meant that we were not. Mark had breezed up the track, leaving Jake and me panting in his wake. Furthermore, he seemed intrigued by the castle, although we couldn't really tell if he wanted to go in, for his facial expressions gave nothing away. And then, when he offered to buy us an ice cream, we were totally thrown. 'An ice cream?' I thought to myself. 'But we never buy ice creams.'

I instantly felt an intense appreciation for Jake. That's not to say that Mark was a bad person. He wasn't. In fact, he was a lovely person. But, as I conjured up Annika's words from back in Abreschviller – 'You can only walk with someone whom you love' – I suddenly realised the fragility of a walking partnership.

We skipped the castle, and to Mark's confusion the ice cream too, and then ascended once more until a sweeping view of Lac de Saint-Point and the Montagne du Laveron range appeared to the west.

'I'm walking the *GR5*,' Mark said with the sort of indifference that suggested modesty.

'Really?' I was astonished. Mark's pack was three times smaller than ours, he had no poles, and instead of boots he wore running shoes. I had assumed he was an ill-prepared day walker.

'I'm an ultra-lightweight hiker,' he replied. 'I don't have a lot, eight kilograms roughly, but the gear is expensive. A jacket that's ten grams lighter is a hundred dollars more expensive. It's all American.'

Mark's tent weighed 800 grams. Jake and I, in one sitting, had regularly eaten tins of fruit weighing the same amount. And our tent, although catering for two, was four times heavier than Mark's. Yet perhaps even more astonishingly, his tent weighed twenty times less than the one used by the German brothers whom we had met a few weeks earlier in Liverdun.

Mark didn't have a stove, which meant he didn't need to carry gas. Instead, he would soak oats or couscous overnight in cold water. It all seemed to make sense. Why walk in heavy boots when there is the option to wear something lighter? Why have hot food when you can have cold? Why have two skins on your tent when you can have one? And why walk twenty-five kilometres with a pack weighing twenty kilograms when you can walk forty carrying eight kilograms?

But where was the comfort? We had a book to read, journals to write, and maps to scrutinise. Mark didn't keep a journal, and he had thrown away the sections of the maps that he didn't need. If the tent was too warm, condensation would drip from the ceiling, and, if it rained, water would seep through the skin. Jake and I enjoyed our luxuries and, though Mark's walking paradigm was one that worked for him, we were glad it was not ours.

'Do you get lonely walking by yourself?' I asked as we followed a forest track along the ridgeline paralleling the elongated lake.

'All the time.' Mark's eyes suddenly glazed over, and I could tell that this was something he thought about a lot. 'I wanted to try it. Normally, I walk with my girlfriend, but I wanted to see how it felt to walk alone. I don't like it. I get scared a lot – really paranoid. The sounds that you hear in the forest should make you happy, that's what it's all about, right? But it scares me when I hear a stick snap and the trees creak.'

'Do you think it would ever be enough to make you turn back?'

'I already have. I was in Luxembourg. I hated it there! It was too predictable, with its hills and rivers, and nowhere to camp. But, anyway,' he continued slowly, 'I was feeling vulnerable and just thought, what's the point? I'm not enjoying it, so I got on a train and went home, back to Holland. But it wasn't long before I started to feel guilty, and a few hours later I was on my way back to Luxembourg.' Mark sniffed a laugh through his nose, though I'm sure it was a memory that haunted him.

'Will you make it to the Mediterranean?' I asked after a few moments of silence.

'Honestly, I don't know.'

All of the rooms in Malbuisson were full, which was odd given that the small lakeside town seemed to boast a disproportionately large number of hotels whilst maintaining a disproportionately low number of visitors. Perhaps they didn't like the way we smelt?

Mark went and pitched his tent in a campsite at the far end of town and then joined us for a beer beneath two horse chestnut trees on the lit terrace of Hôtel Le Lac. Cigarette smoke wisped from the mouths of the old men beside us as we told Mark, with fond memories, about the time I had kicked a stone against a fir cone back in Fesservillers. As it turned out, it was a pursuit Mark enjoyed too, and we spent the next hour or so reeling off stone-kicking memories from the path that perhaps should have been erased.

A white Peugeot swerved into the car park on the opposite side of the road, bridging two spaces with tyres keen to rebel against the notion of parallel parking. The door swung open, and a woman with thick black-framed glasses, ponytailed dark hair, and a cursing Australian accent leapt out of the car. Brenda was like a freed dog that had been kept inside too long, bounding and grinning as she hollered, 'Where's my beer then?' across the street.

It was getting late and, despite the wealth of anecdotes being dished joyously around the table, with each gulp of beer that hit my bloodstream my eyelids grew heavier. Jake, meanwhile, was one notch further along the 'sleepiness scale', and no matter how hard he tried to hold the weight of his head safely on his shoulders, it kept toppling limply to the side.

A waitress tiptoed over and began to clear our empty bottles. 'Excuse me,' she said timidly with a soft accent. I looked up and immediately recognised her. 'You came into the hotel earlier looking for a place to stay, yes?' With long acorn-coloured hair and dimpled cheeks, the petite woman held her shoulders close to her body and spoke with a nervous tone.

'Um, yes,' I replied. 'But the receptionist said there were no beds left in town.'

'Yes, I heard. Did you find somewhere to sleep?'

'No.'

'Well,' she hesitated, 'I wanted to ask if you would like to stay on my mother's farm for the night. It's not far and we have beds for you all.'

I glanced over to see Brenda maintaining her boundless energy, excitement exuding from her broad grin. 'That would be brilliant!'

We dropped our bags onto the bedroom floor as Mauricette, Lea's mother, frantically stretched a sheet over the mattress. A thick head of curly hair fell across her face, and her shoulders and hands painted a life of rural living. 'She doesn't want it looking messy for you.' Lea smiled.

'*Je peux vous aider?*' Jake asked, pulling the corner of the sheet.

'*Non!*' Mauricette instructed, muttering something to Lea.

'She wants you to rest. Now, let's go down and eat. Oh, and give your washing to my mother. She wants to put it in the machine.'

Mauricette struck me as the kind of woman you would be wise to listen to, so we emptied the clothes from our bags and made our way down to the kitchen where we sat around a small candlelit table and were served pasta and beer.

'*Le Petit Poucet*,' Lea said, having somehow got onto the conversation of fairy tales. 'We call it *Le Petit Poucet*. You know, with the children and the breadcrumbs.'

'That's *Hansel and Gretel*!' Brenda objected.

'No, it's *Le Petit Poucet*, with the children and the breadcrumbs and the Ogre.'

'Ogre? There's not an ogre in *Hansel and Gretel*,' Jake interjected.

'But there is in *Le Petit Poucet*,' Lea said.

'Can you tell us the story?' Brenda asked like a child before bedtime. 'Please?'

'If you want me to.'

'Yeah, we do!'

We switched off the lamp and pushed the candle towards Lea, forcing the light of the flame to dance across her face. 'Once upon a time,' she began, 'the Lumberjack and his wife were living in the forest with their seven children. One was so tiny that everybody called him the "*Petit Poucet*", or the "Little Poucet". They were happy, but very poor. Times were hard, and famine was big.

'One night, the Lumberjack told his wife that they couldn't live like this anymore and that they had no choice but to abandon their children into the wood. The Little Poucet was awake and heard this conversation, so he woke up early and went into the garden, where he picked up a handful of small white stones and put them in his pocket.'

'This *is Hansel and Gretel*,' Brenda interrupted.

'Shush!' Jake and I hissed.

'It's *Le Petit Poucet*,' Lea said calmly. 'Where was I? Oh yes, the stones. In the morning, the family went for a walk, moving further and further away from their house. In the middle of the woods, the Lumberjack told his children to gather some sticks. And, while they were gone, the parents left without being seen. When the children noticed that they were alone, they all began to scream and cry, all except the Little Poucet, because he knew how to get back to the house – follow the little white stones.

'The children found their way back to their house. While they were gone, the Lumberjack and his wife went to the village to buy some food. The wife was crying and crying until they came home and saw their children at the door. They were so happy to see them. But they soon remembered that they had no money and decided, for the second time, to abandon their children again, but this time further into the woods. The Little Poucet heard the conversation but, when he went out to pick up the stones, the door was locked.'

A black and white cat had now joined us in the kitchen, arching

208

its back around Lea's chair and nudging at her feet. She lifted the purring ball of fur onto her lap and then continued the story. 'In the morning, the wife gave some bread to all of her children, so the Little Poucet decided that instead of using stones he would use breadcrumbs. They went far into the deep, dark wood. The parents left, but the Little Poucet wasn't worried, for he knew he would be able to follow his trail home.

'Unfortunately, when the children went to find the trail, they realised that the birds had eaten all of the breadcrumbs, so they couldn't find the way back. They were lost, hungry and sad.

'After hours of walking, they eventually found a house. They knocked on the door, and a woman opened it. The children asked for a place to sleep, and the woman said that they couldn't stay because the Ogre was living there, and he loved to eat small children. But the woman was nice and decided to hide the children from the Ogre until the morning.

'The Ogre came back and began to eat. But there was an unusual smell in the air, like fresh meat. It wasn't long before the Ogre found the children. He shouted at his wife and decided that he would eat the children the next day.

'The Ogre had seven daughters. They all slept wearing golden crowns. The Little Poucet, who was really clever, was worried that the Ogre might come in the night and eat them while they slept. So he decided to take the golden crowns from the daughters and put them on his brothers' heads.

'The Little Poucet was right. The Ogre came at night-time and touched the brothers' heads. He saw the crowns and, assuming he was drunk, went to the next room. He didn't recognise the daughters without their crowns and so he killed them all!

'The Little Poucet woke his brothers and they ran away. The Ogre was furious. He put on his *bottes de sept lieues* – they are like magic boots – and went in pursuit of the children.

'With his boots, the Ogre was really tall and fast. But he soon got tired and took a nap. With the Ogre sleeping, the Little Poucet stole his *bottes de sept lieues* and his money, and, with his brothers, ran back to their home. Their parents were so happy to see their children, and all the money.

'They were happy forever.

'The end.'

8

Doubs to Nyon

2,018 to 2,126 kilometres from home

THE FONDUE FAMILY

'I'm not too fussed about walking,' Brenda said at breakfast. 'I've got a car!'

Instead of pursuing our initial plan to give Brenda a taste of life on the path, we spent the next three days with Lea, Mauricette and a profusion of other family members and pets.

The family lived on the edge of a small village called Doubs – built on the banks of the Doubs River – which shared its southern houses with the larger town of Pontarlier. Mauricette owned a second house behind the one we had slept in, beyond which lay a large shed and expansive fields of grazing cattle. It was a busy time of year for Mauricette. Up with the sun, or a little before, she worked until dusk, turning the grass to keep it dry, whilst baling and milking twice a day. The milk from the farm was sold to a nearby *fromagerie*, where it would be cultured, coagulated, scalded and ripened, eventually producing a hard cheese with roasted-nut aromas and a sweet finish, known as *Comté*.

Madeleine, or Mamie as she was known in the family, was the grandmother of the house. She used to work the farm but became too old. With her life of graft behind her, she now spent her hours filling the sugar cube pot in the kitchen and rattling down the farm track, Zimmer frame in hand. Christine, Mauricette's sister-in-law, was the jester of the family and the household singer, humming as she cooked and whistling as she washed, whilst her two children, Silvio the chef, and Iris the English whizz-kid, were quiet and attentive. In amongst the personalities and binding them lovingly together were the extended kin: Minet, a black cat with

210

a fear of strangers, and Charlie, a boisterous sheepdog who craved attention and normally got it.

In the days that we spent with the family, Jake and I must have put on as much weight as we had lost since leaving Bristol. As well as an array of home-made jams, salads and stews, we were treated on our second evening to a *Comté fondue*, cooked by Silvio.

In the low light of the kitchen, we sat around a small circular table, centred by a ceramic *fondue* bowl. The heat from the bubbling sauce was impressive and, with each of our shoulders hugged up against our neighbours', it wasn't long before our cheeks were glowing with resounding warmth. Blending *Comté*, mustard, garlic and wine, the *fondue* smelt rich and sweet.

'To the Fondue Family!' Brenda mumbled through a mouthful of bread, raising her glass of wine into the air.

'We have a tradition,' Iris said, after receiving a poke from her mother. She tore a piece of bread from a baguette and skewered it with her fork. 'You put the bread in the *fondue* and if it falls when you pull it out, you are in trouble.'

'Trouble?' Brenda said with anticipation.

'Yes. There are three punishments. You must choose one. First, you can wash *all* the dishes, second, you can sing a song,' Christine suddenly burst into melody, 'and third,' Iris called over her mother's trilling voice, 'you get thrashed!'

Of course, Jake, Brenda and I thought the final chastisement was a joke, but our laughter was soon cut short as Mauricette unveiled a long black whip from beneath the table.

Thankfully, the only person to lose a piece of bread in the melt was Christine, though I'm pretty sure singing in front of the family was not exactly her idea of a punishment.

Already feeling the effects of the spiced Juran wine, my palms suddenly became clammy as a bottle of clear liqueur was brought to the table and shot glasses handed out. Yet more apprehension came as a sugar cube, dished out by Mamie, was dropped into our glasses.

'It's to disguise the taste,' Lea said with raised eyebrows, suggesting we should approach with caution. The drink – worryingly referred to as *goutte*, or more commonly known as *gentian* – was a home brew and possessed a rather hearty alcohol content of sixty-five per cent. Made from the roots of the yellow gentian

flower, goutte is famed for two things: its ability to remedy digestive problems, and its appalling bitterness. Mamie vouched for its
healing properties with her life (or her bowels, should I say). But
we shouldn't have trusted her.

'So?' Lea quizzed as Brenda and I swallowed the liqueur.

The goutte tasted like alcoholic earwax and, regardless of
Mamie's assurance of its curing qualities, I couldn't hide my
disgust. Brenda, of course, quite liked it. 'Yum!' she shouted, with
watering eyes.

During a rare break from both cooking and eating, Lea
bundled us into her car and drove us across the Swiss border to the
sandy shores of Lac de Neuchâtel where Jake and I finally showed
our thighs to the sun as we hurtled into the water.

At thirty-eight kilometres long and eight kilometres wide,
Neuchâtel is of significant size. Indeed, it would have taken us four
days to circumnavigate the mass of water. I was startled to realise
that our path through the Jura had paralleled the lake just fifteen
kilometres to the west, but we had never known. Were we that
unobservant? Or were we not walking through Western Europe at
all, but merely an inconsequential, narrow dash from one point to
the next? It was a sobering thought, but one that I quickly forgot as
I turned to see a beach ball tear through the air and land painfully
on my nose.

I assumed, from his apologetic smile, that Jake had thrown the
ball. Perhaps he had spotted my musing face from across the water,
inferring from it unsettling thoughts, and summoned up a perfect
throw. Or maybe the excitement of being prematurely amongst the
waves had gone to his head. Either way, I was glad to forget my
foolish contemplations.

Never one for a quiet departure, Brenda was almost knocked
out by a ceramic ashtray as she stood outside the Pontarlier train
station. 'Merde!' a little girl had squeaked after bumping the
dish from her windowsill, sending it spiralling towards Brenda's
head. Thankfully, the ashtray narrowly missed her and was left
to smash into a thousand tiny pieces as it hit the pavement at her
feet.

'Gunna be a close one getting to my train on time, if I even
make it there alive,' Brenda laughed, hugging us both before

climbing into her car. Swerving out from the parking lot, she wound down the window and called out over her shoulder, 'Guess I'll see you in some far-flung country sometime. Now hurry up and get to that bloody sea!'

TAKING THE DOG FOR A WALK

'Can we walk with you?' Lea asked at breakfast as the smell of Jake's freshly made bread dispersed around the sun-washed kitchen. Usually a late riser, Lea's eyes looked tired, but her cheeks dimpled as she smiled. Mauricette's lack of surprise and expression of anticipation made me think that Lea's request had been discussed and presumably approved the previous night.

'We?' Jake questioned.

'Yes, me and Charlie. I've never walked more than a few kilometres, and I think Charlie would like it, wouldn't he?' she said, kneeling down to ruffle the black and white coat of the sheepdog now at her side. 'It'll be fun!'

'Are you trying to kill me? *Putain!*' Lea gasped after a twenty-minute ascent through the forest to the east of Malbuisson.

Charlie, on the contrary, couldn't have been happier: one moment at our sides, and the next bounding up the track, where he would disappear for a minute or two and then return soon after with half a tree branch between his jaws, panting with pride.

The path soon levelled, and Lea's enthusiasm returned. We left the shaded puddles of the forest and their resident newts, bowing gently south into a valley of farms and small towns – Le Touillon, Loutelet and Les Hôpitaux-Neufs – where Charlie's persistent thirst was momentarily quenched by a cow trough here and a *lavoir* there.

'This is where I used to come with my friends to party,' Lea said, pointing towards a line of train carriages overgrown with grass and brambles, and sprayed with graffiti. It was a hot day, and the rusted metal of the crankpins and the rods flaked and crumbled, whilst blue tits chirped and busied themselves amongst the wreck.

'And here,' she said, as we passed Métabief to its east, 'we camped somewhere around here for a festival a few years ago.'

On the lower slopes of Le Morond (1,419 metres) in an open

wood of ferns and sycamore, we set up camp, cooking Lea our delicacy, walkers' risotto, before ambling through the trees to a prairie of mown grass which looked out to the west and the setting sun. All was still, save for the cruising planes that sketched the sky and the leaping silhouette of a tireless sheepdog.

Indeed, it was the tireless sheepdog that woke us in the morning with a serenade of barks.

'Well, that was a nice alarm,' Lea mumbled, rubbing the sleep from her eyes as we dropped through the trees and back onto the woodland track, streaked with sun and shade like the keys of a grand piano.

Charlie had helped himself to our water supply during the night, and Jake and I were glad to find a trickling stream not long after leaving camp. In fact, the rambunctious sheepdog seemed altogether keen on mischief. He continued to tear away at the forest's saplings and wildflowers, growing tired from time to time, when he would return to our company, trotting awkwardly between our legs. He was scared of loud noises too – aeroplanes, machinery, and even the jingling sound of a goat bell that Jake had pushed into his side pocket after finding it beside the path. Running for cover, he would sink into whatever undergrowth he could find to escape the sounds, only returning to the path at the sight of a truly magnificent stick.

Beyond Le Morond, the ground maintained its height, but fell away acutely to the east and into a soup of haze to form the Mont d'Or ridgeline. Gathering several handfuls of white pebbles from the path, we laid them out onto the grass to mark the milestone: '2,000 kilometres'.

Jake and I stared at the number for a minute or two before agreeing that, aside from the pebbles looking rather pretty against the backdrop of lush grass and daisies, the occasion felt entirely insignificant. Indeed, our level of emotion was no greater than the moment we had completed our first kilometre, or second, or eleventh, or, for that matter, our one thousand and thirty-fourth.

At any rate, we were not the only ones to have reached a point of significance. Lea, who had been busy with her own pebble creation, grinned proudly up from the floor. 'Sixteen kilometres!' she chirruped. 'That's the furthest I've ever walked!'

We left Mont d'Or through a swathe of highland meadows, where Charlie continued to flirt naively with danger. At one point, he was so eager to retrieve a stick from within a group of resting cows that we were soon running full pelt towards the safety of a stile with the herd snapping clumsily at our heels. Charlie, of course, with his quick feet and irrepressible energy, was never under threat, and we found him on the other side of the fence with the branch between his teeth, resting beneath a splaying oak.

By the time we reached the Source du Doubs and the town of Mouthe, both Lea and Charlie were waning. Intimidated by the clatters and screams of playing children, Charlie refused to go on, so we tied him to a tree in the shade, poured the last of our water into his bowl and then made our way down to the source.

Water rushed plentifully from a small cave within the vegetated limestone cliff, falling several metres over a ledge and onto a flat riverbed of algae-smeared boulders and pebbles. The water was sweet and, at no more than 7°C, numbingly cold.

'You know, it's obvious you're English,' Lea said later that night as we sat in the Pizzeria l'Arlequin having met a relieved Mauricette and Mamie as dusk fell. Jake and I presumed they wanted to thank us with yet more food for not letting Lea and Charlie die of exhaustion – although it must be said, Charlie was probably close. 'I know you're English because you go up to the bar to order your drinks. The French are lazy. We wait in our chairs!'

In 1985, Mouthe recorded a temperature of -41°C, making it the coldest commune in France. Thankfully for Jake, Ted and me, it was July, and despite the condensing air balling from our mouths, the day was warm, and the town's ominous nickname, 'Little Siberia', fell redundant.

Through my misty breath, I watched two ducks chill their bottoms on the icy river as it swashed downstream through a dewed and twinkling landscape. We were sad to be leaving the Doubs River and the people that fell within its catchment. We felt flat, yet appreciative – no more, we guessed, than post-holiday blues.

From deep green forests, the land opened up. Jake had kindly given me the last *Gout Noir de Café* – now ranked as the best scroggin ingredient – sending the taste of creamy coffee delectably through my mouth. Tractors, circled by flocks of hungry crows, turned the damp grass, leaving clumped braids behind their drawbars. Butterflies, horseflies and the ruby wings of a cardinal beetle eddied majestically between the shoots and petals of the bountiful wildflowers – pink bistort, dandelion heads, gentians and the earthy scent of mountain thyme.

By mid-afternoon, the day had grown hot, and we stopped in Chapelle-des-Bois beneath the shade of a *lavoir* shelter to cool. With sweat saturating our T-shirts, I went in search of refreshments, leaving Jake to push our poles into the ground before hanging our damp garments out to dry, a trick Gabrielle and Yannick had taught us back in the Doubs gorge.

'Milk?' Jake grumbled as I returned from the store with both hands full. 'It's 30°C and we're running out of water. Why did you get milk?'

'I thought you would like it,' I replied pathetically, suddenly appreciating the stupidity of the purchase.

My blunder was further acknowledged as we trudged wearily out of the village and into a patchwork of bogs at the foot of a towering cliff, seemingly our last opportunity to pick up water for the night. It was mid-summer, and with the exception of a drifting rivulet that ducked beneath the track, the marshland was dry. We bottled the yellow-tinted water, loaded it with purification tablets, and then climbed up 250 metres of hairpin bends, finally reaching the flattened crown of Belvédère de la Roche Champion.

Unable to resist the temptation of a night above the valley, we unrolled Ted next to a crumbled drystone wall, supported at its base by dozens of heaped ant nests. A whimsical walker would have pitched their tent across the national divide, sleeping with their head in France and their feet in Switzerland. But we were tired, and novelty was the last thing on our minds.

The valley was quiet, save for the screams of playing children and the jangles of the cows which found our ears with the rising air.

'It's odd,' I said to Jake as we dangled our legs over the edge of the lofty bluff and watched the crested moon rise over the Jura Mountains to the north. A meadow brown butterfly – dark on its wings but for a faint orange eye – landed on my plastered toe, distracting my attention momentarily as it unrolled its proboscis onto the damp dressing. 'It's odd,' I continued, 'we spend the whole day looking at maps, sometimes the night too.' I opened the *Lons-le-Saunier Genève IGN*, our thirty-seventh map, and, with the light from the half-moon and the dimming sky, noted a huge body of blue water in the bottom right-hand corner of the page. The butterfly rolled up its trunk and took to the air. 'When was the last time you looked at one of these maps and thought about where we were? I mean in Europe, in relation to home?'

'I don't know,' Jake said, picking a daisy and dropping it over the cliff edge.

'I haven't done it for weeks. I see the rivers, the tracks, the mountains, the borders, but I never put it into context. We go from one hamlet to another, and then maybe we pass a town, or even a city. But it's just the same as the last: we buy food, postcards, maybe we pay for a bed. But where are we?' Just in front of Chapelle-des-Bois, I spotted the grooves of the small river which we had collected water from earlier in the day. But, beyond the town, the hills and forests looked much the same. 'I don't even know which way we've come from.'

'North?' Jake joked, perhaps trying to lighten the mood.

'Yes, thank you,' I replied. 'But look,' I tapped the area of blue on the map in an attempt to regain his concentration, 'this puts it into perspective – Lake Geneva, Lac Leman. I know exactly where Lake Geneva is, and I know what it means.'

'The Alps,' Jake said slowly, his face awash with contentment.

It was 14 July, Bastille Day, and to commemorate we ate a *pain au chocolat* each and then continued south along the bluff through mixed woodland. Birds courted beneath balls of mistletoe, and the threads of the forest spiders and caterpillars veiled our faces.

Of course, being French National Day, we were moving somewhat against the grain as we arrowed towards the border town of La Cure and, evading the anticipated strip search at the control station, crossed into Switzerland. A road sign read '*Nyon 22km, Geneva 40km*'.

'Twenty-two kilometres,' Jake announced. 'It's going to be a nice short day into Nyon tomorrow. We'll be there before Nan and Gramps!'

After our recent visit from Brenda, and the company of Lea and Charlie on the path, we had pushed our grandparents' imminent visit to the back of our minds. Jake and I had often talked about how important our grandparents were as an inspiration for our journey across Europe, for they too were keen adventurers. Indeed, at the age of eighty, our granddad still hiked and sailed. 'They'll be here in less than a day,' I beamed, unable to hide my elation.

In spite of our route hugging the Swiss-Franco border, it was clear that we had arrived into a different country. Amongst Douglas fir trees and immaculate lawns lay neatly positioned chalet-like houses, each wrapped in a wooden balcony and decorated with hanging lanterns, beams of varnished wood and, almost invariably, a large red flag centred with a white cross.

Through a pristinely trimmed hedge on the eastern fringes of Saint-Cergue, we spotted a man purposefully clutching a remote control. The chap had a well-maintained comb-over of silver hair, an austere expression of tight lips and focused eyes, and a striped polo shirt. It was not until we got closer and managed to peek over the hedge that we realised his entire garden was covered with a network of miniature railway lines, bridges and commuters. A train moved safely through the grass carpet, never in danger of falling from the rails and always, both Jake and I assumed, arriving at its destination perfectly on time.

Initially stunned at having to pay thirty euros for a patch of grass at the town's campsite, our displeasure quickly evaporated at the sight of a child-sized football goal and an invitation to a game of *pétanque* later that night. After an hour of kicking a football back and forth, we were eventually driven away from the playground by a ten-year-old boy with a snotty nose. 'Guess we'd better go and give this *pétanque* thing a go,' Jake said, taking one last shot at the goal, much to the annoyance of the little boy.

Joined by another Englishman, Jake and I battled woefully against the locals, all of whom seemed to have no problem hitting the jack with a flick of the wrist. We, however, were simply glad if the ball left our hands without thudding into the kneecaps of any on-lookers, who quite frankly were standing far too close to the action.

In all, the opposition were merciful and allowed us a point here and there when their lead became stretched. There was one character, however, who clearly believed that, when it came to *pétanque*, shows of compassion were for the weak.

Pierre – with his thigh-high denim shorts, leathery skin, beady eyes, wiry hair, and an irrepressible scent of olive oil – reminded me of a mad scientist after two weeks in the sun. He was an exceptional *pétanque* player and threw the metal *boules* with grace and precision. But, unlike the other players, he was not in the mood for humouring us.

With Donna Summer's 'Hot Stuff' echoing out from the toilet block and the sun edging down, Pierre eventually decided that enough was enough, picked up his *boules,* and, five minutes later, left the sand for bed having single-handedly thrashed the English by eleven points to three.

ROAD CLOSED

We had both woken in the night, startled by the sound of footsteps close to our tent. It wasn't until Jake unzipped the porch that we realised it was not a forest that surrounded us but a gathering of motorhomes.

Sleeping in new landscapes every night played with our senses, and we rarely got through a camp without waking to confusion. A barking dog at a campsite back in the Vosges had Jake thinking we were about to be attacked by an angry landowner, whilst both of us had woken on a number of occasions with the thought that the tent was infested with crawling ants, waking suddenly in our sleeping bags and frantically brushing the imaginary insects from our bodies.

But when morning came, the night-time's disorientation was forgotten and our bearings were confirmed: we were fourteen kilometres from Nyon and, with that, Lake Geneva.

Now in Switzerland, the waymarking had once again changed. We followed a succession of yellow and black *Tourisme Pédestre* signs into town, but were prevented from going any further by a blockade of grunting machinery and roadworkers.

'*La route est fermée,*' a large man in a plastic hat said sternly, holding his arms out to the side to prevent us from passing.

'*Pour aller à Nyon, s'il vous plaît?*'

'*La route est fermée,*' he repeated. 'Road closed!'

'*Oui, mais y-at-il une autre route?*' I pointed at the map, hoping for a little help. Instead, he nodded at a diversion sign on the roadside.

Knowing that we had extracted all that was possible from the gruff roadworker, we left Saint-Cergue with the diverted cars, feeling their wing mirrors flash by our shoulders and tasting the road fumes on our tongues.

Having only just acquainted ourselves with Switzerland's *Tourisme Pédestre*, it was a shame to be leaving its guidance so soon. Without waymarkers, and with little help from our ambiguous 1:100,000 *IGN* map, our chances of getting lost suddenly increased. We now had no other choice but to rely on passers-by for directions, which, given our track record with locals, was well and truly a last resort.

Yet, somewhat uncharacteristically, with each stint of pointing fingers and briskly spoken directions, accompanied by several dubious spins of the compass, we were guided onto the next obliging stranger – '*La première à gauche, la deuxième à droite, continuer tout droit.*'

Bouncing from one local to the next, we zigzagged through woodland, over railway lines and across fields, until eventually, after an eleven-kilometre detour, we reached the masonry of Trélex. Greeted by an ebullient *lavoir* and its ballet of red geranium petals that spun daintily on the water's surface, we dipped our hands into the cold bath before addressing the map.

'We're back on track,' I announced, pointing towards a *Tourisme Pédestre* diamond nailed to a wall of blooming violet wisteria.

Although we still hadn't seen the lake, we knew that we were close, and our steps quickened along the tarmac road that led from Trélex to Nyon; through crops of golden maize and their dining sparrows, and past fields of flaming sunflowers, each beaming obligingly to the south and the early afternoon sun.

Cars and trucks rumbled above our heads as we passed beneath the A1 motorway (connecting Geneva, Bern, Zurich and Switzerland's eastern border) and into Nyon's western suburbs.

It wasn't long before a glint of shimmering blue water caught our eyes from between the narrow streets, and Lake Geneva opened out in front of us.

We leant over the railings of the lakeside promenade, between flower boxes and plane trees, and peered into the water as it rolled against the rocky shoreline. Across the lake, with the glare of the sun masking the horizon, we could just make out the lower foothills of the Alps. A drop of sweat ran down my brow, bonding momentarily with the tip of my nose before falling into the water below.

'Now, your granddad did warn them that you may be a bit scruffy, so don't worry about that,' Mum said down the phone as we stood on the waterfront outside Le Beau Rivage, an opulent fifteenth-century hotel, grander than any we had stayed in on our journey so far.

Whether he didn't like the idea of touching our unkempt belongings or, more likely, our granddad had told him specifically not to offer assistance, the porter at the reception remained motionless and watched on awkwardly as Jake and I hauled our packs over our shoulders and set off up the stairs.

Within thirty minutes, we had turned the immaculate hotel suite into an odorous mess of gear, dirt and aging food. Ted hung from the lake-view balcony, along with washed socks, underwear, T-shirts and sleeping bags. Meanwhile, the interior of the room was submerged in unfolded maps, books, leftover consumables, roll mats and, of course, several different species of creepy-crawlies.

Leaving no freebie unused, I cut my hair with the luxury of a mirror, bathed using the complimentary shower wash, and then cleaned my teeth with the miniature dental products that sat in a basket by the sink.

With a bottle of spring water in one hand (I had already managed to break the coffee machine) and an individually wrapped biscuit in the other, I lay on the bed in my white robe and matching slippers watching the television, which, quite hospitably, had welcomed us to the room by name. The only thing that we had not abused was the complimentary shoe polish, although I did see Jake eyeing it up.

'You've got a better view than us,' Gramps said, after knocking on our bedroom door and peering into the suite with Nan standing patiently at his side. Unlike Jake and me, our grandparents, who were three times our age, appeared fresh and boisterous, both with a glint in their eyes that reminded me of their modest wisdom.

'Oh, it doesn't matter, Ted,' Nan responded, putting two pairs of spotless walking boots onto the bed. 'I hope they're the right ones, boys.'

'They had better be,' added Gramps. 'They took up half the luggage space!'

'Oh shush, Ted!'

Along with the boots, I was given a new journal which delighted me no end, swapping it for my old one whose final pages I had filled at our stay in Doubs.

'I have some letters too, and your granddad thought you might need this chart.' Nan handed Jake a small wad of envelopes and a map. 'What's the map for anyway, Ted?'

'The what?' he replied, not for the first time requiring the question to be repeated.

'The map!'

'Well, it's of Mont Blanc, isn't it? I thought the boys might be interested. Bit old, mind, but it got me around the massif well enough, so they'll be fine.'

'You had to be taken away in a rescue helicopter, Ted!' Nan interjected.

'Well yes, but it wasn't my fault,' Gramps protested jovially as his eyes shone with reminiscence through the thick lenses of his glasses. 'We were on the Combe de la Glière on the Aiguilles Rouges. It was early. In fact, we'd only just left the *refuge* on the western side of the Chamonix valley. Something must have disturbed the rocks above us – another walker or a chamois perhaps. Anyway, a piece of debris came bouncing down and hit me on the head.' Nan rolled her eyes disapprovingly. 'I wanted to carry on, but the others insisted on getting the helicopter in!' A slight smile had found its way onto our granddad's face. 'They took me to Chamonix in the helicopter!'

Nyon wasn't the town I had expected it to be. Raised above the lakeshore, a cluster of medieval structures – amongst others, L'Église de Notre Dame and Le Château de Nyon – looked down upon the town's gardens and a host of restaurants, whose food, drink and music filled the wide pavements. It was a lavish town, where wealthy businessmen and families on a break from the bustle of Geneva came to drink expensive wine and to shop.

With salmon-coloured trousers, a light striped polo shirt and copper-brown skin, Gramps fitted in well. As did Nan, who spoke French when she ordered her food as her silver-dashed hair blew gently in the lakeside wind. Jake and I, on the other hand, looked conclusively out of place.

On the second evening, we ordered *Fondue de Cheval*. Unwilling to be made fools of, we refused to wear the tuxedo-

222

printed paper bibs that the waiters tried to place around our necks. However, the bibs were not a novelty for children, nor a garment to chastise gullible tourists, but a vital form of defence against a dish of hot spitting oil. After skewering a lump of raw horse meat, we were then instructed to dip our forks into the spluttering fat. But this only made matters worse as a fresh bout of effervescence flung licks of scorching oil onto our hands and cheeks. It was far from an enjoyable, cultural experience, but one which was comfortably alleviated by the Juran wine, the sound of a bowing violinist, the vastness of the lake, and the ornamental clouds that sat upon a mantelpiece of mountains towards our southerly horizon.

Adamant on losing as much luggage weight as possible before setting foot on our final mountain range, Jake siphoned through the gear, ruthlessly putting aside unnecessary items: old boots, maps, a guidebook, my used journal, notes, memory sticks and the goat bell that we had picked up from the meadows beside Le Morond. I was impressed with the gear cull, though I'm not sure the same could be said for Nan and Gramps, whose expressions of disbelief suggested that they were less pleased to be carting the load home.

On the morning of our departure, I woke early and stepped onto the balcony. Two men sat in a small wooden fishing boat, silhouetted by the rising sun that lit the water with an amber hue. In spite of the room's perfect temperature regulation, the feathery pillows and the absorbing mattresses, I had slept awfully. Perhaps it was the horse meat causing discomfort in my stomach, or maybe it was the sight of the looming mountains that were soon to take our feet.

Desperate to calm my heart rate, I ran a bath and lay beneath the surface, feeling my washed hair drift in slow motion through the water. The sound of the town was stifled, distancing me from the external world. I listened to the movement of air through my body, the gulp of my pharynx, and the closing valves of my heart: *lub-dup, lub-dub, lub-dup, lub-dub.*

'Now, what was that poem again?' Nan said over a lunch of *croque-monsieurs* and green salad, not long before we were due to board the small ferry across the lake. 'Oh yes, *Sea Pictures*!'

223

'*Sea Pictures?*' I said.

'Yes, I wrote it when you were little. It's about the sea. Now, how did it start...?' Nan's eyebrows crumpled and her lips clamped together in thought. 'That's it:'

> *Who will be the first to see the sea?*
> *"It's there, it's there." A distant sparkle of sun on water*
> *As the car winds down the hill to the beach.*
> *An explosion of bodies, buckets, bags and baskets.*
> *Shrieks of delight as little legs race down*
> *To the shining smiling sea.*
> *Howls of anguish as sea urchins stick swords into tiny feet*
> *Amongst the seaweed dreadlocked rocks.*

> *"Where's the sea? It's gone, it's gone."*
> *Veiled in a cold damp chilling mist*
> *Only the salty smell of seaweed*
> *Booming foghorns of ghostly ships*
> *Quarrelsome cries of seagulls*
> *And the crunch of feet on pebbles.*

> *From the cliffs the sea is green and blue shot taffeta*
> *A white border brushing the rocks*
> *Decorated with seabirds*
> *Enjoying the gentle motion of the waves.*
> *Far out the wind makes patterns on the sea*
> *Then changes like a silk sheet drawn across a bed.*

> *There goes the ferry like an overweight bride*
> *Trailing her lacy white train behind*
> *On the magnificent moody sea.*
> *Waves destroy themselves in a fury of white smoke*
> *Against the rocks*
> *Hurling many coloured pebbles*
> *Onto the promenade.*

> *When darkness throws its mantle over the earth*
> *The sea would disappear again*
> *Until a full moon casts a silver pathway*

On the water
Revealing lights of ships under a starlit sky
As waves lap gently on the sand.

Tomorrow the sea may smile again
Disclosing secret gardens in rocky pools
Alive with sea urchins and baby crabs.
Who knows what the sea will do next?

We waved goodbye to Nan and Gramps as their ferry chugged off to the west and ours to the east. Finding a spot on the upper deck, we leant over the railings at the stern of the boat and stared hypnotically into the spuming wake. Nan's poem must have been written twenty years ago. In fact, I remember Jake treading on the sea urchins and hobbling out of the water with tears streaming down his face. Yet, despite the age of the words, it felt like Nan was pre-emptively describing the end of our walk to the Mediterranean:

"It's there, it's there", a distant sparkle of sun on water
Our legs wind down the hill to the beach
to the shining smiling sea.

9

Nyon to Modane

2,126 to 2,458 kilometres from home

INTO THE ALPS

Rather like the body of a colossal shrimp, the Alps mountain range spires and ripples across 1,200 kilometres of Central Europe. The rostrum and the eye of the crustacean lie in Austria, whilst its antennae protrude to the south and the east into the Republic of Slovenia, with the tapering ranges of the Julian Alps, the Kamnik-Savinja Alps and the Karavanke chain. Germany, Lichtenstein and Switzerland make up the abdomen of the giant creature, whilst its legs paddle through North Italy. Its tail, fluted and muscular, twists beneath the body, through the south-eastern regions of France – Rhône-Alpes and Provence-Alpes-Côte d'Azur – and into the Ligurian Apennines of Italy.

Spending much of its earlier life on the seabed, it was only recently, geologically speaking, that the shrimp came to rest on the land mass of Europe. Sixty million years ago, the two continental plates of Africa and Eurasia converged, rapidly reducing the sea between them until its creatures had nowhere left to go but up. The shrimp was forced out of the water and heaped onto an enormous pile of buckled rock. And so it remained.

We were to break into the exoskeleton of the range from the north-west, burrowing through the dorsal abdominal artery and past Mont Blanc's western aspect. Our route would then take us through the lower tract of the shrimp's intestine and into the brawny national parks of the Vanoise and the Queyras, before traversing the nerve cord and rocky massifs of the Parc National du Mercantour. Maintaining the metaphor, after roughly five weeks of glorious mountainous dissection, we hoped to drop painlessly out of the shrimp's anus and into the Mediterranean Sea.

We were only 300 kilometres from Menton, yet our convoluted passage through the Alps was to take us on a route two and a half times this distance. We also had 40,000 metres of mountains to ascend, an obstacle that would see us climb the equivalent of Mount Everest four and a half times.

Since leaving Bristol, we had accumulated just 20,000 metres of ascent. How would our fitness cope with the rising terrain? Would our joints see us through to the end? And, even if our bodies remained strong, would Jake's debilitating vertigo, a condition that had already presented itself in the Benelux region and the Vosges, impede our 'grand traverse of the Alps'?

Intriguingly, these were questions that weighed lightly on our minds. They were concerns, of course, but ones that we felt we could deal with when the time came. We had walked 2,200 kilometres. Surely we were ready for the Alps? And if Jake's vertigo struck then we would muster the strength to walk around the mountains.

Instead, our anxieties lay elsewhere, not least with our desire to camp. We had heard rumours that wild camping was heavily restricted in the national parks of the Alps, and fines were not uncommon. Mark, who would now be midway through his Alps traverse, had even warned us that, if caught, the park rangers had the right to confiscate our gear and send us home. This seemed an unlikely affair, but how were we to know its veracity? Although we had enjoyed our *gîte* experience with Yannick and Gabrielle back in the Jura, we were not ready to make a habit of it. Having spent much of our budget during the first month of our journey, we couldn't afford the price of the accommodations, some of which were as much as 100 euros a night. Furthermore, we were comfortable with our own company, and many of our best memories had come from our camps beneath the trees, watching the bugs tinker in the sunlight across the roof of the tent, and listening to the rustles of a black squirrel or the song of a sparrow. It seemed that we had no choice but to camp, a fact that made us uneasy yet, in undoubtedly contradictory terms, wholly content.

Things felt different. We woke the next morning after a night of heavy rain in the Forêt de Thonon, a couple of kilometres south of Lake Geneva, only then realising that we had returned to France and were now in the region of Rhône-Alpes. In our haste to find a pitch after disembarking the ferry at Thonon-les-Bains, we had not appreciated how quickly the mountains were upon us. We were only in the lower foothills, yet the scale and extremity of the nearby peaks already felt like a step up, so to speak, from anything we had seen north of the lake.

Leaving a dry patch of rusty beech leaves on the forest floor where Ted had lain, we set off through the Chablais region, once more hunting down the Swiss border and, with it, the limestone peak of Les Cornettes de Bise which lay two days to the east.

'I feel taller,' Jake said, as a swarm of mosquitoes drove us out of the forest and into an open meadow of horses and beehives. A rough track led us through the fields and up to Armoy, a small commune of angled streets and stone houses surrounding the pyramidal roof of the village church. 'It's the boots. Just shows how worn down our old ones were.'

'I'm not sure you're entirely used to them yet, Jake.'

'What do you mean?'

'Well, we've only been walking for an hour, and you've tripped over about ten times already.'

'Eight, actually. But, yes, you're right. Hopefully, we can shave a bit off the soles before we get to the big mountains!'

The sound of a recorder spiralled from the open shutters of a house at the eastern end of Armoy where vegetables coloured the gardens, the tune fading into the darkness of a hazel wood that swallowed the path.

When we emerged from the trees at the village of Reyvroz, we realised it was not just the forest that had darkened but the sky too.

'Sun in the morning, rain in the afternoon – do you think perhaps that there is a pattern forming?' I voiced as we looked across the Vallée de Dranse to what should have been the slanted pinnacle of Dent d'Oche, with Les Cornettes de Bise beyond. Instead, cloud flooded the view, and as we lost height into the valley, the landslide-scarred path reinforced our thoughts that rain was likely to be a theme of our traverse.

In spite of the bruised sky, sweat poured profusely from my skin, stinging my eyes and drying my mouth. With our hopes of rehydration pinned on the Dranse Rivière, we were disappointed to find that its waters were the colour of milk.

'I've devised a weight-loss programme,' I announced, breaking the silence as we left the torrent empty-handed and passed through a string of hamlets – La Plantaz, Les Clouz and Vinzier.

'Have you now?' Jake humoured. 'I really thought we had discussed everything.'

'Nope, not this. It's inspired by walking.'

'Now there's a surprise. Go on...'

'Well, I got the idea a while ago when I realised that we are basically eating absolute crap and losing weight. Sweets, cake, bread, biscuits, crisps, pastries, fatty meat – it's all terrible food, and on top of that, we hardly ever touch fruit and vegetables.'

'That's because we're burning 5,000 calories a day!' Jake interrupted.

'Exactly, so the appeal of my weight-loss programme is that you can eat whatever you want, you can have the worst diet in the world.'

'Not everyone has the time to walk across Europe, Dan.'

'I'm getting to that!' I said impatiently. 'The programme can be applied to someone with an office job, or a teacher, or anyone – that's what's so good about it. So, just like us, they can only go shopping once every few days. But they won't be allowed to top up until the next big shop. The trick is they have to carry the supplies in a rucksack wherever they go. Vehicles can only be used if the distance is truly insurmountable, in which case an additional walk would be required as a forfeit. Water is allowed at any time. The pounds would fall off!' I triumphed.

'So, an office worker would have to wear their pack to meetings and whilst they're at their desk?' Jake queried.

'Exactly.'

'That's stupid,' Jake concluded, abruptly ending the conversation.

We eventually found clear water at the Ugine River, where we filled our bottles before rising out of the valley and onto an exposed *alpage* brimming with wildflowers.

With the intention of injecting a little luxury into our first full day in the Alps, we had wrapped the leftover *croque-monsieur* from the previous day's lunch in a paper serviette. But, just like much of the sedimentary rock that had metamorphosed beneath heat and pressure to form the Alps ridgeline, the grilled ham and cheese sandwich had undergone a transformation. Half its previous size, the *croque-monsieur* was now a dense wodge of soggy bread and cheese with a sheet of fluorescent-green serviette welded to its outer layer. Unable to remove the paper, we ate the sweating sandwich regardless, feeling it thud into the pit of our bellies.

We climbed slothfully towards Mont Baron at the top of the *alpage*, rounding its base where the roots of a pine forest gripped courageously to the rock. The hour was early, but twenty kilometres lay between Mont Baron and the next patch of forest, so we decided to set up camp.

'My back's been bad today,' Jake muttered after crawling into the tent.

'Why didn't you tell me?' I urged.

'What good would it have done? We'd still have walked.'

Jake often kept quiet when he thought that vocalising the problem wouldn't remedy it, but I was a little upset he hadn't told me. 'Maybe we wouldn't have pitched Ted on a heap of tree roots and molehills in the middle of what, I can only assume, is a river gully!' I said with more care in my tone than anger.

Thunder sounded and rain fell as the afternoon turned to night, yet despite having pitched between the banks of a dry river, Jake appeared to be happy, and I drifted off to the sound of him singing Roger Miller's 'King of the Road'.

AN IRISH FRIEND

We woke to the buzzing sound of thousands of flies and the glow of sunlight on the tent. On emerging from our sleeping bags, we were glad to see that the river gully had remained dry and the skies were clear. The Dent d'Oche that had eluded us a day earlier now stood boldly to the north, its talon-like peak clawing at the sun.

We brushed past the foaming white petals of hogweed, the small sunflower heads of mountain arnica, and a mat of sparkling webs strung across buttercup-dotted grass, soon arriving at the rounded crest of Tête des Fieux.

'Mountains, mountains, mountains,' I mumbled as Jake strode out in front of me towards the edge of the flowered bulge. Falling from his feet, the land disappeared out of sight only to rise with purpose a kilometre later in pine forest and high pasture, beyond which lay the white limestone *arête* of Mont Chauffé. Staggering onwards yet further still were the jagged ridgelines of the Réserve Naturelle de Passy, and then the Mont Blanc Massif whose summits, a week's walk away, were snow-drenched and bathed in a subtle apricot hue. With our sights set, we took one last look at the villages to our north and the flat waters of Lake Geneva, and then turned with the *GR5* to the south.

Two million years of glacial erosion saw us pass from one cirque to the next, dipping in and out of the tilted bowls with banks of snow at our shoulders and lakes at our feet. On a particularly tough scramble through boulders and loose rubble, we spotted the silhouette of a chamois standing in the gap of Les Portes d'Oche (1,937 metres). An eagle called and, when we reached the pass, the chamois had gone.

'Stay there,' I said to Jake before running off into the next sweeping basin.

'Where are you going?' he called after me.

'I want to try something. Just stay there.'

Half a kilometre later at the Col de Pavis, I turned to Jake, put my hands to my mouth and shouted across the valley, 'Can you hear me?' My voice bounced from boulder to boulder, swooping around the scree slopes and down to the turquoise lake at the bed of the cirque.

'Ha!' Jake returned. 'You don't even need to shout.' He then lowered his voice. 'Danny smells.'

'I can hear you!' I replied. 'But I agree, so that's alright!'

Mountain ibex sat on a ledge high above the track, their muscular necks and curved horns cutting black into the sky. A little further along the path, there were more. At about a metre tall and the same again with their impressive headpieces, five or six males stood lethargically around a sheath of snow, dropping to their knees from time to time to lick moisture from the surface. The ibex seemed to enjoy instability, herding on steep terrain above the snowline, a lifestyle choice that was certainly less applicable to Jake and me.

The dappling of snow on the surrounding slopes gradually increased and, though it was only our second day in the mountains, a patch had slumped across the path with the midsummer heat, presenting Jake with his first taste of vertigo in the Alps.

'It wasn't too bad,' he concluded once back on dry, solid land. 'Head down, no talking, that's the trick.'

Through the afternoon, the path lost height and the skies

clouded over. We spent the night in the ski resort town of La Chapelle d'Abondance, where a thunderous *météo* report pinned to the door of the tourist information office scared us into paying for shelter. I watched the storm from the window as it crashed through trees on the valley side where we had been planning to pitch, whilst Jake lay on the bed, wrapped in a purple towel and eating streaks of Parma ham straight from the packet.

A man in a blue T-shirt and white shorts pulled high around his waist passed us early the next morning as I stopped to make notes beside the flow of the Dranse. The divine smell of outdoor living was in the air – burning wood, wildflowers, and the earthy aromas of water on rock.

Several hundred metres up the river, we bumped into the man again as he stopped at the bottom of a steep track and unclipped his walking poles from his pack. His legs were thick like tree trunks and his chest broad, whilst sunglasses sat atop a balding head of short grey hairs.

We should have guessed by the milky complexion of Kevin's skin – and perhaps, more revealingly, the green, white and orange flag jutting from his bag – that he was not a local. 'I'll join you, if you don't mind,' he said politely, with a strong Irish accent.

The path was steep and muddy, and led us up a drying wood of steaming tree roots, banked with ferns and wild strawberries. Kevin was attempting a grand traverse of the Alps just as we were, yet his intentions were far more ambitious than ours. 'I'm hoping to get there in three weeks,' he said confidently.

'Three weeks?' Jake blurted. 'It's going to take us five!'

'Well, I don't believe that for a minute,' Kevin objected. 'You're far younger than I am and you're far fitter.'

As we learnt more about Kevin, the assured optimism that he had about reaching the Mediterranean in such an impressive time gradually became more understandable: he was an adventurer and an achiever. He had hiked in Europe, Africa, South America and Antarctica, including an expedition to the South Pole, on top of which he ran his own business back in Ireland, employing seventy people. Kevin preferred to walk alone: it gave him control, and, in the event of a mishap, he liked to have only himself to blame. But, for the time being, he seemed happy with our company and keen to learn about our experiences on the path.

Immersed in conversation, I hadn't noticed the rather fatigued-looking man heading up the wooded track in front of us until we were almost upon him. 'Oh,' he wheezed as we grew rapidly closer, 'it's not often one hears an English accent in these parts.'

Now by the man's side, I realised just how exhausted he looked. With thick square glasses, swept-over brown hair and, to put it politely, an unshapely body, it was no wonder his ears were dripping with sweat and his lungs gasping for air. 'Harold,' he said with a smile, pulling a handkerchief from his pocket and wiping the perspiration from his face.

I had no doubt that it was not only Harold's physique that was making him suffer, but his attire too. His shoes had collapsed to the side – like a child who had played for too many hours in their favourite pair of trainers – and his jeans, surely an undesirable choice of clothing anyway, repeatedly dropped below his bottom, requiring him to stop every few minutes on the pathside, where a monumental hoist returned them to their intended position. However, it was Harold's pack that confused me the most: dumped crudely over his round shoulders, the straps slumped over his arms, and his hip belt flapped redundantly at his sides. 'Yep, I'm doing the GR5 too,' he said, pulling his jeans up once more.

'Really?' I retorted sincerely, although perhaps – and certainly for the best – he assumed my question to be rhetorical.

'Well, I'm doing it in four parts. This is my last, Lake Geneva to Chamonix.'

Harold was either a liar or a fine example of self-deception and perseverance. I sided with the latter, and was soon learning of his tribulations over the previous sections. 'I got chased on three separate occasions by bulls. Utterly terrifying. They appear to have something against me. I've never seen anyone else being chased by bulls. Anyway,' he continued, with a sign of relief, 'they seem more docile here in the north, so I'm happier.'

Ahead on the track, Jake and Kevin had got on to the topic of Mont Blanc, which of course Kevin had climbed a few years back.

'Oh yes, do tell us about that,' Harold called from behind me. 'Is it worth doing?'

By the time Kevin had finished his rundown of the ascent, poor old Harold had dropped off the back of our walking convoy and disappeared out of sight. We spent the rest of the day – as we wound through the cattle-trodden high pasture of Les Mattes, where shepherds called their sheep and alder shrub rooted the ground – glancing curiously over our shoulders. But no matter how far back up the path we squinted, we never saw the plodding silhouette of the determined Englishman.

Noting the increasing exposure of the path, we pulled into camp early, leaving Kevin to walk on to the Swiss Refuge de Chésery, several hours further south.

Clattering into a thicket of brushwood below the path, I followed Jake's calls, eventually emerging into a steep-sided prairie surrounded by young conifer trees. We pitched on a ledge of grass looking out over the Swiss mountains to the east.

I shed down to my boxers and lay in the sun with my head beneath the grass, surrounded by a hidden kingdom bursting with life. Ants and beetles filtered along shrunken pathways above the roots, and grasshoppers leapt from shoot to shoot. In an enchanting canopy of blue gentians, buttercups, and the fanned lilac petals of alpine asters, I watched cardinal beetles clamber, butterflies drift, and wasps spin in the air like a squadron of Red Arrows, courageous and controlled. A hoverfly lingered above the opened map that lay on my stomach, its hum, its cockpit eyes and its drifting shadow a helicopter above the two-dimensional Alps. With such a wealth of terrestrial invertebrates swarming over my near-naked body, I was surprised, and perhaps even a little disappointed, that our tick count didn't experience a sudden inflation. In fact, since leaving Lake Geneva, our tally of burrowing arthropods had stagnated entirely. My count now sat at 78 and Jake's a blood-curdling (or should I say blood-thinning) 117.

I woke in the night clutching my stomach and scrambled for the loo roll. Below a sky of dazzling stars and above the twinkling lights of a small village deep within the valley, I collapsed onto the roots of a pine tree. Desperately nauseous and no doubt as ashen as I felt, I used the trunk of the conifer to support my lurching body until I had nothing left to give.

By sunrise, we were back on the path and, after a second bout of vomiting, began to make our way through a bog of pink and purple orchids and onto the promisingly named *Sentier de*

Fantastique. Unable to stomach any food, my steps were slow and laboured and, with a pang of guilt, I found it difficult to appreciate the stillness of the Col de Chésery and its broad crest, where the sun and a mottling of globe flowers turned the hillside yellow. High above Lac Vert, whose waters were indeed green, slabs of snow dripped like overflowing gutters onto the path, their splashes cooling our ankles and wetting our boots.

On reaching the Portes de l'Hiver (2,096 metres), Jake checked the map. We had walked just eight kilometres, yet I felt like I had climbed Mont Blanc. 'What do you think it is?' I slurred to Jake, who was becoming increasingly concerned.

'I don't know. We've not eaten anything dodgy. It must've been that stream water we bottled at the farm. But, if you can't eat, you need to at least keep drinking, Dan.' He handed me a bottle.

'Now there's a double-edged sword for you,' I muttered, sipping the water and then holding it up to the light. 'It's the cure and the cause all in one.'

With eyes half shut, I followed Jake from the pass, winding down between stone farmhouses as empty ski lifts swung eerily in the breeze above our heads, leaving rippled shadows on the gullied ground.

My head was pounding, and my stomach screaming. In a bid to release a little pressure from my midriff, I loosened my hip belt, but soon found the weight on my shoulders unbearable and was forced to stop.

'Right, seeing as you're insisting on continuing, here's the plan,' Jake ordered. 'Let's cover all bases, OK? We're not drinking crap anymore, we've ridden our luck far too much as it is. Only water from fast flowing, high altitude streams and village taps is going to be bottled, and it'll all be purified. Dehydration and sunstroke will be prevented by drinking lots, wearing hats,' he pulled his from his bag and put it on his head, 'and lots of sun cream. And to rule out food poisoning, those salami sandwiches are going.'

By the time we reached Samoëns, one of the lowest alpine communes on our route, we had walked thirty-seven kilometres and fallen almost 2,000 metres – an agonising descent, far worse than a climb of equal elevation, which left our bones screaming and our muscles wrenched. I collapsed beneath a tree in the town's suburbs whilst Jake went into the centre to find supplies.

Returning some minutes later with his pack filled with fruit and bread, he hauled me to my feet before guiding me along Le Giffre River, where scores of ambling holidaymakers chattered and laughed beside the churning torrent.

'In here,' he gestured, skulking off the well-walked track and into a small patch of compact pine, their lower branches spanning the gaps between the trunks. It was a bad place to camp: a network of roots corrugated the ground, and we were clearly in some sort of holiday reserve. But I was beyond caring, and Jake knew it.

As the trees grew denser, my movements became listless. Stumbling over the rough ground, I began to slow until, soon, I was brought to a grinding halt as a loose branch swung across my route, whipping me across the face and sending my hat to the floor. I dropped my poles to the ground, gritting my teeth with exhaustion and rage. It had been one of the worst days of our walk so far. I was fatigued beyond anything I had ever experienced. Jake took my rucksack from my back, and I stood motionless in the forest, staring into the trees ahead.

Ten minutes later, I was lying on my back in the tent as the alpine thunder began to groan. It was not yet six, and through the trees I could hear the muffled voices of children playing and dogs barking. Several tears rolled slowly from my eyes, and I drifted into a blissful sleep.

ILLNESS AND THE SPECTACULAR

'Fourteen hours you slept for!' Jake grinned. 'And you really didn't hear the rain in the night?'

'Really.'

'Or the thunder? It's only just stopped!'

'Nope.'

'And you didn't hear the birds this morning? Or the kids screaming down the river on their rafts?'

'I honestly heard nothing. Maybe we should be ill more often!'

'Well, my belly's started to feel a bit odd too,' Jake said, rubbing his stomach. 'Let's hope it's just sympathy pain. Hungry?' he chirped, offering me a handful of apricots and a tub of yoghurt. 'You haven't eaten for almost forty hours.'

'Starving!'

I could only manage a couple of apricots and half a *pain au chocolat*, hardly an adequate breakfast for the 1,800 metres of ascent that lay imminently in front of us. By the end of the day we would have equalled the three weeks of accumulated ascent that we had achieved in Belgium.

'I can't think of many worse ways to commemorate our one hundredth day on the path,' I said resentfully. 'Let's just get this over with.'

Three hours later we emerged onto the northern edge of a flat valley between raised massifs and rested beneath the shade of an alder tree. Abandoned boulders, torn by glaciers from the mountainside, scattered the expansive pulpit, whilst the deep pink petals of alpenrose blushed the blanketing grass. To the east lay Tête de Villy – its rounded black ridgeline stained with the enduring snow of last winter's fall, like the hind of a Friesian cow. Whilst to the west, Tête à l'Âne – an imposing limestone *arête* – jutted 600 metres from the valley floor. Like the body of a dormant beast half buried in scree, the spine of the ridge swept southwards through the valley with a profundity and beauty that belittled us.

'That,' Jake began, 'is the best cliff face I've ever seen.'

We revelled in the flattened terrain, weaving between the scarred boulders towards a dip at the head of the valley, the Col d'Anterne. A dainty tornado of lavender butterflies corkscrewed about a warm rock, slowly dispersing as our steps grew closer and then returning as we moved on. We spotted a marmot as its bucked teeth nibbled on the sweet buttercup shoots close to its burrow, watching it raise its head from beneath the grass to inspect our threat level before returning to its feast.

But as the sky turned from blue to grey and the first few drops of rain began to fall, the marmots backed up into their lairs and the butterflies were gone. The downpour came as we made our way along the flooded shorelines of Lac d'Anterne. Dozens of burst streams fed the lake, leaving us with little choice but to wade through the channels, soaking our feet. We were now amongst snow and ice. A chute of water broke from beneath the freeze, plunging over the lip of a gully and into a chasm below, whilst the slopes that flanked the steepening path were damaged with the trails of rockfalls. We followed a line of footprints through the snow, with each step forward slipping a little back, finally arriving at the Col d'Anterne (2,257 metres) after almost two kilometres of vertical ascent.

'There it is,' Jake said, his eyes fixed to the south. 'It's so close.' In front of us stood the Massif des Aiguilles Rouges, a succession of needle-like peaks rising in the north-east with the Col de Montets and falling in the west with Le Brévent. Beyond that lay the crags, the glaciers and the muscular deltoids of Aiguille du Midi, Mont Maudit, Aiguille du Goûter, and the White Mountain, Mont Blanc.

Jake spotted a band of light scrub at the foot of the valley, and within a couple of hours we were lying in our sleeping bags with the porch door open gazing up at the summit of Mont Blanc. We had found a small patch of boggy heath – seasoned with orchids, daisies and cotton grass – between a scattering of stunted alder and mountain ash.

Both feeling out of sorts, we ate our dinner of mashed potato and soup, quietly watching a busy wagtail as the clouds migrated across the sky.

At some point in the night, we woke and unzipped the tent. The skies had cleared, and a full moon sat above the White Mountain and its neighbours. In the low light, the crests appeared unintimidating and humble.

LE BRÉVENT

Our Casios beeped at 5am, and we got ready in the dark before continuing deeper into the soundless valley, where the pinched heads of the dandelions were yet to wake. Rather spoiling the serenity of the morning, and without warning, I was forced to drop my pack and run into the bushes where I quickly learnt that the symptoms of my illness had not abated like I had hoped.

We reached the base of the valley as the light strands of cloud above our heads turned pink, and crossed the turbulent waters of La Diosaz Rivière, stepping onto the toes of the Massif des Aiguilles Rouges. My eyes followed a rocky track up the western side of the range, where it gradually faded into a muddle of bluffs and boulders.

A gentle breeze ushered us up the slope, through pockets of warm and cold air, over springing streams, and by slabs of snow whose crimpled edges reminded me of the curve of a child's paper fan. The path grew steeper, passing foraging marmots and the clashing, silhouetted horns of a herd of chamois high on the rock above us, until eventually, at 2,368 metres, we crested the snowy Col du Brévent where Mont Blanc sat imposingly on the opposite side of the valley. The peaks of the massif were pure and white, whilst their guts spewed with stained glaciers, churning waterfalls and sweeping ravines.

'Five million steps for this view,' I said, feeling a lump rise into my throat. Jake had climbed to the top of a stone cairn to the south of the small col and seemed quiet and contemplative, so I abandoned the rest of my calculations and joined him.

We sat for some time.

I led Jake the wrong way off the col along a thin ridge after spotting a rusted ladder in the rock ahead. By the time I reached the corroded metal, I realised my error and turned to inform Jake, only to see that he wasn't behind me. With the improvised path dropping steeply away on either side, I quickly realised the precariousness of the situation. Unclipping my bag and pushing it into a jagged nook, I scrambled back down the southern face, soon finding Jake clinging to the rock, breathing heavily as sweat poured from his face. 'I can't move. Help me, Dan.'

With one hand secure on the granite and my boots wedged into a fissure, I reached down and grabbed Jake's pack, heaving him up onto a platform beside my shoulder. 'I'm sorry, Jake,' I said as he collapsed onto the ledge. 'We took a wrong turn.'

From our vantage point, we could see a muddied path above the snow running around the base of the ridge. 'Now that looks like a safer option,' Jake announced as his composure returned.

Descending across a steep slope of lichen-painted gneiss, we soon joined the track and followed it up the side of the mountain towards the 2,525-metre peak of Le Brévent.

The summit was brimming with crowds of people. We found a step amongst the throng and unlaced our shoes, drying the sweat from their soles in the sun as the sound of the loaded cable cars clunked rhythmically to our sides.

From the hubbub of outdoor enthusiasts, it was clear that we were not far from Chamonix. Known by some as 'the mountaineering capital of the world', and to others as 'the death-sport capital of the world', Chamonix sounded like a town populated with expensive beds, both hotel and hospital, neither of which we had any intention of visiting. Instead, our sights were set on Les Houches, Chamonix's unassuming neighbour and birthplace of Marie Paradis, a poor maid and servant who, in the early nineteenth century, humbly became the first female to climb Mont Blanc.

A descent of 1,500 metres took us down a stony track, shadowed by the canopies of a dozen paragliders, towards an elongated sprawl of infrastructure at the foot of the valley. The path was well used despite the hard-working cable car, and we nodded at the continuous stream of hikers, mentally congratulating them as they puffed resolutely in the opposite direction. In fact, there were so many people using the route that we spent much of the descent stepping awkwardly to the side of the precarious track whilst groups of children, old-age pensioners and even a chihuahua marched enthusiastically past. (It's worth noting that, although the chihuahua did seem to be finding the climb surprisingly easy, it was being carried by its owner.)

With our knees and ankles on the brink of turning to dust, we were relieved to reach the valley floor, greeted by an obstacle course of thoroughfares – the Chemin de Fer tourist railway, L'Arve River and the pulsating E25 motorway – that took us noisily into Les Houches.

It was a town under construction. Yet, ignoring the cranes, the clanging girders and the pneumatic drills, it was a spectacular place to spend a night – an alpine cliché of wooden chalets overshadowed by snowy *aiguilles,* where there were as many pairs of walking poles as there were legs, and as many hotels as there were walking poles. Jake must have agreed for, within two minutes of our arrival, he had found a cheap hotel at the far end of town.

Our room was much the same as the facade of the building: made entirely of wood and more unpleasant, on closer inspection, than first impressions suggested. Thankfully, we were used to washing and toileting in the forest, so the curious absence of a bath plug (which we overcame by bunging the drain with our Shammy cloth) and the non-existence of toilet paper (which we solved by looting the downstairs lavatories) didn't prove too much of an issue.

*

240

With my belly sounding like an old plumbing system, churning and bubbling until the pipes could take no more, we were forced to stay in Les Houches for two days. I spent the majority of the forty-eight hours staring at the Artex on the wall opposite the toilet: like a winter snowstorm, the plaster stippled and swirled around buried cabin roofs and the humps of mountain peaks. For every fifteen minutes that I was on the toilet, I had one minute off, giving me just enough time to reach my bed, at which point I would swivel quickly back towards the loo. I summed up the experience by jotting a few notes into my journal: 'Ill, bored, frustrated; toilet, bed, toilet, bed, toilet, bed. Chased two flies around the room. Stubbed my toe. Toilet, bed, toilet, bed. Flies pissed off to annoy other resting walkers. Toilet.'

'How did it go?' I asked Jake after he returned from a trip to the pharmacy.

'Good and bad.' He threw another handful of toilet paper onto the bed.

'In what way?'

'Well, they didn't speak English,' he replied, with a little bitterness in his voice. 'Which is odd, considering that the mountaineering capital of the world is literally five kilometres down the road. Anyway, I got the drugs.' He handed me a pack of Imodium and another of Nifuroxazide.

'What happened?' I couldn't tell if Jake was ashamed, embarrassed or upset, but something was wrong.

'They made me act it out.'

'Act what out?'

'They couldn't speak English, could they, and my French isn't the best, so they made me, you know, act out what the problem was.'

'Oh!' I said sympathetically, trying to hold back the laughter.

'And, trust me, when your panel comprises three pharmacists and a shop full of customers, it's not as much fun as charades with Nan and Gramps at Christmas.'

FREEDOM TO CAMP

'Great!' Jake declared, switching the mobile phone off and tucking it back into his bag. 'Phil's coming in a few days. He wants to walk too!'

After spending a day on the trail with us back in England, Phil was keen to sample more. Jake had first met Phil – a man of adventure and experimentation, with a bushy head of hair and bountiful energy – at Aberystwyth University on the rough and rugged west coast of Wales when they were both nineteen. After realising that they shared interests – exploring the surrounding countryside, playing football, and running unclothed up and down Aberystwyth's seafront promenade – it was clear that friendship was only a matter of time.

With enough food for three days, we hoped to be in Landry, one of the few towns en route with a train station, just in time to meet Phil and make another resupply.

'Is there a shop in Landry?' I asked the curly-haired man behind the desk at the Les Houches *office de tourisme*.

'Should be,' he said vaguely, flexing large biceps as he stretched his arms behind his head.

'OK,' I replied, a little dissatisfied with his ambiguity. 'And what about Montchavin? Is there a shop there?'

'There should be.'

'We need to resupply on food somewhere in that area. Can you look on your machine?' I pointed at the computer in front of him. 'All we need is a small supermarket, or a shop.'

'Nah, I'm pretty sure there should be a shop.'

'Great,' I said, 'you've been very helpful.'

Thankfully, however, our frustrations with the ambiguous information clerk were short-lived, and within a few seconds he had us back on his side. 'You know, if you're above 1,600 metres and you're caught out in the dark, you're allowed to pitch your tent out in the mountains for the night. You won't get into trouble.'

'Really?' Jake beamed, before adopting a more austere expression. 'I mean, not that we were planning to be caught out, but we can camp anywhere?'

'Sure, why not, right?'

It seemed quite clear to Jake and me that the clerk's repertoire of knowledge was not so much based on written rules but hearsay from a mate of a mate. Nonetheless, we took his guidance gladly, grateful for the peace of mind that a representative of the tourism authority had just granted us permission to camp pretty much wherever we pleased.

By dropping into the Chamonix Valley our path had united with the Tour de Mont Blanc, a 170-kilometre circuit of the Mont Blanc Massif, and arguably the most popular long-distance hike in Europe. We had thought about adding the loop onto our journey – Gabrielle and Yannick, along with our granddad, had talked so highly of it – but within minutes of joining the path, and with an ample injection of walkers' snobbery, we were ready to leave it.

'Honestly,' I complained as we reached the Col de Voza (1,650 metres) on Mont Blanc's western aspect, 'it's not the same with all these people.'

'A few days ago, you said you loved the fact that everyone was enjoying the outdoors!' Jake objected. 'You were even glad to see that chihuahua, and you hate chihuahuas. The ugliest dogs on the planet you called them!'

'They are ugly! But, yes, you're right, I'm a serial hypocrite,' I confessed. 'I think I was being a little ignorant. From far away, Mont Blanc just looked a little more...remote, I guess. You couldn't see all this.' A tram chugged to a halt beside a restaurant in the middle of the col, emitting teams of excited climbers, each with ropes around their shoulders and a helmet clipped to their pack.

On a clear summer's day, such as the day was, the Mont Blanc summit feels the feet of more than 200 people. In fact, it was likely, as we weaved between the circles of chatter, that there were more climbers in our current view than we had seen on our entire journey. And it wasn't only the slopes that were overloaded, but the skies too. Paragliders swung through the trees whilst scenic flight tours and the chopping blades of resupply helicopters blemished the air.

I was still having problems eating, and knew that the banana sandwich I had struggled through earlier in the day wouldn't get me much further. We were therefore relieved, after grinding out an arduous twenty kilometres, to see the camper van rooftops of Le Camping Pontet, just south of Les Contamines-Montjoie.

For many of the people embarking on the Tour de Mont Blanc, Le Pontet was the first scheduled overnight stop. We were early and, though the campsite was already brimming with tents, we were able to find a nice spot beside a bench and beneath a larch tree.

Not far behind were the Scouts. Young, noisy and enlivened, the teenagers seemed too old to have their shirts stitched with symbols, and their cream shorts pulled high. Indeed, a large number of the group had beards.

Then there was the 'Lone Ranger', old and wise, quiet and content. I watched as he carefully considered the lay of the grass, the angle of the sun, and, most importantly, the point furthest from any other tent. Satisfied with a patch at the far end of the site, the Lone Ranger unrolled his shelter, and then crawled inside for a nap.

It must have been quite a shock for the poor chap when he woke an hour later to find that his small segment of peace and quiet had been turned into something quite the opposite: the 'Quechuans' had arrived.

The Quechuans, as Jake and I referred to them, were a breed of trekker attracted to the temptations of the low-cost and easy-to-assemble nature of a Quechua Shelter. In the event of snow, wind, rain or low temperatures, it would have been more comfortable sleeping on the horns of a chamois than between the walls of one of these pop-up tents. But, as it was, the sun shone, and as the tents sprang cheerfully out of their bags and into an upright position, I thought them to be rather appealing. The Lone Ranger, I observed, must have felt otherwise. Rising from his slumber, he stood amongst the community of bulbous blue tents – like a field of giant bubble wrap – and considered his options. Decisively, he dropped back into his shelter, where he grabbed a bottle of wine and a pipe before making his way across the lawn to a solitary tree. With his head against the trunk, he lit his pipe and then began to drink solemnly from the bottle.

Walkers' midnight, it seemed, was a term little used in Le Camping Pontet. It wasn't until 11pm that a group of screaming children stopped kicking their plastic football against our tent, and the Scouts, despite their impressive plethora of colourful badges and their apparent transference into manhood, seemed ill-practised in 'helping others', being 'courteous', and remaining 'clean in thought, word and deed'. Instead, they sat themselves on the bench two metres from our heads, yelling, blaspheming and howling with laughter until the early hours of the morning.

*

Since the downpour at the Tête à l'Âne a few days earlier, the air temperature had been gradually increasing, and in spite of our early start and the shade of the river gorge, I could feel sweat dripping from my brow onto my arms. We rose onto a track between *alpages* of cotton grass and grazing cattle, joining a string of hikers that pushed and pulled up the slope towards the Col du Bonhomme (2,329 metres).

We had only walked about thirty kilometres since joining the Tour de Mont Blanc, yet we already felt acquainted with many of the ramblers around us: the young women with the baguettes, the pale-skinned, inexperienced English couple, the old man who slalomed along the track so as to ease the angle, even when it was flat, and the super fit French siblings who didn't sweat or smile. But, despite the pleasant nods of recognition dished out as they passed us and we them, Jake and I were glad to reach the ridgeline of Crêtes des Gittes, where the Tour de Mont Blanc swung north to scale the eastern peaks of the massif and the *GR5* continued on south.

'I think it's safe to say I won't be coming back to France to finish the Mont Blanc Circuit,' Jake said as we began to climb up the backbone of the Crêtes des Gittes.

'No, you're right, definitely off the bucket list,' I agreed. 'Unless, of course, there is some sort of nationwide ban on Scouts walking the path. Then I might consider it!'

By the time we had reached the blade of the ridge, the path had narrowed to just a couple of feet, falling acutely away on either side. Thick with snow and ice, we edged along the slender crest with braced bodies and timid steps, as the wind swirled up from the pits of the valleys.

Whilst Jake struggled with his vertigo, too terrified even to talk, I spotted a familiar sight at the opposite end of the *arête*: the green, white and orange flickers of an Irish tricolour.

'I thought it was you two up on the ridge,' Kevin said with a grin as he sat on a bench outside the wooden walls of the Refuge du Plan de la Lai sipping on a beer. 'No one else has got bags that big!'

Jake looked like he had only just recovered from the ordeal and shook his head weakly from side to side. 'It was horrible, Kevin. I thought I was going to fall.'

'I thought you might have a problem, Jake. I loved it though!' He took another gulp of beer.

It turned out that Kevin had also taken a day off in Les Houches, spending the rest of his nights in the conveniently placed *refuges* and *gîtes* that had dotted the path.

'They're alright,' Kevin said as we quizzed him on the accommodation. 'Food's great! Problem is they're busy, and for someone who likes their own space, it's hard to get away from the more sociable walkers. They'll find you no matter where you hide. There's one chap, a guy from Cambridge, who seems very nice and all, but he moans and moans and moans.'

'About what?'

'Anything he can really,' Kevin laughed, checking over his shoulder for fear of being overheard. 'He wants it all to be entirely natural, everything! He doesn't like the roads, the planes, the *refuges* – even though he sleeps in them – and he hates the ski lifts. Yes, the ski lifts get him very vexed. But we're not the only ones enjoying the mountains. What about the skiers, the snowboarders, the mountain bikers? The alpine economy would be buggered if it wasn't for the ski lifts.' All around him, plates of succulent salads, spiced potatoes, and meats were being brought to the table. 'Do you boys want a beer?'

'Don't tempt us,' Jake replied. 'We want to get to the mountain before dark.'

I turned and stared up the path, following it with my eyes as it bent and undulated through a mass graveyard of limestone slabs that jutted a hundred metres from the ground before climbing towards the pyramidal peak of Aiguille du Grand Fond.

'Thirty-six minutes,' Jake said in the morning, pointing at his Casio. 'That's how long it takes to pack our lives away.' We had slept at the bottom of a damp slate-fall overlooking the turquoise waters of Lac de Roselend, and began the day with cold noses and ears. The crimson sky led us south, past spying marmots and the cruising silhouette of a golden eagle, before losing its colour to the rising sun. Scarves of waterfalls draped down the mountainsides, their velocity turning them as white as snow, and their echo sounding across the valley like 10,000 chirping swifts.

At 2,469 metres, after clambering up a rubble slope overshadowed by turrets of metamorphic rock, we arrived at the Col du Bresson, where a young Italian family threw snowballs and a stiff breeze blew. To the south, the view was vast: dipping into the Vallée de la Tarentaise before soaring with the peaks of the Parc National de la Vanoise, and, beyond that, the Piedmont region of Italy.

Led by the Ormente River, we lost height into the Tarentaise basin, from time to time passing slumps of snow that lay across the turbulent water. Spotting a particularly large heap, we dropped down to the flow and peered beneath the structure. Despite the obstacle, the river continued to run, carving out an underground ice cave large enough to park a London bus. The walls and ceiling were textured with ribs and dimples that dripped with water and fragments of ice.

Jake walked into the cavity and brushed his hand against the wall. 'I don't understand how this is still here. It's so bloody hot.'

A shard of snow detached itself from the entrance and crashed into the river beside me. 'Well, it's definitely on its way out. Let's go before we get axed by a lump of ice,' I urged.

Between the sunken slate roofs of Forand, Les Fours and La Lance lay banks of primrose-yellow foxgloves, deep blue spring gentians, and the rubbing thighs of a thousand grasshoppers. The decrepit sheds soon grew larger, and by the time we reached Valezan, a beautiful village of hilly streets, flowered gardens and fruiting cherry trees, we were amongst grand farmsteads where the clinking sounds of cooking escaped through the open windows.

We ducked our heads into the village *lavoir* and splashed the backs of our knees before pushing on into the base of the valley and up the other side, where a 500-metre ascent took us through Montorlin and towards the mountaintop village of Montchavin (1,250 metres).

After collecting some supplies from the village store, we were directed to a campsite, where a woman with a husky voice and grinning eyes walked us through the grounds. The heat of the day was quite something, and I was not the least bit surprised as we passed a thermometer on the wall of the toilets to see the mercury sitting proudly above 40°C.

'*C'est Mont Blanc,*' the lady announced, distracting us from the temperature gauge as she pointed north. '*Et ici,*' she continued, boastfully raising her eyebrows and swinging her arm to the east, '*c'est l'Italie. C'est magnifique, non?*'

'*Oui, c'est magnifique,*' I agreed.

With my eyes failing to adjust to the darkness, I grappled at the tent door, terrified that death was upon us. The trampling grew louder and my panic stronger. Finally, the zip dislodged from its buckle, and I exploded from the tent onto the wet grass outside. All was quiet. Below in the valley, the lights of Landry glimmered, disturbed only by the subtle lunar rainbow that encompassed the moon above. I looked left and right, only then realising that the dozen or so charging giraffes that had somehow managed to find themselves in the depths of the French Alps were in fact a creation of my subconscious.

'What's up?' Jake whispered after I had slipped back into my sleeping bag and zipped up the tent.

'Giraffes. But it's OK, I scared them off.'

'Right. Night then.'

By the time we reached Landry train station at the bottom of the valley, it was midday. Not a thing moved, save for a ball of tumbleweed that bounced up the track with a hot wind that left my throat dry.

At 12.10pm, a train hooted and the rails began to rattle. The first three carriages were empty, but as the wheels ground to a halt and the doors cranked open, a tall, bearded figure with rosy cheeks and dark hair appeared in the doorway of the fourth carriage.

'An English paper!' Jake snatched the newspaper from within the roll mat attached to Phil's pack and turned straight to the sports page.

'Well, hello to you too,' Phil said in a deep voice, before bellowing with laughter.

'Ready for some mountains?' I asked, stuffing a bag of Golden Delicious apples into his side pocket.

'I guess I'll have to be, seeing as you guys have already assigned me the role of Sherpa!'

In the time that Jake and I had known Phil, he had done many things that most people would consider unwise: he had cycled naked through the streets of Brighton; stuck a safety pin through the lobe of his ear; and, in the latter years of his higher education, ate a droplet of sheep excrement, subsequently making him host to a rather nasty organism known as campylobacter pylori (although, in his defence, he didn't know it was sheep excrement).

But alongside his long list of daring endeavours, Phil was also a man of endurance. In 2011, accompanied by two wheels, some panniers and a rather large pair of thighs, Phil cycled for sixty-three days from San Francisco to Manhattan, covering thirteen states and 5,000 kilometres. Having proven himself through the barren central states of the US with nothing but a bike for company, Jake and I were interested to see how Phil would fare climbing through the European Alps. Was it merely a case of adapting, or were our ventures incomparable challenges tuned finely to a particular mind and body?

As misfortune would have it, Phil's first day on the trail comprised two testing factors: a 1,000-metre ascent through the Ponturin river valley and searing heat. The unfamiliar wind that we had felt earlier in the day had strengthened, and so too had the clouds that now began to fill the sky between the deep valley walls. With tiring legs and a great unwillingness to pitch in the rain, we began to search for a tent site.

'*Vous campez ce soir?*' a mother and her two children questioned after stopping us on the track.

'*Oui.*'

'*Attention!* There is a thunderstorm coming. You are scared, no?' she said, concern in her voice.

'Now we are,' Phil chuckled.

The mother frowned. '*C'est dangereux, attention,*' she said before putting her arms around her children and continuing on down the path.

After some time searching, we found a hilly spot amongst thinly packed pine. Through the gaps in the trees and across the valley to the east were the decisive peaks of Mont Pourri and Dôme de la Sache. The upper reaches of the mountains dripped with glaciers, each emitting half a dozen chutes of water that toppled over the rock ledges and into the Ponturin River beneath.

It was the steepest pitch we had made since leaving Bristol. In a bid to counter the slope, we piled our rucksacks and clothes at the foot end of the tent, a surprisingly effective strategy that saw us sleep comfortably through the night. Phil, on the other hand, was to have quite a different experience.

Never one to overindulge, Phil had assumed that a trip to

Southern France in the middle of the summer would be a fair-weather experience. He had thus brought what could only be described as minimalistic sleeping items.

'That's not a bivouac!' Jake laughed.

Phil looked up from the ground where he was preparing his bed. 'What's not?'

'You said you were bringing a bivouac.'

'I *have* brought a bivouac!' He stood up and pointed at his bed on the floor.

'That's not a bivouac!'

'What do you mean?'

'That's a plastic bag! It's not a bivouac!'

'It's kind of a bivouac.'

'Are you going to sleep in that?'

'Well, it's more of a base layer, you know, to stop the water from the ground getting me wet.' Phil crouched to the floor, climbed into his sleeping bag, and after a little rearranging, let out a satisfied sigh. 'This is the way to do it – the tree canopies swaying, the waterfalls, the stars. Beautiful.'

It was 4am when I woke to thunder. I opened my eyes and saw a flash of lightning bounce around the tent walls. Rain began to fall.

'You alright, Phil?' I called out a few minutes later as the storm intensified.

Through the resounding rain, I could just make out a muffled reply: 'Yeah...'

When morning came, the sound of tapping droplets still rang out on the flysheet, and I pulled the door open to reveal the sodden outline of a suction-packed Phil. At some point in the night, he had wriggled into the plastic bag, which I now noticed had been repaired in several places with crosses of black duct tape. Having consumed his air supply, the bag clung devotedly to his body and was puddled with rainwater. I was relieved, after a small poke, to see the body move.

The gradient of the path eased onto a glaciated valley of stranded boulders and scattered larch between swirls of black rock and white snow. Threads of water poured from the mountain spires that appeared and disappeared with the dynamism of the cloud. Visibility was low, and the network of ambiguous trails that cut the landscape was impeding our route-finding.

By 9am, we were soaked through to the marrow and unsure of our whereabouts. Through the thickening mist, we caught sight of a silhouetted figure on a nearby rock ledge. Hooded and motionless, the statue appeared to be watching us as we struggled through the weather, but once we got to within shouting distance, he turned slowly and disappeared into the fog.

After another hour of speculative turns, a second shape appeared through the translucence. 'I think we're on track,' Jake shouted from within his hood. 'It looks like a *refuge*.'

We peered in through the small porthole windows of the hut. Warmly lit and heated by a crackling fire, the *refuge* was filled with stranded walkers who seemed quite happy conversing by the flames with pots of tea and saucers of soup on the burning stove. Jake and I could see that Phil was tempted, as we were too, but knew that if we stopped we would never leave. I pulled the compass from my bag.

'The col is that way.' A Frenchman pointed through the thick cloud after spotting us analysing the map beneath the shelter of the porch. We thanked him and then continued on as the gusts increased, reaching the Col du Palet (2,652 metres) a few minutes later where my teeth chattered and my breaths grew deeper.

The cold had thrust me into a foul mood, and I marched ahead of Jake and Phil who, despite the impenetrable cloud, had slowed to absorb the view from the col.

'You could have just put your trousers on,' Jake remarked as we lost height, making our way into the modern ski town of Tignes le Lac.

'I don't have any! And, at any rate, we haven't worn trousers once. I'm hardly going to do it with just a few weeks left!'

None of us were particularly enjoying the morning, and with a hint of guilt, we all agreed that 10.30am was a reasonable time to begin looking for a place to stay. Embracing the laziness of our ten-kilometre day, we checked into the first hotel we could find, spent sixty-five euros on fresh fruit and vegetables, and then finished a bottle of Old Nick rum before the sun had gone down.

OVER THE APEX

Our walk in the rain the previous day had seen us enter the Parc National de la Vanoise, an area dominated by the Massif de la

251

Vanoise and celebrated for its diversity – scree slopes and moraines, glaciers and snowfields, moors and wetlands, pinewoods and meadows. Our path was to follow an S-bend through the park, kissing the Italian border, before meeting Modane, a town to the south of the Vanoise known for its transport links – most notably the Fréjus Road Tunnel, connecting Modane to the Italian town of Bardonecchia. Phil needed to be back in England by the weekend, meaning we had three days to get to the town.

On two wheels, each no wider than twenty-five millimetres, Phil's balance was impeccable. An assumption would have led you to believe that such accomplished balance was a transferable skill. It wasn't. Within a few hours of leaving Tignes, he had racked up as many stumbles as Jake and I had since leaving England, miraculously steering clear of harm's way. However, as we navigated around the high pasture of the Pointe du Lavachet, amongst grazing horses and beneath the emerging sun, a particularly hazardous section of the path saw Phil twist his knee awkwardly between two rocks.

With all-year-round snow, ski towns in the Vanoise are plentiful, and we soon arrived at Val-d'Isère where, thanks to the dangers of the surrounding slopes, we were spoilt for medical choice.

Phil stepped out of the *pharmacie* with a broad grin on his face. 'I'm officially a long-distance hiker now!' he rejoiced, yanking a newly purchased white support up his thick calf and around his knee.

We left the town alongside the Isère River and began our ascent up the northern face of the Col de l'Iseran. Holding up the back of our three-man convoy, I couldn't help but find amusement that between six knees, three were strapped with braces. To passers-by, we must have looked like the walking wounded or, perhaps less courageously, a trio of attention-seeking hypochondriacs.

Unfortunately for Phil, his woes were not over, and it wasn't long before the path delivered its next blow: blisters.

'Boots off,' Jake ordered, retrieving the medical kit from his bag. Small fluid-filled bulges populated Phil's feet, whilst the tops of his toes were raw and bleeding. Thankfully, with a high pain threshold, Phil was happy to continue walking, and after crowning the col – at 2,770 metres, the zenith of our walk – we sank into the Val d'Arc, where blankets of violet-coloured meadow cranesbill veiled the mountain slopes, and young marmots wobbled tentatively from their burrows.

'I think I might need some sun cream,' Phil suggested between conversations as the afternoon sun dropped below the protection of our caps. Holding out his arms and twisting his legs to reveal the backs of his calves, I saw that Phil's skin had taken on a dangerously vivid crimson tone. He slapped on a handful of cream and, in spite of the air temperature which now lay somewhere in the mid-thirties, then pulled on his only long-sleeved garment – a thick cotton hoodie.

We spent the night amongst a band of hazel trees rooted to the banks of the Arc River, and then continued on the following day under radiating skies, pitching at a campsite twenty kilometres downstream in Sollières-l'Envers. When morning came, a glance at the map revealed that we had surplus time to get to Modane.

Our pace slowed. We sat on a beach of schist and quartzite pebbles beside the Arc River, skimming stones across the braided channels as we discussed pop music, Tony Blair, colossal squids, and, quite dispiritingly, the reaction society would exhibit when told that, by the end of the month, the world would explode. We ate melon amongst the colourful market stalls of Lanslevillard, then left the town to the west, passing the red and yellow marquee of the Cirque Atlas and its band of camels, llamas and a lonely donkey.

Le Verney, a little further downstream, was no different from any of the other alpine communes we had seen. It had the usual display of geraniums, tarnished window shutters, and a stone *lavoir*. But after spotting a wooden bench in the shade of a small cobbled square, we found ourselves stopping in the village for some time. A man with wellington boots and dirt on his clothes filled his watering can in the town's fountain, and two children rattled by on a plastic scooter, narrowly missing an old lady as she stepped slowly down the street. '*Ooh la la!*' she cried, before breaking into an affectionate smile.

'It's tough,' Phil said after I quizzed him on his thoughts of the experience so far. 'But I don't think I've shamed myself too much. Of course, my body might suggest otherwise – the first-degree burns on my hands, arms, legs and ankles, the knee, the bleeding toes and all that – but I'm enjoying it.'

'What was it like when you cycled across the United States?' Jake asked.

'Well, the snow on my bare knees was pretty horrible! Some days were good, others weren't.'

'Were you immersed in the challenge – the lifestyle of cycling?' I probed.

'I think I was. Particularly some of the middle stretches through barren, featureless Nebraska, when I was cycling dawn 'til dusk and camping in thickets, and only meeting the odd few people in diners – I really got into the swing of things. I didn't see a single other cyclist in the entire state! I find it difficult to work out how I occupied my mind. Fifty miles would go by, in misty cornfields, identical towns with grain elevators and windmills and roads that never turned, and I think my mind was almost asleep, just awake enough to turn the pedals, like a dolphin – if Flipper could cycle. Make sense?'

'Totally.'

We dropped into Modane through the dust of the marble works on the northern fringes of town. A series of roads and train lines frayed across the valley floor, calmed only by the presence of the Arc River that had been channelised to accommodate the town.

We had hoped to celebrate our completion of the Vanoise with a kebab or a greasy burger, but after finding a campground on the northern flanks of the valley with a view of the Fort du Replaton, we cooked a saucepan of gnocchi and watched the sun go down.

The company of another walker – the refreshing conversation and observations, and even the tone of a new voice – had proven a welcome distraction from the trials of our journey. But as Phil said goodbye and disappeared off down the hill to the station, we began to feel our focus and eagerness for the path return.

Under the dimming light, we watched an old man with a proud belly creak awkwardly from his Challenger Campervan. Wearing nothing but a pair of small black Speedos, with a saucepan in one hand and a colander in the other, he hobbled over to a nearby tree and drained the pasta over its roots. Returning to his camper van, he climbed back up the steps, took one last look at the darkening sky, and swung the door shut.

'Just the sea left now,' Jake mused as a Mediterranean-scented breeze flittered through his hair.

10

Modane to Menton

2,458 to 2,843 kilometres from home

SPIRITUAL

I brushed my teeth in front of the mirror as 'Stayin' Alive' by the Bee Gees rang out from tinny speakers in the corner of the washroom. The sun and wind had cracked my lips, my chin was bushy with hair, and dirt lay in the wrinkles around my eyes – I looked weathered and unfamiliar.

There were other changes too. We had finally grown sick of the cured sausage baguettes that had been at the heart of our diet for months, and moved on to jam sandwiches. The taste was refreshing, and we were appreciative of the opportunity to eat a little fruit, even if it was submerged in buckets of sugar. The scroggin had also evolved, now containing muesli, foam bananas, pumpkin seeds, and a handful of blue and pink sweets that tasted, quite disturbingly, of washing powder. But, perhaps most prominently, we had begun to notice a change in the path. Hints of the shifting climate flecked the alpine landscape: grasshoppers sprang from the arid ground, lizards bathed by the trackside, and the smell of baking larch resin filled the air.

'Interesting-looking chap.' Jake nodded his head towards a man with a silver ponytail who had slept in a bivouac close to our tent. 'He looks kind of spiritual, doesn't he?' His rough and wrinkled skin, the colour and sheen of a well-polished table, was covered with a moth-eaten, sun-faded T-shirt and a pair of dusty white Bermuda shorts. We watched him as he left the campsite under the weight of a modest and well-worn terracotta pack. He walked with a lengthy stride and his chin held high, and in his right grip was a hand-carved wooden walking stick that fluttered with feathers. There was something powerful about the man, no doubt aided by his wizard's staff, and we had the distinct feeling that it wouldn't be long before our paths crossed again.

The *météo* outside the Modane *office de tourisme* predicted several days of clear skies and relentless heat. But, for every 200 metres that we gained alongside the Ruisseau du Charmaix and up through the valley towards the Col de la Vallée Étroite, one degree was knocked from the air. Eventually, at 2,434 metres, we crested the pass, where a pleasant atmosphere of no more than 25°C cooled our perspiring skin.

The climb to the col had been steep, and one of incident. Midway up the valley, after passing the hamlet of Les Herbiers, Jake had been forced to stop by an unwelcome infliction of chafing high in his groin. He smothered the spot with Vaseline and we continued on. However, after no more than 500 metres, he came to a standstill for a second time. 'It's not working! What should I do? It's really painful.'

I shrugged my shoulders pitifully, unable to think of a suitable remedy.

Jake unpacked the first-aid kit and, in an act of experimental desperation, picked out several plasters that he proceeded to apply to the areas of abrasion. Much to my surprise, and Jake's delight, the operation was a success, and we were able to continue unhindered until lunch.

On the grass of a flowery meadow, we looked lethargically down upon a dammed section of the Ruisseau du Charmaix, finishing a jam baguette each before starting on a bag of carrots. A cyclist appeared at the water, parking his bike against the banked stones and untying his laces. Gradually, the layers fell away until soon he was down to just his tan lines, at which point he waded into the pool and began to wash with a small flannel.

'He must know we're here,' Jake whispered.

'Perhaps that's why he's doing it. He's an exhibitionist?'

Having focused on his face and armpits for several minutes, the man switched his concentration to the less accessible parts of his body, contorting into unusual positions as he delved for a nook here and a cranny there. He washed with vigour and precision, swivelling his hips to create the optimum stance, whilst every now and then refreshing the flannel with a decisive dunk and a wringing of the cloth.

'Look!' Jake's posture elevated with excitement. Unbeknown to the cyclist, who was now thrashing enthusiastically at his bare bottom, a second man had surfaced on the path beside the dam. 'He's really been caught now.' Much to our surprise, and indeed disappointment, neither party seemed at all fazed by the encounter, and the hygiene assault continued whilst the pair exchanged pleasantries.

By the time we were down to the stumps of our carrots, the second man had moved on, and the cyclist was reluctantly stepping back into his clothes. Entertainment over, we called an end to the lazy lunch and hoisted our bags onto our backs.

'I don't believe it!' Jake said, tapping me on the shoulder. 'Look!' Despite redressing moments earlier, the cyclist was once again bare-skinned and splashing about in the water with as much enthusiasm, if not more, than he had the first time. 'Some people really love bath time,' Jake concluded, treading onto the stony path and marching off up the hill.

We left the Col de la Vallée Étroite via its southern aspect, winding into a deep basin lipped at its west by the turtle-backed peak of Mont Thabor (3,178 metres) and to its east by Roche Bernaude (3,153 metres), a deep grey, scree-footed ridgeline, striated across its length with ribs of quartzite. The sound of gushing water attracted us to the cusp of a grassy, larch scattered hill, where a view into a narrow gorge spilling with flumes of crashing water tempted us into an early camp.

Once Ted was pitched, we lay on the floor amongst needles and shoots. The sounds of the churning gorge filled my ears, and the taste of couscous filled my mouth. Through half-opened eyes, I watched the low evening sun splay through my eyelashes. My reverie was broken a little later as a fly dropped dead from the sky and landed on my foot. Within minutes, an army of ants was carrying the deceased away. The ants gradually dispersed from my feet. I returned to the sun to see that we had lost its light to the shell of Mont Thabor.

A WALKER'S FAUX PAS

For three days, we moved with little incident under clement skies across a rugged landscape of glacial rivers, high tarns, and exposed rock, tinged red with iron deposits. Between the pinched cols of

Thures, Pertusa, Dormillouse and Lauze, the route dropped into great meadows, where cattle-trodden terraces bloomed with sleepy buttercups, whilst huddles of gossiping mushrooms whispered beneath the shade of their golden caps.

Losing yet further height, the path fell into vast prairies of grassy tussocks – like the manes of a thousand sleeping lions – where the pink cactus heads of cobweb houseleek grew between the rock cracks, and swathes of lilac lupins stood tall amongst ruined farmhouses and crumbled stone walls.

Rarely without the Clarée River for more than a few kilometres, we spent successive nights beside the torrent, glad of the opportunity to wash before bed and wake with the sound of bubbling water and its resident birdsong.

Feeling torpid, and with lunchtime approaching, we took a rest stop on the shores of a small, lonely lake as dragonflies, damsels and the mustard wings of a swooping butterfly danced about the water's surface.

In need of a wee, I walked a little way from the lake and began my business, only to realise mid-flow that we were not alone at all. The startled couple, who had just laid out a rather delicious-looking picnic no more than a few metres from where I stood, were very reasonable about the whole affair, and I was glad to leave the lake with little other penance than blushed cheeks and a heightened sense of awareness.

As we grew closer to Briançon – the highest town in the European Union and our opportunity for a night beneath a roof – forts began to appear in the rock and atop the ridgelines. We crossed the arched stonework of the Pont d'Asfeld, 168 *pieds* above the Durance torrent, before filtering between ramparts, through the Fort du Château and into a labyrinth of medieval streets.

SICKNESS IN THE QUEYRAS

Raised high above the confluence of the Durance and the Guisane Rivers, upon the southern plateau of the Crête de Payrolle, Briançon's old town was the perfect place for us to spend a night.

We ambled up La Grande Rue beneath a string of red and white flags which adorned the walls of the narrow, teetering houses alongside the cobbles. At one moment, I caught a glimpse of Briançon's humble past, as children splashed joyously in the gutters and old men puffed on their briar-wood pipes. But as we edged closer towards the heart of the town, a more realistic modernity emerged: colourful souvenir shops, revving coffee machines, postcard stands, and overweight tourists draped with the usual array of electrical appliances – cameras, smart phones and GPS gadgets.

Following the guidance of the *office de tourisme*, we made our way to the Pension de Rampart at the far end of Briançon. Led past peach-coloured walls, a terrace of plastic chairs, and a faded red and white awning, we were shown into a small, dimly-lit bar kept warm by a flat-capped man nursing a glass of dark amber beer. At thirty-five euros a room, it was the cheapest place in town and one that clearly attracted a particular type of clientele. 'Is that...?'

'It is!' Jake said in a hushed voice. 'Spiritual!'

After seeing 'Spiritual', as he was now known, back in Modane, we had spotted him for a second time a day or so later speaking to a couple on the trackside. With a kind, gratified face, dusty clothes and his long wooden staff, we suspected that Spiritual's motives for being on the path ran far deeper than a physical challenge. Whatever his reasons, it felt comforting to see him again, and though we didn't converse as we saw him turning the lock in the door next to ours, we reciprocated each other's smiles – from one unknown journey to another.

In spite of its price, the room was wonderfully equipped – a double bed, television, sink, kitchenette (somewhat incongruent with the *'Ne mangez pas dans la chambre s'il vous plaît'* sign stuck on the wall beside it) and a balcony overlooking the town's ramparts and its resident herd of foraging goats.

The partitions between the rooms were, however, thin. 'Blimey,' I sighed, as the stamping feet above our heads and screaming baby next door intensified. It was, unquestionably, an irritating blend of resonances, but it was a curious one too. 'I think Spiritual has a baby,' I proposed after establishing my bearings in the room.

'Well, given that there is definitely a baby next door and Spiritual is definitely next door, I think you might be right,' Jake concurred with a hint of sarcasm. 'Dan,' he said, changing his tone, 'I'm feeling quite tired. Do you mind resupplying without me?'

I left the hotel in the heat of the afternoon, winding down through the intricate streets of the old town into Briançon's contemporary centre. Jake's absence, coupled with the discovery of a rather large supermarket, appeared to be a recipe for needless procurement, and I returned to the room several hours later with an undeniable surplus of food bulging from my rucksack. But in the hours that I had been gone, Jake's fatigue had evolved into sickness, and in spite of the banquet-like spread – brioche, apricots, ham, watercress, tomatoes, cheese, olives and chocolate mousse – the only thing to acquaint itself with Jake's digestive system that night was a handful of Imodium tablets. Not exactly the feast he was craving.

The drugs worked well, and, with Jake's bowels successfully bunged, we were able to leave Briançon early the following morning. But with his low energy levels and the food-filled bags, progress was slow, arduous and, for Jake, though he barely mentioned it, entirely miserable.

'If it's not me, it's you, isn't it?' I said in a bid to cheer him up. Getting little response, I returned to the discomfort of my weighty pack, wedging my thumbs beneath my shoulder straps to relieve a little pressure.

Not for the first time, we had trouble rediscovering the path as we left town. After several wrong turns, we soon gave up on our map and compass, and reverted to a more unorthodox form of navigation: stalking. Having latched onto two hikers, who we followed down several streets and up a hill, we soon saw another pair heading in the opposite direction and began to stalk them instead. But it wasn't long before we realised that the second couple were merely on a tour of the town, and had we continued to pursue their steps, we would have ended up back where we had begun.

Eventually, after spotting a geared-up chap with short silver hair and a tamed beard, reassuringly referring to a blue 1:25,000 *IGN* map, we were led away from the buildings and into a hillside of allotments. The smell of smoke and earth filled my airways, reminding me instantly of my childhood, and I watched joyfully as an old man pulled a carrot from the ground, eyeing it proudly up and down before placing it into his basket. We managed to lose our guide somewhere amongst the vegetable plots, but it didn't matter: we were back on the map.

We climbed further into a heat-oppressed forest of thirsty pine, where banks of flowers reached across the track as if offering themselves to aid Jake's drained muscles. Stubborn and refusing their help, he pushed them aside.

Morning turned to afternoon, and, with Jake's pain enduring, we stopped early for the day in the Parc Naturel Régional du Queyras, pitching Ted in a forest beneath the arrowhead of Pic de Cros. Thunder rumbled but the rain didn't come, and after helping Jake into the tent to rest, I found a log to sit on in the sun.

My mind started to wander. I thought about a question a friend had asked me before we had left Bristol: 'Won't you get bored?' It was a good question, and one that I had had difficulty answering, even after we had started the walk. But, as the afternoon progressed and the hours fell away, I soon had an answer. I had spent an hour snapping twigs into a small heap on the forest floor. I wasn't making a fire, and I wasn't building a tiny house to shelter the many ants that were surveying our tent. I was snapping twigs for the sake of snapping twigs. I then spent another hour after dinner flapping the washed dishes through the air with the vague objective of drying them. I could have used our towel, or left them to drain on our bags, but I didn't. To an observer, these actions could be seen as proof of boredom. But I wasn't bored. In fact, I was inspired. Suddenly the notion of under-stimulation seemed absurd, and I went to bed that night hypothetically responding to the question: 'Bored? Of course not! Have *you* ever tried drying dishes by waving them through the air like a disruptive toddler? No? Well, let me tell you this, it's glorious!'

Under sullen heavens and racing winds, we continued on through the Queyras, along the Torrent de Bramousse, and up to the Col Fromage (2,301 metres) where my hat blew from my head. Defying gravity, arrows of raindrops and white dust soared up from the crumbling Ravin de Rasis that fell away steeply to our south. Dotted sparsely along the pathside stood the slouched trunks of a resisting conifer forest, the gale playing its woodwork like an orchestra of eerie pipes.

Jake's stomach was sore, his muscles weak, and his mood defeated. His skin was pale and his eyelids heavy, his hair bushy and untamed, and the subtle grin that so often resided upon his face had dropped to an expression of lasting discomfort.

The storm grew stronger, persisting for a day and a night.

The ridgelines above the path came and went with the churning cloud. The chap with the *IGN* map, who had unknowingly led us out of Briançon a couple of days earlier, sat on a rock beside a footbridge over the Ruisseau de la Pisse. With a cigarette stuck to his lip and his hands smoothing the contours of the boulder, he struck me as a man whose comforts were modest and whose way of life was simple. Still unsure of his nationality, we nodded as we passed, and then, noting his calm expression and silver beard, named him the 'Kind-eyed Scot'.

Mist flowed across the glacial tarns, each lake looming with the spotted heads of their resident rainbow trout. And a *pastous*, a shepherd dog of the high mountains, sat nobly on a distant rock above its flock of grazing sheep. Indeed, the nip in the air and the bleakness of the sky were so great that even the crowns of the *alpage* wildflowers remained in their slumbers – coiled, tucked and clasped shut from the world.

Conversation had become stifled, and our pace had slowed. I was worried about Jake, but no matter what I said, his response remained the same: 'Let's just walk through it.'

Since leaving Bristol, I had developed a method to gauge the severity of Jake's afflictions. The most telling sign – above nausea, diarrhoea, lack of appetite, short temper and heavy breathing – was his unwillingness to take a photo. At the height of Jake's mood, the camera would seldom leave his hands, and we often arrived into camp an hour or two later than we could have, courtesy of his unremitting trigger finger. Conversely, to pass a feature of even remote splendour without him stopping for a photo suggested that he was in considerable discomfort. So, what better way to test the state of his illness than by summiting the Col Girardin (2,706 metres), where a vast view of alpine massifs dominated the north and the rusty hues of the Mediterranean mountains the south? Indeed, even the ground beneath our feet provided a valiant test as an inhabitation of marmots scurried playfully through the rock slabs, pausing with a sniff and a twitch before diving into a hole, only to bounce out again seconds later.

I turned to observe Jake's condition. His face was drained and weathered, and his slumped shoulders led to hands that gripped weakly at their walking poles. He looked gormlessly at the marmots before rotating slowly to face me. 'Camera?' he said softly, at which I smiled and gladly retrieved it from his pack.

Jake didn't sleep well. Slow punctures, inflicted upon our roll mats in the previous weeks, had caused our beds to deflate slowly through the night, until soon we were lying on a rough ground of stones and branches. The evening had been cold too, and not long after finding our slumber in the early hours of the morning, a chorus of barking deer had woken us. Jake's real angst, however, came with the inexorable cramps that had pulsed through his stomach from dusk until dawn. He was still ill and still struggling.

I conjured a couple of *pains au chocolat* from my pack for breakfast, hoping that food would improve his mood. But they were old and rubbery, and had become contaminated in my pack with the smell of damp clothes. Our bread was stale too. With its preservatives out of date, it had been pulverised into a bag of crumbs. A far cry from the morale-boosting breakfast I had envisaged, we might as well have been eating old flip-flops and sawdust. I was thus grateful for the wild strawberries that we found on the pathside, which pleased our bellies, and the splendid sight of the gliding vultures that circled above our heads on the Col du Vallonnet (2,520 metres).

A long day had seen us pass from the Queyras into the Parc National du Mercantour, and we woke the next morning amongst sun and flowers, between the verge of a conifer forest and the noisy Ubayette Rivière.

I lay with my head on a pile of clothes, absorbing the busy world around me as light dripped in through the porch. The undergrowth was tall and dense. Cow parsley, buttercups, globe flowers, meadow geraniums and dandelions hugged the sides of the tent, whilst spider threads came with the light and went with the shade. We had spent many hours observing the crawling, slithering and leaping creatures of Europe's forests, and had become rather well acquainted with their habits and personalities. Zany Zack – with six legs, a dark brown exoskeleton and rotating antennae – appreciated his personal space, never letting us get too close. An attempt to interact would provoke Zany Zack into an enormous leap, spiralling him across the tent like a tiny cannonball. Nostalgic

Nigella was dull-witted, yet content. It was clear from the way her flat round body moved – almost in slow motion like a shrunken tortoise – that her mind was elsewhere. And then there was Timid Tricia, undoubtedly the smallest of the creatures, like the head of a pin, with a deep black complexion and otherwise imperceptible physical characteristics. Shy at first, she would gradually build the confidence to climb aboard our lazing bodies. Unfortunately, Timid Tricia had not mastered the pitfalls of overconfident foraging, and as she moved from a hand, up an arm and intrepidly towards a face, she would, more often than not, become the recipient of a nasty swat.

'Right, I can't take these insects anymore,' Jake blurted as he sent Timid Tricia flying across the tent. 'Let's get walking!'

It was a chill morning, and my nose dripped like a broken tap into my moustache as we passed banks of twinkling cotton grass frozen in the shade of the mountains. With six days of sweat and dirt coating my face, I was thankful to hear from Jake that we would be spending the day amongst a number of glacial lakes, finally presenting an opportunity for a wash.

By mid-morning, we had arrived at a dip in the valley, at long last feeling the sun on our shoulders. The Lac du Lauzanier (2,284 metres), one of the park's most visited lakes, was dotted with bathing day walkers and picnic baskets, amongst which we found a patch of grass and came to rest.

Though the scene was busy, we soon spotted the decorative staff and silver ponytail of Spiritual, who had propped himself conveniently against the post of a *GR5* sign beside the track. With eyes resting shut and his chest bare, it would have been easy to assume one could pass the dozing man unnoticed. But with each walker that trod by, one eye would peek open, accompanied by a broad smile and a few words. I concluded that Spiritual was not only profoundly sacred but a master of fleeting social interactions.

'The Kind-eyed Scot is here too,' Jake said, pointing to a heap of boulders on the far shore of the lake.

Having found a little solitude away from the basking walkers, the Kind-eyed Scot pulled his baselayer over his head to reveal an impressively built torso for a man of his age. He dunked the garment in the water and thrashed it dry with powerful beats that rung out around the cirque walls.

We left Lac du Lauzanier, sharing a few words with Spiritual before climbing through barren rock, its striations as crumpled and folded as the pages of an exercise book at the bottom of a school bag. Scree slopes and snow led us steeply up to the Pas de la Cavale (2,671 metres), where we ate lunch amongst a host of tottering cairns that mimicked the towers of sandstone stamping the horizon to the south. In the valleys between lay the lowland pastures of Salso Moréno – mustard green and mottled with grazing sheep that flocked hypnotically from one shape to the next like bacteria beneath a microscope. A golden eagle soared above our heads, releasing a feather from its wing as it rose with a thermal over the col. The plume twisted and eddied for what felt like minutes before coming to rest in a torn up slope of boulders and rubble somewhere down the mountainside. Out of reach, I thought begrudgingly, knowing that it was likely we would never witness such a sight again.

From the steep shale combe, we spotted two chalky blue pools of water some way down the path, the Lacs d'Agnel, and after exchanging affirming glances, deviated from the path towards them.

The small craters were not quite as tropical as they had looked from afar – with muddy cattle-trodden banks, scores of bathing frogs, tadpoles and dragonfly larvae, and a sludge of sunken detritus at their beds – but we were hot, smelly and desperate for a wash.

Leaving my clothes in a heap beside the water, I leapt into the deep pool. Bubbles raced past my ears as I sank, drifting slowly downwards before kicking away from the darkness and back towards the surface. I opened my eyes to the glare of the sun, shielding my face as Jake's pale body flew through the air towards me, crashing into the water, and surfacing with a cry of delight: 'Waahoo!'

It was an exhilarating feeling, and, for the first time in a long time, Jake's smile was genuine. Indeed, our elation was so great that we soon forgot our proximity to the path, and as Jake came running towards the water once more, leaping gleefully into the pond, I couldn't help but feel a slight pang of discomfort for the startled onlookers who had just emerged on the brim of the small hollow.

265

After a short day of walking, we arrived into Bousiéyas, a tiny community of half a dozen corrugated iron houses built jauntily into the rock above La Tinée Rivière. Jake's condition had improved so much that we decided to treat ourselves by buying dinner at the local *gîte*, where the owner, a young woman with a freckled face and a string of daisies through her hair, told us we could camp in the cemetery.

I left Jake to pitch the tent and walked down to the river to fill our bottles. Spotting a rapid beneath a footbridge, I made my way across some fluvial rubble, waking from my stupor as a head turned from atop one of the river's boulders. Just as Jake and I had seen a week earlier, the Kind-eyed Scot was lying across a rock balling cigarette smoke from his mouth. We nodded at each other, and then I bent down to the water and held a bottle in the flow.

'I hear you've come a long way.' I swivelled on the ground as the man blew more smoke into the air before turning to face me.

'Yes,' I replied, bewildered. 'How did you know?'

'The Irishman told me.'

'Kevin?' I said, unable to hide my intrigue. The Kind-eyed Scot nodded. 'When did you bump into him?'

'Oh, a few times, in one or two of the refuges and on the path.' Now that I could hear the man's accent, it was clear that he wasn't Scottish but English. He spoke softly with considered words and a mild case of rhotacism, pronouncing 'refuge' as 'wefuge' and 'river' as 'wiver'. 'We'll be a few days behind him now though. He stormed ahead back in Tignes, that place with all the ski lifts. Horrible things they are – really spoil the view.'

Although we had only walked with Kevin for a few hours, it was sad to think that we might not see him again, and without having exchanged contact details, we likely never would. 'That's a shame,' I added, noticing that the Kind-eyed Scot's solemn expression matched mine.

'I know, I mean the mountains should be left alone instead of scarred with eyesores like these bloody *télésièges* and ski lifts.'

Ignoring the misunderstanding, I nodded and shook my head in one movement so as to assert my opinion of *téléski*, *télésièges*, *téléphériques* – and for that matter, all manner of *télé-things* – as entirely neutral. 'Anyway, you know everything about us by the sounds of it. What about you?'

'Arthur, from Cambridge,' he said confidently. 'I started at Lake Geneva, but am undecided on my finish. Menton is supposed to be a nicer way to end, so I'll probably choose that over Nice.'

Officially speaking, the *GR5* ends (or begins) in the centre of Nice. However, adopting a similar view to the Kind-eyed Scot, or Arthur as we now knew him, Jake and I preferred the idea of a more picturesque finish. In a couple of days' time, we would branch east, away from the *GR5*, and join the *Grande Randonnée 52 (GR52)*, a route that was to add several more days to the journey.

'You ought to be careful drinking that water,' Arthur warned, raising his eyebrows towards the bottles in my hands. 'I don't drink anything below 2,000 metres and certainly nothing below the cattle line. You'll get sick.'

'Yes, we've learnt that the hard way,' I said, hearing my belly gargle with protest at the new water supply. 'We're using purification tablets, but it doesn't seem to stop us getting ill.'

Arthur stuck his hand into his pocket. 'Here,' he passed me a packet of pills, 'these are the best you can get, but I wouldn't rely on them. Get your water from a tap if you can.'

'Thank you.'

'Where are you sleeping tonight?'

'The cemetery.'

Arthur chuckled. 'Yes, I saw that was an option. It's the *gîte* for me tonight: nice bed, a nutritious meal. Are you eating well?'

'No. Not at all,' I confessed. 'Our diet is awful. We bought a salad from the *gîte* earlier. It was the most nourishing food we've had in weeks.'

Arthur's expression was telling. 'You've got to eat well,' he said, shaking his head.

He was right, of course, and we had known that from the start. Jake and I had agreed that we wouldn't short cut on nutrition. If we wanted something, we would buy it, no matter what the cost. But, in practice, we found expensive meals difficult to justify, and the temptation of another cheap packet of instant noodles, or a box of couscous, would often prevail.

'I made my mistake in the Pyrenees. No fruit or vegetables, just things that I could carry, like bread and sausage. But I lost a lot of weight, and then became ill. You've got to eat well,' he reiterated. 'Drink well and eat well.'

Arthur's words stayed with me as I walked back up the road to the tent, where I found Jake lying on the grass reading Nicholas Crane.

'So Arthur is the moaning man from Cambridge that Kevin was telling us about?' Jake said after I told him the gossip from my trip to the river.

'Yep!' Another gurgle resonated from the pit of my stomach. 'Jake, I know we haven't got much toilet paper left, but I think I may have a problem again.'

'Are you joking?'

I shook my head as Jake passed me the roll, and then ran off back down the road towards a small patch of forest. Unfortunately, and with the added woe of our heavily depleted toilet roll and Imodium supplies, this set the pattern for the night: return to the tent, lie down, wait five minutes, stand up, run down to the forest, then stagger back up the road to the tent.

The baton of illness had been passed seamlessly from Jake back to me, and, as I sat with my back to the tree for the umpteenth time, closing my eyes with exhaustion, I accepted my condition. Regardless of our physical state, stubbornness would see us through to the end.

C'EST POUR LA DIGESTION

'Water. It's all about water,' I said to Jake the next morning. We had woken early and left the cemetery with deep blue dawn skies overhead. Gradually, the light turned from cobalt blue to violet, before smothering the surrounding rocky hills with a golden incandescence that warmed the slopes of fragrant lavender and the bodies of the waking lizards. 'It's a constant battle. If we don't drink it then we'll suffer from dehydration, but if we do we'll probably catch a bug. And even if we know the water we have is clean, we'll be afraid to drink it because we don't want to deplete our supplies unnecessarily. It's the nature of long-distance walking: you drink when you don't really want to for fear of not having another opportunity, yet you don't drink when you have water, even if your mouth is dry with thirst, for fear of running out.'

'That's how a lot of people in this world live, Dan – not knowing when they'll next get clean water, or whether it will make them ill.' Jake was right. Our struggles with water represented the daily challenges facing much of the world's population. Suddenly, the true significance of WaterAid and the money we had raised for the charity held more meaning. 'Mum said we've got over £7,000. Not bad for a quick stroll across Europe.'

With our early rise, we made quick progress between the shrubby meadows of the shallow valleys, crossing dry stream beds, and brushing the wilting heads of the summer's wildflowers before reaching Saint-Étienne-de-Tinée by lunchtime.

Since leaving Bristol, we had not felt the pressures of time, aside from reaching the forest ahead of the rain, or the next town before our food ran too low. But a recent phone call home had changed all that.

On 20 August, just ten days from the terracotta roof tiles of Saint-Étienne-de-Tinée, we would be meeting Claudia and Rose in Menton. Of course, this was a thrilling thought, but it had changed things. We were ahead of schedule. Seven days of comfortable hiking would see us into Menton, but we had ten to fill. In theory, the idea of a lazy stroll towards the finish line sounded great – extended lie-ins, long lunches, afternoon swims in the cooling lakes. But surplus time to an addicted walker is a difficult pleasure to embrace, and as we entered the grounds of the Camping du Plan d'Eau with six hours of daylight still remaining, I suddenly felt less certain of my recent response to the question, 'Won't you get bored?'

With an artificial lake at its centre – accompanied by flumes, inflatable balls and fountains – the campsite was busy with bronzed bodies and animated children. Gérard, the camp owner, walked us through the holiday park, greeting guests with one-liners and nods whilst plucking dead petals from the blooming flowerpots that fringed the path. Gérard – short in stature, with tanned skin and a small island of grey hair above a sun-beaten scalp – struck me as a man who rarely sat still. Pushing fifty, his body and bounce seemed more reminiscent of a man in his mid-twenties. He showed us to a splendid mat of grass beside the ablutions block and then returned down the path, calling back as he went, 'If you need anything, just ask!'

The effects of our last two Imodium tablets that I had taken in the morning were beginning to wear off, and I spent the next hour sitting on the toilet.

'I wouldn't mind it at home,' I said to Jake after returning to the tent. 'You can relax more, and it doesn't matter if you're in the bathroom for hours. But there are only two toilets here and a bloody queue of people waiting outside them. It's embarrassing. I'd rather be in the forest!'

Jake was as sympathetic as always, but he was also the voice of reason. 'Maybe we would be better off in the forest, but we haven't got any food, so I'm afraid we're staying.' It was a Sunday, the day of rest, and everything in Saint-Étienne-de-Tinée was closed. Suddenly, my chances of finding a new supply of Imodium and, more pressingly, toilet roll were dashed. We were stuck in a beautiful town of chapels, frescoes, cafés and fountains, yet all I could think about was the logistics of a lavatory queue and the best way to prolong the use of the twenty sheets of toilet paper. The latter quandary, I quickly concluded, was plain: there was no best way.

As the afternoon ticked slowly away, glimmers of hope came and went. Arthur, who had joined us on our patch of grass, spent a few minutes rummaging around in his pack in a bid to find a remedy, but soon became distracted after pulling out a pair of socks. 'They're double-layered. See,' he said, rubbing them together, 'they rub against each other instead of your skin.'

'I'm sorry, I have to go,' I interrupted, fleeing to the toilets just as Arthur began to slip the garments onto his hands for a more thorough demonstration.

Momentarily relieved, I left the restrooms with my head down, but before I had reached the taps, I caught sight of a beaming smile in the corner of my eye.

'Hey,' Spiritual said cheerily, '*ça va?*'

Holding my stomach, I shook my head. '*Pas bien.*'

'*Votre estomac?*'

'*Oui.*'

'*Pourquoi?*'

'*L'eau,*' I pointed at the tap water, '*mais dans les rivières.*'

'*L'eau!*' Spiritual looked genuinely concerned and a frown of craterous wrinkles began to congregate on his forehead. '*Pas bon,*' he muttered, putting a large weathered finger on his chin before springing suddenly to life. '*Ah!*' Hesitantly, he raised his hands towards my shoulders. '*Je peux vous faire un massage? C'est pour la digestion.*'

270

Usually a sceptic of treatments such as a diarrhoea-abolishing massage, I was surprised to hear my voice jump at the proposal: '*Oui, s'il vous plaît. Merci.*' I must have been desperate.

In the middle of the bustling ablutions block, with his chest bare and his expression one of deep in thought, Spiritual ran his hands over my shoulders and down my arms. He then took my hands and began to rub my fingers. I presumed, though I daren't have asked, that he was drawing the stomach bug away from my suffering gut, through my arms and, like an icing sugar piping tube, out of my fingertips.

The massage ended ten minutes later.

'*Merci...*' I said, hinting for a name.

'*Pierre.*'

'*Ah, merci Pierre.*'

'*C'est mieux?*' he said, rubbing his own belly and then pointing at mine as it bubbled with intent.

'*Oui,*' I lied. '*Absolument.*'

Some hours earlier, Jake had ventured into town hoping to find an open shop, and it wasn't until dusk began to fall that he finally returned. In one hand, he held a four-pack of toilet roll, and in the other, several boxes of medication.

'How?' I said, breaking into the tablets. 'Where did you get these from? You've been gone hours.'

'Gérard, the camp owner, said we could ask him if we needed anything, didn't he? So I did. He drew me a little map.' Jake passed me a piece of paper covered in small lines and dots. 'Then he told me to follow the directions to the hospital. When I got there, I was instructed to go upstairs. A nurse with a big grin was waiting for me. "Jake?" she said. I nodded, and then she gave me the medicine and told me to take it to you. Turns out she was Gérard's wife.' Jake looked particularly proud of his successful quest and lapped up my gratitude with vigour. 'So, what have you been up to? Apart from sitting on the toilet, I mean.'

'Not much,' I replied, casually shrugging my shoulders. 'Spiritual gave me a massage, but that's about it really.'

'What?' Jake cried, dropping to the ground beside me. 'Tell me everything!'

BACK NORTH

We left Saint-Étienne-de-Tinée after two days of illness having learnt three things: Arthur prefers double-layered socks to single; Spiritual definitely has a baby (although we were still unsure as to how the child kept appearing); and massage does not have anti-diarrhoeal properties, but nonetheless feels good, even when performed in the middle of a communal washroom by a topless man with a ponytail.

Our forty-first and final map (*Nice-Draguingnan 1:100,000 IGN*) led us south-east, across the Tinée Rivière and through a forest of steep, zigzagging bends, towards the ski town of Auron. However, far from a reward for a difficult climb, the town was arguably the most gaudy of all the alpine communes we had passed through.

'Wow, Arthur is really going to hate this,' I said, after finding a bench in the middle of the concrete town square. Like a giant pincushion, the surrounding slopes were stitched with the large metal needles and cable threads of France's hard-working ski lifts. Meanwhile, the town, as bilingual as any we had seen, comprised a host of garish neon lights, the irrepressible odour of frying fat, and dozens of amplifiers, each of which had their own playlist.

'I actually quite like it,' Jake said, as the sound of Adele's 'Someone Like You' cut through the drone of half a dozen other songs. 'Good music, lots of hustle and bustle, and these sandwiches are nice too.'

'*We* made the sandwiches,' I objected, turning towards Jake to see that he had now closed his eyes and joined in with Adele's chorus.

Although Jake's dismay at Auron was not as great as mine, we were both glad to return to the more rural side of the Alps where our feet took us briskly away from the town and over the Col de Blianon (2,014 metres).

From the pass, we descended steadily into the Vallée de la Roya-Bévéra. Rose bushes and lavender scrub filled the drying terraces that notched the surrounding slopes, buzzing with the clumsy red and black wings of burnet moths and the legs of golden grasshoppers. Long forgotten stone farmhouses lay derelict on the stepped hillsides, their walls being torn slowly to the ground under the strain of untamed raspberry tendrils and their muscular

272

roots. We reached the bottom of the valley, passing between the overgrown gardens of the hamlet of Roya, where children played in the dirt and clothes hung from drooping washing lines, before following a turbulent river against its flow up a narrow gorge of limestone cliffs.

Flat ground was proving hard to come by, and it wasn't until we had scrambled back and forth through the steep terrain for almost an hour that we eventually found a camping spot between a huddle of boulders beside the river. Since arriving in the Alps, this had become part of our routine. Unlike the previous sections of our trip where our only real obligation was to find a forest, we now had the added requirement to find a level plane on which to put Ted, or at least somewhere close to level. But, perhaps somewhat patently, finding horizontal terrain in Western Europe's most expansive mountain range often proved difficult, and an hour-long search for a decent night's sleep was not uncommon.

Our spot by the river was not ideal – we had to fill the small trenches beneath our sleeping bags with spare clothes to even out the surface – but the view of the limestone overhangs and stacks through the larch branches, and the rumble of the river left us satisfied.

I sat against a tree and stared at the lichen that enfolded its trunk. Dark in colour and split into circles and polygons, the tessellating growths reminded me of cracked clay. An ant crawled across the lichen with waving antennae, before moving on to the crumbs of powdered soup from our dinner which dusted the nearby roots. Soon there were scores of ants, and as I watched the bodies traipse off back towards their nest, I imagined the queen's pleasure at the sight of the army's delicious find. Once the soup powder had been cleared, my attention turned to our socks that were hanging from Ted's guy ropes. For an hour or so, I picked grass seeds from between their stitches, glad to remember the stimulation and habitual enjoyment of such ordinary activities.

'It says here that you can see the sea from the Col de Crousette.' Jake took his eyes from our guidebook and peered up to the pass. We were standing in the middle of a sweeping plateau between the Vallon de la Maïris and the Col de Crousette, a dip in the side of the narrow-ridged crest of Mont Mounier. It was mid-morning, and though we had been walking for several hours, an arched run of precipices that lipped the plateau's south-western aspect – like a boulevard of high-rise apartments – had only just caught the light of the sun. Sporadic paint licks guided us through a marsh of cotton grassed ponds to a scree slope below the pass where a shaggy *pastous* watched us from above.

The day was hot, and the skies appeared clear, but after picking a path through the rubble and emerging onto the Col de Crousette (2,480 metres), a thick jumble of clouds assembled on the southerly horizon. 'No Mediterranean today,' I said, slumping onto a rock and reaching into my pack for a bag of scroggin.

'You can smell it though, can't you?' Jake stuck his hand into the bag, pulling it out and inspecting the mix of muesli, foam bananas, pumpkin seeds and French Werther's Originals. I drew a deep breath. The mountain thyme, which had been with us since the Vosges, was aromatic and earthy, whilst the rose bush scented the air with a sweet balsamic resin that made me think of the sea.

'It really peters out to the south. They look more like hills than mountains,' I said, pointing down to the diminishing peaks beyond our feet. We had been in the Alps for a month, and in all that time I had never seen a view as modest as the one before us now.

'Well, we're not going south. Take a look over there.' Jake pointed to the east and the Franco-Italian mountains, where a charge of tumbling cumulonimbus clouds had begun to stampede through the brawny 3,000-metre peaks of Cima di Brocan, Cime du Gélas and Mont Bégo. Our next four days of walking would take us away from the water, north-east through the Mercantour National Park to the Italian border. Having stepped into our eighth and final country, we would then veer south and follow the mountains to the sea.

But with just sixty kilometres separating us from the French Riviera, were we risking resentment by opting for a scenic route that took us a week off course?

Sitting quietly on the warm rocks looking east, we watched as vultures cruised through the sky, and lines of diverging cattle spread across the lower slopes. Resentment, I instantly decided, was the last thing on my mind. 'Only a week to go,' I said solemnly.

Although Spiritual was walking alone, we rarely saw him without company. At the Refuge de Longon – a slender stone building with a corrugated iron roof set at the base of an open, grassy valley – we spotted him talking to a young Spanish couple on a bench beside a water trough.

'*Ah! Bonjour!*' He grinned, bidding his new acquaintances farewell before joining us next to the water as we filled our bottles.

'*L'eau...*' I swashed my hand through the trough and looked inquiringly up at Spiritual, '*c'est bon à boire?*'

'*Oui, c'est bon!*' He bent down to the trickling water and slurped it from within his cupped hands. '*C'est bon!*' He then pointed at my stomach. '*Votre estomac, bon?*'

'*Oui merci,*' I said sincerely, only then realising that both Jake and I had miraculously been bug free for almost two days. '*Mon frère aidez moi,*' I added, nodding at Jake.

'*Et vous?*' Jake said. '*Où avez-vous dormi la nuit dernière?*'

'*Ah!*' Spiritual raised a finger before pulling a small map from his bag and leaning it on the side of the stone bath. '*Ici.*' He pointed at a red circle he had drawn on the map. '*J'ai campé ici.*'

Jake and I were amazed to see that over the past two weeks, give or take a few kilometres, Spiritual had slept in the same places that we had. If the weather was good, he slept out in the open on top of his bivouac, and if it was raining, he slept inside. Much like Arthur and Kevin, Spiritual preferred to walk alone (though he loved to talk), and he adored watching the stars from his sleeping bag with only the land for company.

'*Un moment!*' he said, just as our French vocabulary began to run dry. He put his hand into the pocket of his sun-faded T-shirt to reveal a walnut-sized piece of dolomitic limestone that he had picked up from the valley earlier in the day. '*C'est bon pour votre coeur.*' He pointed towards his heart and then smiled warmly, rolling the knobbly stone between his fingers before offering it our way. '*C'est pour vous.*'

We left Spiritual to rekindle his conversation with the Spanish pair, and continued on into the valley where the path fell steeply into the Forêt de la Fracha. For its size, the stone that Spiritual had gifted us was remarkably heavy. Having snapped our toothbrushes in half back in Luxembourg to reduce weight, I found it difficult to drop the rock into my pocket without questioning its necessity. But, after a brief consultation with Jake, we agreed to keep the limestone on the basis that its weight, which was no more than 100 grams, was far lighter than that of two unhealthy hearts.

By late afternoon, we were beginning to tire. 'Wait here,' I said to Jake, leaving him to guard our packs as I pulled myself up onto a bank beside the path.

'We can't camp here. It's way too steep.' Jake laughed.

'You're probably right, but I'm tired,' I shouted back over my shoulder, grappling at the slope's exposed tree roots and tussocks of grass for support.

After half an hour of searching, I still hadn't found a suitable spot and was beginning to lose energy. With my frustrations growing, I returned to a small gully discovered earlier in my search.

'I know it's not perfect,' I admitted to Jake after calling him up from the track, 'but I couldn't find anywhere else.'

'Not perfect is an understatement, Dan. I could barely even get up here. Oh well, I'm sure it will be alright once we've cleared some of the rocks.'

The clouds that we had seen in the morning were now sprawled across the sky above our heads and had transformed from a bashful white tone to one dark and overbearing. A bolt of lightning suddenly lit the forest, followed swiftly by a crack of thunder.

'Let's get the tent up,' Jake announced, spurring us into a frenzied assembly that left Ted looking like a half-inflated hot air balloon.

We leapt inside for cover, already drenched from the pouring rain, only to realise that water was streaming in through the upper corners of the tent. Jake plugged the leak with our towel whilst I climbed back out to investigate.

Marbles of rain dashed through the pine trees, knocking cones into the air and pushing branches to the ground. It didn't take me long to realise that the small threads of trickling water that were flowing over the rocks and logs were all gravitating towards one gully. 'We're in a bloody river!' I yelled through the storm, crawling back into the tent to gather our belongings. We packed up with speed, swung our bags over our backs, and then hauled the sodden tent over our heads and slipped clumsily up the hill. Thankfully, the gradient soon improved beneath our feet and with it our chance of pitching on dry land.

On day 124 of our walk, we witnessed a quartet of events that answered four of life's most pressing questions. Firstly, is there anything more disconcerting to wake up to than the sound (and then sight) of an Amazonian-sized slug sliding and scratching its way down the wall of your tent just two centimetres from your head? The answer, I now believe, is no.

Secondly, is there anything more beautiful in the natural world than a steaming, sun-bathed pine forest the morning after a night of heavy rain? After picking the molluscs out of our shoes and from the pockets of our bags, we continued on through the Forêt de la Fracha. Drapes of sun fell faintly through the canopies, lighting the wings of flies pirouetting above a forest floor of glittering grass. I crouched to my feet beside a congregation of cappuccino-coloured mushrooms, depressed in their centres, and sheltering an underworld of edaphic bugs. No, I thought, stumped for an alternative, it's probable that there is nothing more beautiful.

My third question concerned the *GR* waymarking. Flicked onto a vacant fence post or a conspicuous stone, the *GR* symbols are impressively widespread. France alone has over 100,000 kilometres of footpaths, most of which are marked. Who paints these tiny symbols? I had always assumed it to be the national park authorities or hiking organisations. But, as we wound along a dusty white track between the decrepit sheds and farmhouses of Rougios, we found the answer: two old men, dressed in tattered denim dungarees, skin dark and wrinkled, stood next to an aging larch tree beside the track. The men were covered with red and white flecks, and the pockets around their waists were filled with brushes. The first man dipped a brush into his dented tin of red paint and then carefully ran it along the trunk of the tree, before the second man repeated the process, but this time with a streak of white below the red. Of course, I wasn't so foolish to assume that the two old men in front of us – who were now touching up their paintwork with a smaller brush – were responsible for the entire nation's GR waymarkers, though they *were* old enough, but perhaps these were the kind of guys who did it: landowners, local communities or, in fact, anyone with time on their hands and spare paint under the stairs.

The fourth and final question came to mind as we followed the drying paint of the two old men down the track towards a small river amongst the trees: who makes those opportunistic-looking river crossings, comprising conveniently heaped stones and rocks that always seem to reside just where they are needed? What sector of society is so giving that it spends its valuable time dropping rocks into a river for the sake of keeping somebody else's feet dry? The answer, I now know, is children. Ahead on the rising path, a mother and father waited patiently for their brood, all of whom had stalled in the shallows of a rushing brook in the valley. Two boys scampered from one rock to the next, heaving them from the river bed and dumping them onto a pile, where their sister neatly arranged them into a line, forming a two-metre wide passage for dry feet. We stepped gratefully across the stones whilst the children continued to work, thanking them for their perseverance before overtaking the parents at the next bend. 'So, it's children who do that!' I exclaimed to Jake, delighted.

We spent the morning descending for half a kilometre into the Vallée de la Tinée, only to see our path cross the basin floor before climbing another 500 metres back up its eastern aspect towards the village of Rimplas.

For a few moments, it felt as if we were breathing English air, as we passed beneath the shadows of oak and fruiting apple trees, shielding our warm cheeks from the heat of the sun. But then came cherry and fig, and the perfume of drying olive leaves, corrupting our nostalgia and reminding us that familiar countryside was far from close by.

The figs became riper as we climbed higher, past dog rose, hazel and the delicate spindles of sweet pea, its flowers blushed pink amongst tussocks of feathery grass. Sweet chestnut husks scattered the ground like tiny balled hedgehogs and, as the woodland gave way to the exposed bluffs of liver-hued slate, blackberry bushes flourished with fruit in the rising sun.

We had sighted Spiritual in the distance an hour earlier and figured, given the possibilities for social interactions in Rimplas, that we would soon see him again. Washed with hollyhocks, lupins and the divine smell of plums that hung heavily from branches ready to snap, we wound up the village's stone streets, passing pastel walls and terracotta roofs before spotting our friend on the street ahead. Pushing off from his staff beside the garage of an unrendered house, he joined us for a few paces, finally giving us the chance to ask him about his walking stick.

The top end of the staff had been carved intricately into the shape of a clutching hand. To him, it represented spirituality and a higher belief, encompassing all religions: '*Hindouisme, Islam, Christianisme,*' he said, with wide eyes. '*Toutes les religions!*'

Below the hand was the symbol of the *Camino de Santiago de Compostela.* Jake and I had seen these markings several times on our route: a few weeks earlier just north of Briançon, in Luxembourg as we left the capital, and in the Belgian Ardennes. With many of the signs depicting a blue backdrop and nine yellow lines radiating out from a semicircle, we had always assumed it to represent a sun: enlightenment gained by pilgrims on their journey to the shrine of St James in the Cathedral of Santiago de Compostela.

But, as Spiritual explained with a show of familiar, flamboyant gesticulations, the symbol of the *Camino de Santiago* is in fact a scallop shell. To some, the significance of the shell is rather trivial, no more than a device once used by pilgrims as a vessel for drinking water alongside the path. It is also seen as a representation of the many medieval routes that cut through Europe towards Santiago. Yet for others, and most certainly for Spiritual, the symbol holds deeper meaning. One story describes how, following St James's death, as his body was being shipped towards the Iberian coastline and the burial site of Compostela, a storm struck. Thrown into the ocean, St James was lost. However, as the storm subsided, St James's body was found washed up on the Galician shores covered in scallop shells.

Tied beneath the engraved symbol of the *Camino de Santiago* were a number of feathers. Although he didn't say as much, I guessed that the tethered plumage was more of an aesthetic display than an emblem of profundity. '*Et voilà!*' he concluded, bashing the staff into the ground to show its strength.

Leaving Spiritual in our tracks, we pushed on through the afternoon and climbed steadily to Saint-Dalmas, an unusual village of sparsely built houses dotted upon open grassed terraces. With each property cruelly boasting a smoking barbecue and a cooling swimming pool, the sight of Camping à la Ferme Miel was well received, and though it didn't have quite as many frills as its neighbours, it did have a shower and a gas stove, so we were happy.

The opportunity to wash and save on camping gas was a relative luxury, but Saint-Dalmas held more significance. The commune, far more poignantly, represented the divergence point of the *GR5* and our new path, the *GR52*. For ninety-three days, the *GR5* had been our home. With the exception of just a few mornings, we had woken each day to a new landscape, yet one constant remained, evoking reassurance and comfort: the unquestionable knowledge that we would set foot onto the same path that we had trodden one day earlier. Regardless of our physical or mental state, we had the momentum of the *GR5*, and this gave us strength.

Tomorrow, we would be uniting with a new path, and though we presumed it would possess many of the same characteristics – red and white waymarkers, friendly hikers, and an impressively well-chosen route – we felt sad to be leaving the highs and lows of the foot-wide abrasion that had been our home for more than a quarter of a year.

A glance over the map suggested that we would struggle to find food for the next four or five days, meaning a bulky shop was in order. The local convenience store was expensive, but knowing it would be our last major resupply before reaching Menton, we ignored the prices and bought with our taste buds.

'OK, so this is what we have.' Jake dropped the two shopping baskets to the floor and began to siphon through the packages and tins. 'Honey and ginger cake, crisps, chocolate, bread, jam, couscous, soup, scroggin, stock cubes, tinned fish, and a hundred packets of biscuits.'

'Doesn't sound like much when you put it into words, apart from all the biscuits, of course. Do you think it will be enough?'

'It'll have to be. There's no way we can carry any more than this.'

The sounds of a group of excited, playful children filled the campground until sundown, soon replaced by the strident laughs of two beer-fuelled Frenchmen and the rolling snores of our neighbours. A band of creaking air mattresses joined the wheezing breaths, taking our restless night through to the early hours of the morning. And then, at 5.30am and with the stars still twinkling, a family of holidaying Italians woke with enthusiasm and voice, apparently happy with their decision that the best time to pack away a twenty-kilogram tent – which included the flatulent-like blasts of their slowly deflating air beds – was when everyone else was still sleeping.

'At least the blackbirds sound nice when they wake us up early in the forest,' Jake said grumpily when we finally rose with the rest of the campers.

TIME FOR AN ARGUMENT

Over the previous few days, we had begun to notice a change in the mountains around us: their stature sank towards the Mediterranean coastline. But, as we joined the *GR52*, veering back on ourselves and climbing steadily north towards the Col du Barn (2,452 metres), we were thrilled to see – with the angular peaks of the Franco-Italian frontier breaking our horizon – that we still had one final obstacle to complete.

Our first night away from the *GR5* was spent in a forest of open larch, quilted with a bed of low, woody bilberry shrub. Jake filtered through the trees along a series of faint deer tracks, searching the higher slopes alongside the cliff walls of Mont Archas (2,526 metres) whilst I stuck close to the path, hoping to come across a flatter pitch where the land lay more favourably. The hardy prongs of the bilberry were too sharp for Ted's baselayer and so too were the stony gullies that on a wetter day would have run full, draining the gneiss crags of the higher mountains. I could hear Jake's boots stepping through the ravines somewhere further up the slope yet, closer by, something was watching me.

Between the larch trunks, I caught sight of a pair of dark eyes and a fiery coat. Against the banks of verdant shrub and bone-white bark, the roe deer shone like beech leaves on a sunny autumn day. After two or three minutes of watching each other, we both returned to our duties – she to graze the flourishing bilberry shoots, and me to locate a bed for the night.

'Dan!' Jake's voice called lightly through the trees. 'Up here.'

Jake had found a splendid spot on top of a small hump in the hill. With the ground lacking purchase, we lashed the guy ropes to the surrounding trees from which we hung our sweaty clothes to dry. The rest of the afternoon and early evening was spent trying to determine the optimum-sized gap in Ted's door, big enough to allow fresh air in to cool the sauna but small enough to deter the wealth of biting mosquitoes and irritating flies that apparently found our flesh impossible to resist.

'*Tiou – ouiich*! *Tiou – ouiich*!' The spitting calls of a black grouse roused us at dawn. I opened my eyes to a marvellous display of silhouetted moth wings spread across the outer layer of the tent, and then climbed from the porch to see a familiar pair of eyes staring at me through the trees. It was the same roe that I had spotted the day before.

'Another beautiful day,' I whispered to Jake, who had just emerged from the tent as a patch of sunlight fell upon the deer's tawny coat.

We ate honey and ginger cake as the path moved further into the valley, past a man in a flannel shirt stirring a bonfire, and his small herd of smoked-out cows that stretched lazily across the track. Soon the path began to climb, breaking free of the trees into a barren land of stony mountains, their escarpments flickering with the black wings of a muster of crows.

Despite our resupply two days earlier, the modesty of our rations was already beginning to show. The energy from the cake we had eaten for breakfast had already worn off, and so too the biscuits that we had consumed at mid-morning after leaving the forest.

'We got any bread?' Jake mumbled.

'We've had our rations for the morning already,' I lamented, feeling my stomach moan at the thought of waiting any longer.

'How did we get it so wrong? We've been on the path for more than four months. We should have known better.'

With straining eyes, I glared up at the trail ahead. Winding through a landscape of broken rubble and sparse woody shrub, the track climbed steeply to the Col de Fenestre, a craggy dip in the skyline connecting France with Italy. 'Maybe we could have a little jam?' I offered desperately. 'I'm running out of energy.'

Escaping the wind, we huddled between two large rocks and pulled the pot of jam from my pack. It was a distressing moment. Feeding tiny spoonfuls of sugar into my mouth, I was sure that I was swallowing more dust from the dry air than I was food. I began to worry about the coming days, and as Jake screwed the lid back onto the pot, I could see that he too was concerned.

'Right,' Jake said abruptly, after several minutes of silence, 'we've got two options.' Scrambling to his feet, I could see that he had made a decision. 'Either we turn back and retrace our steps, something I certainly don't want to do, or we quit feeling sorry for ourselves and push on. I vote we keep moving. There are people far worse off than us.'

'You're right.' Adopting Jake's enthusiasm, I pushed off the rock and stood up into the wind. Without another thought, we slung on our packs, rediscovered the trail, and made decisively for the Italian border.

'Italy!' Jake exclaimed with a sigh, as we climbed the final few steps of our ascent. 'Our eighth and final country, although I'm not really sure we can count it.'

'What do you mean? We've crossed the Italian border,' I said, pointing at a stone beside us. 'There's an "I" on this side and an "F" on that side.' I looked out beyond the 2,474-metre pass and down into the wild valleys of Parco Naturale delle Alpi Marittime. 'We're in Italy, even if it's only for a few minutes, so we're counting it!'

'Alright, alright,' Jake conceded happily. 'Shall we celebrate with some food?'

Dividing a small piece of bread in two, we ate the slice slowly to prolong the satisfaction. I had never really thought about the taste of bread before, at least not in so much detail. Holding it on my tongue, I was amazed at how sweet the dough became as time went on, and how delicious the tiny grains were as they split between my teeth.

Ten minutes later, we were back in France, jinking down the winding track and towards a *refuge* at the eastern end of the Vallon de la Madone de Fenestre. With an access point and car park, the busy shelter made our heads spin. We thought about asking for a little food from the chattering day hikers, a notion that soon fizzled out as our pride prevailed, and we swiftly fled the *refuge* entirely, past the crammed car park and into a forest beyond.

Below the peak of Mont Cavale, we called it a day and slept, for the second consecutive night, with bilberry close to our shoulders.

*

'I love these early rises,' Jake said the next morning, after returning from the *refuge* with a full water bladder and bottles. 'It's so fresh!'

Just down from the shelter was a large bank of grass strewn with dozens of tents. I watched as one of the doors fell open and a head popped out. The lady looked up to the sky, and then with closed eyes took a deep breath of air and smiled. 'And we're up before all of the Quechuans too!'

We had realised just a few days into the Alps that the days usually began clear and crisp, and then darkened in the afternoon. Thus, to see a rush of thick, lurching cloud building to our west so early in the morning suggested that rain was likely to find our skin at some point in the day. But for the time being, with the sun gradually creeping down the mountainside, we were in high spirits and began to ascend an awkward shelf of boulders and rock slabs at the foot of Mont Ponset (2,828 metres).

With my body held close to the rock, I was taken by the swathes of green and mustard lichen that hugged its surface, the symbiosis of the fungus and its photosynthetic partner spreading the organism in various shades along grooved arms. 'It looks like a bird's eye view of the Amazon!' I panted to Jake as he waited for me at the top of another scramble.

'I'm not sure I'd say that,' he replied, looking out over the jagged valley of broken rock.

'No, I mean...'

'Argh!' Jake cried, tripping on the ground and then reeling off a string of curses. 'I'm fine,' he lied, continuing on up to the slender pass that had appeared in the ridgeline of Mont Colomb ahead of us. 'I keep tripping today. My toes are killing me!'

Struggling to summon the right words to ease Jake's frustrations, I was thankful when we sighted two nearby chamois grazing on a small patch of grass up to our right. But the distraction was only momentary, and less than five minutes must have passed before he began to limp again, this time from a pain in his knee.

The topography of the Pas de Colomb, at 2,548 metres, was almost sheer, and we squeezed through the gap in the rock with our shoulders scraping the walls, greeted on the other side by a magnificent show of irradiance in which beams of light fell between the jutted ridgelines of Mont du Grand Capelet (2,935 metres) and Mont de Merveilles ou Caïre des Conques (2,729 metres).

Crossing from snow to scree, the path fell abruptly for several hundred metres into a valley and towards Lac de la Fous. But before we could reach the water, a rush of stones from behind stole my attention. I turned to see Jake lying on his backside. His initial expression of distress quickly turned to anger, and he rose abruptly to his feet with dust covering his body and teeth gritted.

A solitary thistle, which until this point had been a mere bystander to the incident, was the first to feel the repercussions of Jake's anguish as he decapitated it in one fell swoop of his stick. 'I'm really fucking pissed off today!' he bellowed. As the spikes of the thistle head hit the ground, Jake swung again, this time battering his pole against a pathside rock.

'Jake,' I shouted, 'what are you doing?'

He took his eyes from the stick, which had bent midway down its length, and glared up at me. 'So it's OK for you to be upset when you hurt yourself, but not me?'

I was shocked at Jake's retaliation, but knew it wasn't really me he was upset with. After four and a half months of walking, our feet were bruised and our bones fragile. A stubbed toe was not merely a few seconds of annoyance but a dozen hammers knocking furiously against the foot, resonating along the metatarsus and up the tibia where the nerve cords would ring irrepressibly for an hour. Since leaving the forest four hours earlier, Jake had been tripping and stumbling all the way up to the col. It was likely that his fall moments earlier had triggered the release of several hours of pent-up frustration, or, the more I thought about it, 127 days of injuries and ailments. It was the first time in years that I had seen Jake's temper boil over, and it made me uncomfortable.

Several weeks earlier, we had decided that the best response to a clumsy trip was silence. I found little comfort in Jake's offering of sympathy for such incidences, nor did he in mine. Remembering this agreement, I kept quiet as Jake stared miserably at the ground before putting one foot in front of the other and beginning down the hill with his newly shaped walking pole dragging dejectedly through the scree behind him. Assuming he wanted space, I continued on in front and didn't stop until I had reached the lake twenty minutes later at the bottom of the valley.

When Jake eventually joined me, his expression had changed little. He was clearly still upset. Keen to distract him, I brought his attention to a pair of walkers ahead on the track. Despite our relatively slow pace, we had caught up with a middle-aged couple as we rounded the lake shore below the rugged southerly aspect of Mont Clapier (3,045 metres). The lady, dressed in a dark cap and pink baselayer, led the way, striding ruthlessly away from her struggling husband who was gasping to keep up with his wife's impossible stride. 'I think we know who wears the trousers in that relationship, don't we?'

Jake didn't respond.

With just a couple of metres separating us from the flustered husband, I was alarmed to see him clip his trailing boot on a small rock. Sent into a six-step stumble, the poor man eventually fell to the ground, skidding onto his knees and stomach with his arms stretched out on the path in front of him. His wife, now some ten metres up the track, turned with her hands on her hips, before shaking her head disapprovingly and continuing on.

'Wow,' I said, looking over at Jake, 'that wasn't nice.'

Once again, he didn't respond.

We soon passed the couple, leaving Lac de la Fous for a second lake, Lac Niré, where a small herd of shimmering black horses grazed the grassy shores amongst a jumble of moraine and slumped snow.

'I need a break,' Jake muttered, ending his silence and finding a slab of gneiss down by the water.

Without the distraction of conversation, I soon realised that Jake's nose was running like a tap. Every few seconds, before the mucus had time to drip to the ground, he would draw it back into his airways with a short, sharp breath. It wasn't something that usually bothered me, but with nothing else to concentrate on, I decided to raise the issue.

'Jake, you're sniffing quite a lot. Would you mind doing one of those snotting things?' I said, putting a finger on the side of my nose and mimicking the action.

He looked across at me, disbelief masking his eyes, and jaw clenched. It was clear straight away that I had offended him. 'You're unbelievable!'

'What?'

'You do it *all* the time!'

'I was just asking. You can say no,' I retaliated.

'You're such a hypocrite!' he returned with a raised voice, climbing angrily to his feet. 'You could show a little more sympathy, you know! You just left me back there on the slope. You're supposed to support me, not walk off and leave me to hobble down by myself!'

'I thought you wanted space. That's what we've always done.'

'Yeah, after a slip or a stubbed toe. Not after falling halfway down a fucking mountain!' he blared. 'And then you had the cheek to say that the woman was ruthless for leaving her husband on the floor. You did exactly the same thing half an hour earlier. You're such a fucking hypocrite!'

Jake rarely swore, and he certainly never swore at me. I was stunned by his outrage and felt utterly sick at the thought of upsetting him. But his accusations had incensed me. 'Look, don't take this out on me. I know you're having a bad day, but that's not my problem!'

'You're supposed to support me! You knew I was upset, and then you go and tell me to stop sniffing when I'm already down! Well, if you can't stand me then I'll leave you alone.' He jumped from the rock and clambered around the shoreline, coming to rest where the boulders met the grass down by the water.

With his head in his hands and his knees shaking, I could see his fury. But what had I done wrong? It wasn't my fault that he had fallen over, and I had walked away because I thought he might want some space to clear his head, not because I didn't want to support him. And the sniffing? I was only asking. It doesn't take much to snot onto the floor. None of this was my fault.

For some moments, I sat alone, cursing his outburst under my breath. But as the minutes passed, I began to feel guilty. He *was* having a hard day, and perhaps I should have been a little more caring. And the more I thought about it, yes, it probably was hypocritical of me to highlight the callous nature of the lady in pink towards her husband. Deciding to bite my tongue, I followed the rocks over to Jake and put a hand on his shoulder. 'I'm sorry, Jake.'

He continued to stare into the lake, barely acknowledging my presence, and with that my anger returned. 'For fuck's sake! I'd never do anything to upset you intentionally, you know that!'

'Do I?'

'Yes!' I got up and returned along the rocks to our packs. Boiling with anger, I grabbed a handful of pebbles from the ground and began to sling them into the water, cursing loudly with each throw. I started to hurl the stones harder and harder until soon my shoulder was straining with a self-inflicted pain that only exacerbated my blaspheming.

The hour-long climb to the Baisse du Basto (2,693 metres) was silent, save for the crunching of rubble beneath our boots. I knew Jake was thinking about our argument as much as I was, and decided that there was no point in interrupting his thoughts with more defensive discourse. It was the first fight we had had on our entire journey, coming just three days before we were set to reach the end. Perhaps this should have made me happy. To spend so long in another's company would more often than not have been the catalyst for scores of arguments. We had had just one. But I wasn't happy. I was angry, confused and, worst of all, saddened at the thought that Jake would even entertain the idea that I would act with anything other than his best interests at heart.

Apologies were made and accepted over a packet of pulverised biscuits in a blustery wind that cut across the Baisse du Basto ridgeline, before we strode purposefully across see-sawing rocks and by lakes drifting with ice, dipping down and then up to the Baisse de Valmasque (2,549 metres) across the valley.

'Lunch?' Jake suggested. 'If you can call it that.'

Much like our biscuits, the small loaves of long-life bread that we had bought back in Saint Dalmas had been squashed amongst our unwashed clothes and camping gear. We were glad for the spoonfuls of preservatives added to the loaves, for it meant that they were still relatively fresh, even if they had been demoted to the size and density of a tin of beans. Spreading jam across the shrunken slices, we ate our rations whilst peering south into the Vallée des Merveilles, a scene as wild as any we had walked through yet.

Huge chunks of angled volcanic breccia – like piles of giant Lego dusted purple, green and red – lay on the valley slopes, whilst cliffs and stacks stood gingerly around the basin's towering lip. A slide of rocks clattered down the mountainside to our left. Looking up, we spotted the notched aquiline horns of a mountain ibex. With sure hooves, the ibex scaled the brutish terrain, picking a route that led a few metres beyond our boots, before disappearing behind a crag of rock splattered black and green with lichen, like a large-scale Jackson Pollock painting. It was hard to believe, looking into the chaotic valley of torn rock and debris, that we were about to set foot into one of the largest collections of Bronze Age petroglyphs in the world.

Jake and I were not particularly excited about the prospect of the rock art but, as inferred by the bundles of intrigued trekkers that were congregating on the path below, we were about to enter a site of great significance. Adopting studious expressions, we dropped into the valley down a rugged path where a sign welcomed us into the site, warning that the use of walking poles was strictly prohibited.

The first petroglyph that we saw comprised a couple of lines and a circle, and the second looked a bit like a spearhead or a dagger. By the time we sighted our third etching – some sort of stick man doing a handstand, or perhaps we were looking at it the wrong way round – our concentration began to drift.

Over a period of five years, from the end of the nineteenth century to the beginning of the twentieth century, amateur archaeologist Clarence Bicknell identified 10,000 drawings. I have no doubt that Clarence found great satisfaction in the venture, and so too his archaeological predecessors whose discoveries brought the overall tally to somewhere around 36,000. Yet, in spite of their impressive history, we soon became distracted.

'Let's see how many of these historians care enough about the art to put their walking poles away,' I said as we passed another warning sign, digressing conversation away from the petroglyphs.

Intriguingly, out of the dozens of hikers making their way through the valley, Jake and I, who were almost certainly the least interested in the inscriptions, were two of the only people to have filed their walking aids into their packs. We even saw one of the Vallée des Merveilles tour guides – a short round man with spectacles that highlighted a look of erudition – digging a pair of sticks into the stony path to support his rotund body. For people who seemed to care so much about their past, they didn't take much care.

Leaving the tour groups behind us, we continued towards the southern end of the valley and the Cime du Diable, ominously known as the 'Summit of the Devil', a craggy peak partly obscured by an atmosphere of menacing-looking cloud. We climbed to the Pas de Diable (2,430 metres) just south of the peak, where silhouetted upon an outcrop close to the path we saw a chamois and its suckling kid. The bovids were swamped by the descending mist, and rain began to fall. The vapour moved at a brilliant pace, sweeping over the surrounding contours and across the way, at one moment leading us into a white abyss, and the next clearing to give views of our route south.

Subjected to low visibility and a crumbled landscape, we struggled to find a place to camp, continuing on for another two hours until eventually, detouring from the path, we found a level patch of grass on the edge of a cluster of conifers. We set up camp on the soft matted ledge, unsure of our location, as tracks of cloud washed up the mountainside and swallowed the trees.

'Eventful day,' Jake said as I handed him a bowl of lumpy walkers' risotto a little later on.

'Sure was.'

Jake lifted up his walking pole. 'Shame about that.'

'Yeah, I guess.' We both looked out to the south and into the cloud. 'I wonder what's around us,' I said, neither expecting an answer, nor wanting one.

HUNGER FOR THE END

At midnight, I woke feeling hungry. With our rations all but gone, I opened the tent and reached for a bottle of water that lay just outside the door, hoping that it would fill the void. My movement disturbed Jake, and he sat up with squinting eyes. Moonlight beamed in through the door.

Getting to our knees, we crawled tentatively out onto the damp grass. Like a pair of weary mallards, we wobbled slowly along the grass beside the wood, where a gentle gradient took us to a ledge looking out to the north and west. Numbing the glint of the stars, the full moon illuminated the dips and peaks of the surrounding terrain, transforming the landscape into a mass of crumpled foil, monochrome and lifeless save for the amber glow of a village in the far distance. The lunar radiance was bright enough to read a map, but effortlessly resisting the urge, we returned to the tent and rediscovered our sleeping bags.

I stirred again with a hungry stomach – or perhaps it was a pang of sadness for the final wild camp of our walk – this time a few minutes before dawn. I turned to see if Jake was awake. He was. Nodding to the end of his makeshift pillow of jumpers and T-shirts, I realised that he was watching something. A beautiful green caterpillar stretched lazily on his pillow, and then began to step across the clothing towards his hand. We rose quietly, propping the larva onto a leaf amongst a tangle of brambles verging the forest, before raising our heads to inspect the day.

Cones hung in the nearby pine, glimmering in the low light like Christmas baubles, and clouded yellow butterflies – surely the early birds of the Lepidoptera – fluttered around us in a flight twenty-strong. Now that the mist had gone and the light of day had returned, it was clear, as we looked south, that the land around us had dropped. The rugged mountains of the Vallée des Merveilles were behind us, replaced by an unassuming terrain of forested hills and rounded crests.

'Baisse de Saint-Véran,' Jake said with the map in his hands. 'That's where we are now – 1,836 metres above sea level. I'm not sure I fancy this walk into Sospel.'

'What are we looking at?'

'About thirty kilometres, but with two and a half of descent.'

'Ouch!'

Within minutes, our knees and ankles were feeling the strain of the declining slopes. We lost height along a falling *arête*, past a shepherd and his herd of bleating sheep, and onto a row of ruined barracks overgrown with purple flowers and a host of irrepressible clouded yellows. Passing a *fromagerie*, we smelt the perfume of smoked cheese and a fuming barbecue that mixed blissfully with the scent of the lavender hills.

'It doesn't get much better than this,' I said, filling my mouth with trackside raspberries and wild strawberries. 'I can't wait to get home and have a massive fruit salad!'

'And meat!' Jake added.

'Cheese!'

'Roast vegetables too! Or anything roasted for that matter. In fact, anything that isn't bread, couscous, noodles, or biscuits,' Jake exclaimed.

'Exactly!'

The path began to undulate into a group of trees, where leaf skeletons and sycamore seeds patterned the way, and mushrooms of all shapes and sizes bedded the forest floor – some deep red and dipped in the middle, and others flattened and ochre like a squashed peach.

'Are you excited about finishing?' I asked as I began to think about home.

Jake shrugged. 'Yes and no. I'm a bit scared. Obviously, it's going to be great to see everyone, but once that's died down, what have I got?' He kicked a stone across the path and watched it topple into a ditch. 'No set plan, no job, and even if I get those things, what can be better than this?'

He was right. The strain of being away from home and our loved ones was obvious, but we were coping. We had learnt to manage the distance. But what would it be like when reversed? How would we survive without the small comforts that we had come to love from the path, and with that the grandeur of the animals and trees, the water and the rocks? It was going to be hard to adjust, and, like Jake, I too was scared.

'But saying that, I feel ready to finish,' he added after a moment's thought. 'In two days, we will have completed a challenge greater than anything we've ever done. I've never been prouder, and I'm sure I never will be. It's been incredible, but it can't last forever. Menton has always been our finishing point, and when we get there, I think I'll be ready. I'm not sure I could go on even if I wanted to.'

'Really?'

'Yes...really. Could you?'

'I don't know. I think so.'

'What about Claudia?'

I tried to picture Claudia in my head but was amazed, and a little troubled, to find that I had difficulty remembering her face. It wasn't the features that I struggled to conjure – her dark hair, her smile, and her slate-blue eyes – but her expressions. 'No, you're right, perhaps I couldn't go on,' I concluded.

Through hogweed and purple orchids, the path dipped in and out of the forest, rounding the 2,000-metre crowns of Mont Giagiabella and Mangiabo, before leaving the Parc National du Mercantour and sinking lower into a valley of terraces and olive trees. It wasn't long before the terracotta roof tiles of Sospel began to mosaic the valley floor, and with them the Bévéra Rivière, a wide channel bed of small trees and shrub, braided with water that glugged to gravity's orchestral baton.

We spilt out onto the river where an old man with no teeth called from his veranda of geraniums and petunias, 'Camping?'

'Oui, Monsieur, s'il vous plaît!'

He pointed us down the road and towards a bridge. On one side of the river, a string of four-storey houses dipped their foundations into the water. The buildings looked old and well loved, with sloping roofs, rusted balconies draped with drying clothes, and yellow walls patterned with mustard tiles. On the southern bank, the Avenue Jean Médecin bustled with promenading locals who chattered contentedly and rested on the river's flanking stone walls. Crossing the water, we caught glimpses through the slanted alleyways of playing children, and then the *clunk* of a *pétanque* ball in a nearby park. But in spite of all of these warming shows of culture and heritage, the most thrilling sight of all came with the red, white and green logo of a Spa convenience store, which glimmered through the promenade's plane trees at the western end of the town.

Ditching the stale crumbs of our remaining bread, we bought gleefully – tomatoes, melons, peppers, gnocchi, olives, sweetcorn and, thanks to Jake, a jar of pickled onions – and then left the shop with an orange each in hand.

It took us ten minutes to get from the town centre to the Stade Municipal-Camping at the other end of town, during which time I managed to successfully lacerate an impressive proportion of my legs and arms whilst attempting a short cut through a thicket of blackberry bushes. Had the short cut been obstacle free, I would have saved myself an extra thirty seconds of road walking. However, as it was, the bush stopped me painfully in my tracks like a fly in a web. Jake, who had chosen the longer and undoubtedly more sensible route, was forced to come to my rescue, pulling me, along with a trail of hooked brambles, out of the mess and back onto the road.

'Smooth, Dan,' he said, as small trickles of blood oozed from my skin.

It was 19 August. Claudia and Rose were not due to arrive into Menton for another two days. Yet, according to the map, we were only twenty kilometres from the sea. With a day to spare, we decided to stay in Sospel for two nights, giving us time to prepare for our final day of hiking.

'This is the last time we're pitching you,' Jake confessed to Ted, rolling him out onto the floor before assembling the poles. 'Here,' he said, passing me the longest of the three sticks.

I threaded the pole into the loophole on the outer skin and pushed it through. *Snap!*

'What was that?' Jake exclaimed just as I was about to ask the same question.

'Shit, it's broken!' Pulling the pole back out of the flysheet, the problem quickly became clear: one of the fibreglass segments, midway down the framework, had snapped clean in two.

After a brief meltdown involving a number of clichéd hysterics – 'It's a disaster', 'Why us?' and 'This is not how it was supposed to end' – Jake quickly talked me out of my melodrama, and we began our repairs. Using a combination of parts, including two pieces of rubber from Jake's walking sticks, elastic bands, duct tape (and the cardboard roll it was wrapped around), superglue, a reel of thread, a shoe lace, and one of Ted's pegs, we successfully managed to break the pole further, thrusting it miserably beyond the potential for repair. As a result, we had little choice but to pray that it didn't rain, for not only did Ted look utterly ridiculous, with lopsided limbs and a sagging roof, but the slightest show of precipitation would have led to a leak or, more probable still, total structural failure.

Spiritual arrived not long after us, and though he would have been well within his rights to howl with laugher at our camping mishap, he was kind enough to show sympathy instead and offered his assistance. Remembering the massage in the camp toilets a few weeks earlier, which was supposed to have cured my unsettled stomach, and the stone in my pocket apparently there to ensure a healthy heart, we quickly declined his offer. Although I was curious as to what a man of his disposition would have summoned for a broken tent pole. The acquisition of an iron-rich deposit from a faraway land? The consumption of a local tree root, providing stability and strength? Or perhaps, as a final desperate measure, another topless massage in the toilets?

It didn't rain in the night, and Ted held strong.

As it turned out, an entire day provided surplus time for us to prepare for our arrival into Menton. After buying a baguette and a jar of jam for lunch, along with a bottle of Sospel wine for Claudia and Rose, we were back at the campsite with eight hours of daylight still remaining.

Spiritual had also chosen to stay another night, yet unlike us he appeared to have a lot to do on the final day of his Alps traverse. I found him beside his tent, crouched on the floor with chippings around his legs, scraping enthusiastically at a piece of wood with his penknife.

'*C'est quoi?*' I said, bending down next to him and nodding towards the carving.

He smiled, grabbed his bowl, and pretended to eat, '*Une cuillère!*' A spoon. '*C'est une racine,*' he added, poking a tree root that had ruptured through the grass at his side.

'Argh, it's made from a root!'

'*Oui, oui!*' he agreed, to which I suddenly began to think: perhaps this was the local tree root that he was going to use to fix our tent?

Much like us, Spiritual had slept badly the previous night. However, unlike us, it was neither the yapping dog nor the sound of the moped engines breaking wind through the town until the early hours of the morning, but the unfortunate occurrence of three telephone wires that stretched languidly above his bivouac. Having been woken a number of times by their negative field of energy (or at least that's how I translated it), he was not prepared to endure a second night in the same discomfort. Spiritual thus spent the remainder of the afternoon dragging his bivouac and all his belongings from one patch of grass to the next, looking up at the wires for several minutes before shaking his head and uprooting again.

Meanwhile, Jake and I had our own problems to attend to.

'I might clip my nails,' Jake said pensively. 'Yeah, I'm going to clip my nails.'

'Good idea,' I concurred. 'Perhaps I'll shave.'

'You can't shave until we finish!' Jake protested, glaring up from a particularly gnarly-looking plate of keratin which he was halfway through chiselling from his big toe.

'I was just going to neaten it up a bit, not the lot.'

Even if I had wanted to stride into Menton clean-shaven and fresh-faced, it would have been impossible. The disposable razor, which had remained unchanged since our departure, was rusty and blunt. I dragged it roughly across my checks in front of the toilet mirror, trimming one or two hairs off with each stroke, before giving up. I washed the suds from my face then stood upright and stared at my naked torso in the mirror. My hips, bruised and blemished, stuck out ungainly from my waist, and my ribs corrugated my sides. The muscles in my arms had diminished to little more than skin and bones, and so too the deltoids of my shoulders. I was fascinated to see, however, after pulling up my shorts to inspect my thighs, that much of the hair loss that I had experienced earlier in the trip had now recovered. This suggested something rather profound: we had been walking so long that the hair on our bodies had changed to suit our altered lifestyle, perhaps growing back coarser, or with stronger follicles. We had been on the path so long that we had witnessed evolution.

'What about blisters?' Jake retorted after I ran back to the tent and blurted out my revelation. 'That's the same – the skin changing to suit an altered lifestyle.'

'Oh,' I responded, feeling a little disappointed.

'Now, we need to finish these pickled onions before we leave tomorrow.' He thrust the pickles towards my face. 'Eat up!'

WAVES

At 5.30am, I reached into the pocket stitched to the inside of the tent, silenced my beeping Casio, and then wriggled out of my sleeping bag. Unimpeded by the darkness, I dismantled my pillow, taking my socks, walking shorts, T-shirt and fleece from the pile, before pulling the garments over my body. Though we had washed our clothes the day before with steaming water and a lathering of soap, sweat still adhered to their fabrics – ingrained and undeterred by the boiling suds – leaving my skin feeling sticky and my odour unfavourable.

By now, Jake was awake and had straightened his body towards the side of the tent to allow me more room to manoeuvre. I stuffed my sleeping bag into one plastic carrier bag, my bundle of camp clothes and my roll mat into another, and the remaining items into a third, and then unzipped the door to the vestibule where the rest of our gear lay beneath the shelter of our waterproof rucksack covers. I clambered gently from the tent, slipped on my knee support and my boots, laced up, and then rose to my feet to see that night had now turned to dawn with a deep blue sky and the melodic song of a male blackbird that sat in the branches above our heads.

As the air of Jake's roll mat hissed quietly from beneath his knees, he handed me my three plastic bags, which I then pushed into my rucksack and topped with the cooking stove, maps and my diary. By the time the main compartment of my pack was full, Jake had filled his from within the tent and was now crawling gingerly from the porch.

I skirted round Ted's peripherals, pulling the pegs from the ground and tying the guy ropes, before collapsing the rear pole and the back end of the flysheet. After Jake had packed the final few items away – food, water bladder, sewing kit, toiletries and the bottle of Sospel wine, now tied precariously to the outside of his olive-green bag – I released the broken backbone pole and watched Ted's flaccid body fall weakly to the ground. With the tent bag being used to store our baguettes, I crammed Ted into the bottom compartment of my pack, and lashed the poles and pegs, along with my sandals, onto the bungee cords above.

Summoning our dynamo torch – which on a quiet morning, such as the day was, sounded like the whining alarm of a World War II air-raid siren – we quickly scanned the grass for forgotten belongings, and then glanced thoughtfully at the map. 'Back through town and out to the south-east,' Jake whispered, handing me the chart which I tucked beneath my arm.

The plane trees along Avenue Jean Médecin danced softly in the Mediterranean breeze, which put salt on our cheeks long before we had begun to perspire. The hour was still early, and all but the *boulangeries* were closed.

Passing the bakery vents, we felt the warmth of the ovens waft against our bare legs and with it the smell of yeast and flour. We bought a baguette from the Boulangerie Artisanale aux Nouveaux Pains.

I thought back to our first day on the path and the Split Tin Bakery that we had passed five minutes after leaving our home. It seemed to me that so much had happened between then and now, yet the bread smelt no different. But what was I expecting? To discover a loaf that I had never tasted before, one that overwhelmed me with indescribable euphoria, changing my being and with it my life? No, to me the bread smelt much the same. Yet I was happy, feeling a tremendous sense of achievement to have its scent so close by on our final day of walking. It was a splendid smell – one that made me smile, and one that I knew I would never forget.

In spite of Sospel's altitude of 350 metres, we still had 1,200 metres to climb and 1,500 to fall. Not only did this make for a strenuous end to our journey, but it also meant that the sea, hidden behind the crowns of Cime de Baudon, Mont Ours and Grand Mont, had still managed to avoid our gaze.

A dirt track led us steadily away from the buildings, past elderberry, apple, blackberry and plum. Looking back, I saw the first rays of sunlight ripple across Sospel's terracotta roof tiles before the path fell into a deep forest of holly and beech, clad with hanging ivy.

By noon, the trail had pulled away from the trees and we found ourselves upon a landscape of parched hills and valleys, dotted in places with the last of the summer flowers. Crouching to my knees, I picked a bunch of drying lavender stalks and a handful of mountain daisies, wrapping them inside a broad aster leaf that I had spotted in the forest. Meanwhile, Jake, who had found a small bouquet of white lavender, a few yellow sprigs of Spanish broom, and a spindle of purple sweet pea, was tethering his flowers with a piece of string and the paper bag in which our baguette had been sold. We put the bouquets into a plastic bag and clipped it to my pack, where it bounced buoyantly against the backs of my legs with every step.

Within several minutes, and despite our best efforts to shade the blooms from the burning sun, the flowers had wilted terribly and the arrangements had begun to fall apart. Then, as if to rub salt in the wound, I was forced to watch as our bottle of Sospel wine slipped slowly from Jake's pack towards the stony trail. But the awaited shatter didn't happen, and instead the bottle thudded to the floor and rolled to a dusty halt on the pathside. With dying flowers and a sorrowfully dirty bottle of wine, I was resigned to the fact that our gifts for Claudia and Rose were going to arrive in Menton as weathered and damaged as Jake and me. Perhaps it's better that way, I thought. More appropriate.

Our anticipation, as we climbed side by side to the wooded Col du Razet, was met with an obscured view through a canopy of thick pine.

Neither of us said a word.

For a few moments, I wasn't sure what we were looking at. But then my eyes gradually adjusted to the light beyond the silhouetted branches, and the pastel-blue of the Mediterranean Sea fell into focus. We had made it.

Still silent, we moved a little up the path where a more expansive view opened out in front of us.

'How do you feel?' Jake asked, staring between two valleys and down towards the horizon where the sea met the sky.

After a minute's thought, I looked across at him. 'I don't know,' I said sincerely. 'I don't know how I feel.'

Hugging the Italian border, the path drew closer to the sea, dipping at one moment behind the bulge of a hill or a group of trees before rising once more. With each glimpse of the water, we would stop and stare for a few moments and then continue on until, eventually, after a final climb through the sweltering heat of the afternoon, we were led up to the Col du Berceau (1,090 metres).

On Wednesday 21 August, six million steps, 3,000 kilometres and 130 days after leaving Bristol, England, we sat on the grass and looked down onto the Mediterranean Sea – magnificent and vast. I scanned the shores of the Côte d'Azur where an unbroken embossment of coastal infrastructure stretched as far as the eye could see in both directions. To the east lay Italy – Ventimiglia, Bordighera and the city of San Remo – and to the west, France's fifth most populous city, Nice, and the luxurious apartments of Beausoleil and Port Hercule, where Monaco's million-dollar yachts excreted wakes of wealth onto the shimmering sea.

We emptied a jar of apricot jam into the baguette, split it in two, and then began to descend towards the water down a rugged track past broom and pine.

'Menton, 1hr' read a sign beside the stony path. My heart fluttered, and my legs wobbled. Uncontrollably, we began to run – more a suggestion of our longing for the water than the steep and slippery gradient – kicking plumes of dust into the salted air as we went.

One geranium-laden building became two, and two became three, until soon we were amongst the walls of suburban Menton, winding down narrow lanes and runs of stone-cut steps, intermittently glimpsing the twinkling blue through the bougainvillea-draped alleyways.

With sweat on our brows and sun-blushed cheeks, we fell out onto the Promenade de la Mer, amongst palm trees, hotels, and the sound of bowling waves.

We crossed the road and climbed weakly over a low sea wall, landing on a small crested moon of pebbles. Dropping our bags onto the rocks, we stripped down to our underwear, undeterred by the audience of intrigued French onlookers and the yapping terrier tied to a nearby parasol, and walked calmly down to the sea, where the splashing Mediterranean greeted our bruised bodies.

I caught sight of Jake through the rolling waves, his eyes closed and his expression awash with contentment. As the water lapped over my shoulders, I felt weightless.

Epilogue

As anticipated, it wasn't easy leaving the experience of a lifetime behind. Jake returned to the aquarium, reacquainting himself with his love of jellyfish, octopuses and fish, but invariably feeling as if something were missing. And I – much like my brother, reluctant to let the story end – ignored the calls of a nine-to-five, pulled out my chair, sat at my desk, and began to type.

A year passed by. I moved to Canada to seek my next adventure, but at the end of each day would return to the past, building characters and dialogue, and researching the path, seeing my manuscript gradually evolve. With my mother pulling the strings from home – tirelessly and quietly – drafting, editing, re-editing and polishing, I finally reached the end of our journey, just as the autumn leaves of 2015 began to fall.

Our walk to the water was over.

A little over a year after arriving on the shores of the Mediterranean Sea, Jake was admitted to the Bristol Royal Infirmary Hospital following a week of increasingly fading vision and dull headaches. With the numerous tests and scans that followed, we soon learnt that he had developed a large brain tumour. The tissue had been growing for five years, from the day he had agreed to walk through Western Europe to the moment we reached the Mediterranean Sea.

To the relief of our friends and family, the tumour was diagnosed as benign, and the operation to remove the growth was successful.

On Jake's final day in hospital, he lay on his bed and looked out of the window. Rain fell onto the car park below, and far away on the distant horizon lay a band of fields. 'I know it's nothing special,' he told our mother. 'But it looks beautiful. Everything seems clearer than it did before.'

Acknowledgements

To thank all those who aided Jake and me on our journey through Western Europe would be an undertaking as great as the venture itself. Without their support, our challenge would have been far greater.

Particular thanks must go to those who donated money to WaterAid, and those who helped spread the word of the charity's worth; to the Trail Angels from the path – too many to mention – and to those who supported us from more distant lands.

A big thank-you goes to my family: to my sister, Jessica Graham, for her pride in our endeavour; to my grandparents, Joan and Ted Emmett, and Mary Graham, for their wisdom; to Ben O'Neill for her encouragement, and to my auntie, Lesley Emmett, for her homemade socks; to my father, Stuart Graham, for putting adventure in our blood and showing us the map; and to my mother, Carol Graham, for quelling her worry in support of our journey, for her loyalty to each and every step that we took, and for her skill and determination to help lay our experiences onto the pages of this book.

I owe special thanks to Claudia Collins for teaching me that small is often grand, kindness is everywhere and love, in its truest sense, is, without doubt, infinite.

And, finally, I would like to thank Jake Graham, my brother and best friend, my mentor and walking companion, for, without him, the adventure would have been little more than a walk to the Mediterranean Sea.